SCHOOL ORGANISATION

By The Same Author and Publisher:

- *Educational Philosophies in India*
- *Foundations of Education (2nd ed.)*
- *Education in Ancient and Medieval India*
- *Comparative Education (3rd ed.)*

SCHOOL ORGANISATION

(Highlighting the Basic Principles in Consonance with the Tenets of True Democracy)

S P CHAUBE
A CHAUBE

SECOND REVISED EDITION

VIKAS PUBLISHING HOUSE PVT LTD

VIKAS® PUBLISHING HOUSE PVT LTD
E-28, Sector-8, Noida-201301 (UP) India
Phone: +91-120-4078900 • Fax: +91-120-4078999
Registered Office: 576, Masjid Road, Jangpura, New Delhi-110014. India
E-mail: ***helpline@vikaspublishing.com*** • Website: ***www.vikaspublishing.com***

- Ahmedabad : 305, Grand Monarch, 100 ft Shyamal Road, Near Seema Hall, Ahmedabad-380051 • Ph. +91-79-65254204
- Bengaluru : First Floor, N S Bhawan, 4th Cross, 4th Main, Gandhi Nagar, Bengaluru-560009 • Ph. +91-80-22281254, 22204639
- Chennai : E-12, Nelson Chambers, 115, Nelson Manickam Road, Aminjikarai, Chennai-600029 • Ph. +91-44-23744547, 23746090
- Hyderabad : Aashray Mansion, Flat-G (G.F.), 3-6-361/8, Street No. 20, Himayath Nagar, Hyderabad-500029 • Ph. +91-40-23269992 • Fax. +91-40-23269993
- Kolkata : 82, Park Street, Kolkata-700017 • Ph. +91-33-22837880
- Mumbai : 67/68, 3rd Floor, Aditya Industrial Estate, Chincholi Bunder, Behind Balaji International School & Evershine Mall, Malad (West), Mumbai-400064 • Ph. +91-22-28772545, 28768301
- Patna : Flat No. 101, Sri Ram Tower, Beside Chiraiyatand Over Bridge, Kankarbagh Main Rd., Kankarbagh, Patna-800020 • Ph. +91-612-2351147

School Organisation
ISBN: 978-81259-1132-6

Second Revised Edition 2003
Reprinted several times
First Reprint 2014

Printed in India.

Preface to the Second Edition

In this new edition we have enlarged the scope of the subject by including three separate Chapters on 1. Co-curricular Activities: Importance, Types, Values and Essentials of their Programmes, 2. Importance and Organisations of Dramatics, Educational Tours and Excursion, and 3. Hobbies, Junior Red Cross Society, N.C.C., School Assembly, School Exhibitions, School Publications, Scouting, Girl Guidance and Community Service. It is hoped that this work will further meet the expectations of students of the subject.

Authors

Contents

Preface to the First Edition

The organisation of our modern schools is generally based on the ideals of education as conceived by the British rulers about two centuries ago, as it suited them keeping their administrative purposes in view. Needless to say, now the ideals of our education have changed in consonance with the tenets of our developing democracy since 1947. Hence the basic principles on which our schools should be organised should also be correspondingly modified in view of the fundamentals and directive principles of our Constitution as promulgated since 1950.

It is only a truism to remark that the very vitality of our educational institutions today has been deplorably and adversely affected by such acute problems as (a) student's indiscipline, (b) the defective system of examination, (c) all types of political infiltrations and pressurisation by people bent upon serving their varying vested ends by any fair or foul means and (d) lack of due interest on the parts of students and teachers in their respective roles in learning and teaching situations. In order to do away with these root-eating evils, it is very necessary that in the organisation of our schools a new spirit of selfless service based on democratic principles be inculcated in order that everyone engaged in the pursuits of learning and teaching may take up their task with a missionary zeal to serve the true ends of our educational system.

In this book an attempt has been made to draw the attention of all concerned to the existing evils of the system of our school organisation and to point out the steps that should be taken to strengthen its foundations. It is our earnest hope that this particular feature of this book will merit the attention of the readers. In this context some practical suggestions have also been given to make the school organisational system more effective and meaningful for students, teachers, principals, managers and government education officers and others keenly interested in the growth of our educational system on healthier lines.

Another purpose for preparing this book has been to meet the requirements of students of training colleges preparing for L.T., B.Ed., M.Ed., and M.A. (Educ.) and other degrees, and diplomas in education. Hence in the selection and organisation of materials for this work the main courses of school organisation as prescribed by various universities have been kept in view.

The authors will be thankful to receive any constructive suggestion for the improvement of this book.

S.P. Chaube
A. Chaube

Chapter 1

A New Outlook on Education

A glance over the modern educational literature reveals that great changes are taking place as a result of recent innovations in the sphere of education. The old ideals and methods of education are now fading into insignificance in the dazzling light of the new ones. The changes, however, pose the question whether any new principle or out-look or method has really been adopted. The question is of such a nature that much can be said on either side. Our ancestors in no way lagged behind us in realising the importance of vocational training and giving it a proper place in the system of education. The modern views on child-education found elaborate expressions in the writings and works of Rosseau, Pestalozzi and Froebel. Taking these facts in view, one can venture to say that the modern efforts are only to put the old wine in a new bottle. Yet this much will have to be conceded that even the very well-recognised systems and ideals may appear to be new when considered in entirely a new background or from a different angle.

New Education and Organisation of Schools

As a result of a new system of education significant changes have taken place in the organisation of schools and colleges. Some educationists, in order to describe these changes, go to the extent of remarking that the present system of education has done away with the class-system of education. But on considering this statement impartially one has the realisation that class-system will continue to exist as a unit of the school organisation, though it may or may not retain its separate existence and importance as a unit of education. So far as the social aspect of school education is concerned, that too, cannot be neglected. Stressing the fact that no two persons are equal, education is to plead strongly for the development of the individuality of the child. This implies full freedom for the child, which is not possible in the group or class-system of education. Efforts are being made now-a-days to consider the child not as an element of a group but an independent unit. Giving his opinion in this regard T.P. Nunn says 'Individual is the basis of every thing. But this does not mean that class has got no importance in education.' John Adams in this connection says 'A class contains a sympathetic number. The class is really necessary for subjects giving inspiration.'

The Tendency of New Education

It has already been pointed out that now-a-days the educationists lay great stress on an all-round development of the child. It has, therefore, become the dominating trend of modern education. Two types of education have been recognised under it. One is the collective and the other individual. Of these two the emphasis is more on the second one. Voices are now being raised per force against standardisation in education. People believe that one makes use of an object in accordance with one's ability and capacity. The same object which a person of higher intelligence skillfully uses for his development will be utilized in quite a different way by another of an average ability. It explains that it is the person and not the object that occupies the first place. It is this conception which is at the base of the Dalton Plan and Montessori Method of education.

Activity Based Education—Learning by Doing and Learning by Living

Learning by doing and learning by living have become the watch-words of new education; the school now-a-days is not considered to be a place where information is imparted and the students get only a fraction of knowledge. In fact, it has now assumed the form of a place where students acquire skills of various natures. New education according to Adams provides freedom to some extent to students in order to enable them to do a work in their own way. The main task of education in the beginning should be to keep children engaged in some work and thus enable them to gather experience. It is quite necessary that a child remains engaged in doing something during the period of his or her education. The child, in fact, is to be an active partner of the teacher in the solution of different problems and not merely a passive listener. The absence of activity is nothing less than the negation of development itself.

Activity as the Basis of Education

It is quite clear from the above discussion that activity has become the basis of education and this concept is the latest contribution to the educational world. Now it is thought that the child learns by doing and not by sermons or lectures. Now-a-days the emphasis has shifted from 'what the child learns' to 'what a child does'. The courses of study of the school are prepared with this point of view and the targets to be achieved during the year by a child through different specified activities are also made clear. These things are getting more attention and emphasis than the lessons to be learnt by a child in the course of a prescribed period. The environment in which the school strives to achieve its objectives also helps the child to grasp the facts which are considered to be important for leading him to maximum growth. The teacher has started realising today that the teaching of multiplication and division to a child in a mechanical manner is not so important as to make him understand the implications of these in his actual life experiences. If a child gets inspired to do a work himself as a result of reading or actually working, it is considered to be quite an important thing for him. In a nutshell we can say that child activity has assumed the form of a goal in the new education and the subjects have become the means to achieve that goal.

Child as the Basis of Education

The education of a child depends largely upon his activities. It is not the teacher whose activities form the basis of child's education. It is not so important for a teacher to make a child learn the things which he ought to know. What he should do is to inspire him to know those things himself through constructive activities and experiences. To do so is necessary, as the development and education of a child depends on the reactions born of his own activities, self-expression and experiences of life. Modern education requires that a child should not accept the ready made ideas of others. It is expected of him to acquire all such knowledge and skills which are necessary to face the problem of life successfully.

Discipline

In the changed environment of present-day schools discipline is not so tough a problem as it used to be earlier. It, therefore, does not need the discipline of that sort that existed previously in the school. It, however, does not mean that the necessity of training a student in discipline is no more there. What it actually means is that the rigid sort of discipline that was enforced in the schools in the past is no more needed in the changed environment of modern schools. The main reason for relaxation in the matter of erstwhile rigorous discipline is the great change in the outlook of parents, children and schools. The schools now-a-days are adopting a more human behaviour towards the child than in the past. These changes have naturally resulted in a co-operative behaviour on the part of child in the attainment of the objectives of the school. A similar sympathetic and co-operative attitude is displayed by the parents towards the achievement of the school-objectives. All these lead us to the conclusion that the basis of learning and education is the co-operation between the child and the teacher. The tendency to have pupil-self-government has gained sufficient ground in the educational sphere. Under this arrangement the student himself is both the leader and the follower. The tendency to keep students under easy control is fast disappearing. The teacher to-day is of the opinion that discipline cannot be imposed on students from above as it evolves from within. He is on the look out of an opportunity where it may be easier to teach the child about behaviour. A modern teacher does not do anything for students himself but he lends his co-operation to students in their work. He may be described to be a leader of such a group of children and young men which is motivated by a strong desire to achieve something for itself. He is virtually an adviser, friend, philosopher and guide. He does not impose anything on children on his behalf but gives them sound advice and guides them along the right path.

Freedom and Discipline of Children

Under the new system of education there is no conflict between freedom and discipline. It is practically in a free environment that a child can learn to remain under discipline and develop his personality fully. Repression, on the other hand, can neither infuse the sense of discipline in him nor can it provide opportunities for the germination of healthy thinking and habits. It is, therefore, looked down upon both by the teacher and the taught. Psychological discoveries have proved that the inherent abilities and capacities of a child, if moulded in a right direction, do away with the problem of indiscipline, because the child having got an environment of his liking remains engaged for the most of the time. This is the reason that today emphasis is laid on positive discipline which is also called self-discipline. The punishment, too, has been bidden goodbye, along with the rigid disciplinarian attitude of the past by modern education. The old approach to discipline may prove successful in removing an incorrect answer on some occasion by a student, but it certainly does not produce any such effect on the child which may enable him to give correct answers all the time. Thus we reach the conclusion that a child, under the new educational system, by remaining free in a healthy environment can be brought under discipline in the real sense, but it is difficult to do so by keeping him under the undue control of a teacher.

Emphasis on the Needs of the Child

Play and Pleasure as the Basis of Education

Those days when the child learnt his lessons with tears rolling down his cheeks and sobbing, have become stories of the past under the modern system of education. The child today learns with a broad smile on his face. The reason for this happy mood of a child is the introduction of play and interest as the basis of education. It is an accepted fact now that a child generally does only that for which he has a liking. It has resulted in creating an opinion that a child can learn successfully only when he is given a suitable environment in the school. The child has a natural interest in games and sports. Had it not been so, the child would have never gone to play in the company of his friends, even after repeated punishments and warnings by his parents.

This psychology of children has encouraged schools to make arrangements providing education through the medium of play and games suiting the tastes of children. The text books utilised for child education, too, are full of such pictures and stories as suit the taste of a child. They not only give pleasure to the child but also make him get education without tears. The wailing cries of children that echoed in the primary schools of the past are no more to be found in the present day schools. The cheer-giving atmosphere which has taken the place of the old one is on account of assigning an important place to the interest of the child and play in a modern system of education.

The Child is a Child and not an Adult

Another important feature of the new education is to consider the child a child and not a youth. In other words, it refutes the old theory of education that the child is an adult in miniature. Almost everybody accepts the fact that the things that attract an adult are not necessarily interesting for a child also. We, therefore, have to satisfy the needs of the child—the needs which he feels in the capacity of a child and not that of an adult. It, however, does not mean that new education has not taken into consideration the future likings and needs of a child. It, on the other hand, recognises the fact that the child of today is the father or mother of tomorrow. The teacher today accepts that education prepares the child for the future, but it is in itself no preparation for the future. There can be no denial of the fact that the child is to grow ultimately into a youth and an old man. But it is also true at the same time that the child before developing into an adult needs to be a healthy child. Hence tendency to separate the needs and desires of the adult from that of a child and of laying more emphasis on the present than on the future has developed. These have created a real revolution in the education sphere. Teachers today accept it with one voice that the child has got a unique individuality and needs opportunities in keeping with it for his development. The function of a teacher is only to guide and help a child in the attainment of his goal. The teacher is also to understand fully the individual needs and disparities of children and create an environment in the school keeping those facts in view.

A Study of Contemporary Social Problems

Problems of Real Life and School

The school is a society in miniature. So the child should be given full scope to express his opinion freely at school about the social, economical and political problems. It is due to this approach towards education that teachers even at the primary and secondary stages are expected to give opportunities to students to think over the contemporary problems. Old education, on the other hand, had no room for discussions of this sort. We find in our daily life that even the small children evince a keen interest in current newspapers and magazines. Not to speak only of secondary school students, even those at the primary stage make efforts to utilize their inclination fully. In fact, the reading materials which are being provided by a modern primary school were not given to students even by the secondary schools about a century back. Copious supply of literature even at the primary stage in some countries has enabled children to know a good deal about the facts of life in their very early years. It helps them greatly to understand real life and adjust with it happily as they advance in age.

Subjects and Method of Education

Education is training and not telling. The modern educationists have accepted that education is training and not telling. To put it in other words, now a teacher is not to tell anything himself but make children do things. Almost all the important and recognised methods, such as, heuristic method, Montessori System have self-education as their basis and under these methods it is the child who teaches the teacher and not vice versa. It is the motto of modern education that teachers should tell the student the minimum about any thing and, as far as possible, the latter will derive his own conclusions. According to the Montessori principles the child learns more through sense-experience. Lecture and training are not the same. A world of difference exists between the two. The second one is more important for a child. It, however, is a mistake to infer from this that subjects have been assigned no place in modern education. They still occupy an important place in the modern system of education but with the difference that unlike in the past they are related to life. To put it more clearly, the subjects are not for themselves but are for life. These things prove that education is now regarded in itself as an environment, discipline and life.

The question, whether the educational system as discussed above is simple, is not unnatural in the existing context, and the answer to be given in one word is 'No'. The reason for this negative reply is the need for tremendous resources to create a suitable environment in the school, which is the prerequisite for this kind of education. It is the financial aspect of the system that makes its large scale application in developed or underdeveloped circumstances difficult. Whatever has been done in any country in this regard is not much. But for the above reasons alone the utility of the new education in a child's life cannot be questioned.

An All Round Development of the Child

An all round development of the child is the ideal of the new education. It calls for a balanced development of mind, body and soul. The necessary environment is created in the school to attain these objectives. The subjects are closely related to life. The children are not burdened only with duties today. They are not regarded as obstructions but positive helps in our work. The school aims not only at the making of a student worthy of living by himself but in the company of others also. To achieve these different objectives diversified activities are organised by the school.

Technical Education

An emphasis on technical education is also a speciality of modern education. Every school is expected to strive to provide facilities for technical education and even in the primary classes efforts are made to give education through gainful crafts. The child in respect of the selection of a craft exercises his free will. Our basic education may be cited as a proof in support of this. As the craft selected is the child's own choice, he always displays a spirit of adventure in finding out new things. In such circumstances a teacher his not to instruct. His task is confined only to guiding the child along the right path. He makes efforts to make the subject interesting by bringing it closer and closer to life. It is here that the foundation of the future study of history, geography, physics, chemistry, etc. by the student is laid.

Teacher and Primary Education of Child

We have already discussed that the future of the child depends largely upon his primary education. It is, therefore, necessary that primary education is entrusted in the hands of capable teachers. Only those teachers can discharge the work efficiently and satisfactorily who have not only understood the child fully but are also competent to tackle him with profound sympathy. It is mostly for this reason that primary education of children is being gradually transferred from men to women teachers. The belief underlying the change over is that a woman in comparison to a man understands the child better and is also more capable of sympathetic dealings with him.

Co-Curricular Activities and the School

The co-curricular activities in the new system of education have been given quite an important place. Now the teaching of the three Rs alone at the school is not considered sufficient. Recreation is the fourth and an equally important art, the arrangement for which by the school is as necessary as for the other three. It is held that recreation is not the product of education but education is the outcome of recreation. Extra-curricular activities today have assumed the form of co-curricular activities and have become an integral part of our education. The teaching process today includes all such activities as relate to the mental, physical and social development of the child. The teacher while presenting a subject to students should have a comprehensive view of the subject matter before him and not merely a part of it. The teacher cannot afford to neglect at any moment the individuality and the interest of the child as a whole. The thinking is gaining ground that in order to make education achieve its goal in the real sense, a two-way traffic must exist between the school and the society. To put it in plain words, the school should provide those facilities which the society needs and the society on its part should help the school create an environment needed for the full growth of a child's personality. This objective may be achieved only when the co-curricular activities occupy the same place and importance in the courses as do the basic subjects.

Knowledge of the Child and Education

Under the new education, the teacher before telling anything new to a child tries to get an idea of what the child already knows about it. Thereafter by connecting the previous knowledge of the child with the new one the teacher makes the teaching simple and interesting. He adopts the method of proceeding from the concrete to the abstract. He chooses such devices as audiovisual aids for teaching, as the child has a natural liking for the same. Similarly he makes use of such materials which not only make the teaching interesting but create a desire in the child to learn new things. The duty of a teacher is only to create a desire in the student to know about new things. It is, therefore, the measuring rod of his success. He himself has to do nothing for the child but make the latter do everything. Modern education, as we have already seen, lays emphasis on learning by doing and the child should act and live in accordance with the things that he chooses to learn. He should learn through his own experiences.

Integration and Correlation

The new education also stresses the need for integration and correlation of subjects related to different spheres of life. If this fact is kept in view while teaching, it becomes easier for a child to grasp the subject matter. Keeping this objective in mind craft-centred curricula have been advocated for schools. For example, some practical subjects have been included in basic education. The child through one of the crafts as weaving, knitting, carpentry, agriculture etc., is taught various subjects. In basic schools the emphasis is more on scopes than on curriculum and also on activity than on subjects. There is no difference between art and class rooms in such schools. It will rather be more appropriate to say that the art room is considered to be the best class room.

Directed Learning in Place of Home Study

It was a practice earlier that students learnt thoroughly at home and repeated the same things in the class. Modern education requires that a student should only think of those subjects at home which he has learnt at school. This has resulted in a general remark by some parents that their children do not bring any books home now. This complaint in a way reflects one of the tendencies of modern education. Sufficient opportunities for learning is provided to students at the school by arranging periods of longer duration. But unfortunately in our country, India, today, in most of the schools children are carrying on big load of books to school and bringing them back home everyday.

Socialisation under the New Education

As mentioned earlier, the school and classrooms according to the new education, are today places of recreation for children. They find an atmosphere there which gives them necessary freedom and also opportunity to do what they like. No efforts are made by the school to exercise necessary control over them. Teachers are affectionate towards children and take pains to understand their difficulties. The children are even free to enter the classroom without taking any permission from the teacher and also to go to library and read books of their choice. The children enjoy unrestricted liberty in respect of learning from one another which a generation or two back was considered to be a sinful act. In fact, the schools today have turned into places where student of any age group gather for the purpose of learning. No doubt they seek the help of teachers. The schools also make efforts to arrange subjects related to real life. The teacher considers himself as one, though a more experienced one—among children. He inspires and encourages students to understand and discharge their responsibility in finding out solutions to problems and make a school programme successful. It creates a spirit among children to do a work and own its responsibility collectively. To say it more clearly, schools in this way start the socialisation of children.

Duties of a Teacher

Paedocentric Education

The emergence of a new system of education has completely revolutionised our outlook towards a child. The learning of a child by his own efforts is more important in this system than the teaching by a teacher. Those days are gone when the school was completely under teacher where he ruled like a dictator. Things have now changed entirely. It is now a children's school and the education is child-centred. The old school did not attach much importance to individual interests and differences amongst the children. It is a matter of gratification that the twentieth century is aptly described as a century of the child and education as child-centred education. The child now has become the central figure in education and the teacher has receded to the background. It is not the job of a teacher to infuse external knowledge of any sort in the child. His only function is to help children develop their latent abilities and capabilities. Montessori, explaining the importance of a child has said that one who touches the child touches such a delicate object which has its root not only in the distant past but in the distant future also. She says again that one who touches the child, puts one's finger on such a delicate spot which is the centre of all decisions and which is capable of giving birth to any thing new. It at once brings to the fore that a teacher should tackle the child with great care as his is the most delicate age where both good and evil can take root.

Teacher: Friend, Philosopher and Guide

As in respect of the child so also about the teacher our outlook has undergone a complete change. The teacher today is not regarded as a dictator but a friend, philosopher and guide. His task is to assist the child who is ready to help himself. To assist that child who needs no help is to put obstacles in his way to development. The main function of a teacher and other workers associated with the school is to create such an environment in the school which enables the child to develop his personality himself. In order to succeed in creating such an environment the teacher should not aim at becoming indispensible for children but at infusing a spirit of self-reliance in them.

Place of Teacher in Old Education

The position, was entirely different in the old educational system. Education then was not child but teacher-centred and the teacher did not appear in the role of a friend, philosopher and guide, but in that of a dictator. It was his will and needs that prevailed and subordinated those of the child's. The fact that the child was an evolving being and its needs at the various stages of the evolutionary process were different was completely ignored. The child, on the other hand, was considered to be raw clay which could be given any shape by a teacher. The conception of a teacher brought to the mind a picture of that sort of man who had a whip in one hand and a book in the other. He was considered to be a store of all sorts of knowledge. The art of teaching was likened with the job of filling an empty pitcher with water. It becomes quite clear that to infuse knowledge in a child by any means, was the sole objective and method of teaching under the old education.

Responsibilities of the New Teacher

Though the responsibilities of a teacher in the new education, have been mentioned casually, the subject deserves a clearer and more elaborate treatment. As we have already said, present day education is child-centred, it requires that a teacher should be a teacher of the children and not that of subjects. This aspect of a teacher's responsibility is naturally quite grave as he is to deal mainly not with the subjects alone but with children of active and almost unpredictable behaviour. The experiences of life and the mature thinking of a teacher are to be harnessed to find out ways and means of infusing the discipline of life in a child. It involves the right guidance of a child, the guidance in itself constitutes real education. A teacher needs the quality of maintaining peace and poise rather than delivering lectures to achieve success in his job. The other virtues that will assure him success in his assignments are more about inspection than about teaching and about humility in place of arrogance. Each of these go to make the responsibility of the teacher graver and graver. In fact, the teacher is to assume the role of parents in the school.

Constitutional Head

Under the new education, the teacher in the school enjoys the position of a constitutional head and not that of an absolute king who does no wrong. He has been placed in the school for the right guidance and the fulfillments of the just needs of children. He is to represent both school and society and give them a mould in the right direction. Thus to designate him properly, instead of being called a teacher he should be addressed as an expert adviser or sound counsel. In these circumstances the teacher should avoid helping the child till the latter desires it. All the prevalent methods of child-teaching emphasise unanimously that the teacher should put the least hinderance in the working of children.

Psychological

A Teacher should necessarily be a psychologist. He should understand and appreciate the individuality of every child. He should at no moment think that all children are similar and need a similar treatment. Munish is not the same what Paritosh is, both have got separate and distinct individualities.

Studious and Inquiring

It is essential for a teacher to be inquiring and studious himself. He should possess a strong desire to learn new things. Rabindra Nath Tagore has said in this connection "only a burning lamp kindles another." How can a teacher, himself lacking up to date knowledge, acquaint his students with it? He must possess an inquiring mind.

Is there no need of a Teacher in the Modern Education System

In the context of the topic we are discussing it is quite relevant to ask if the teacher has no place in modern education. The answer is that the need of a teacher in the school is greater today than ever before. If he has lost his importance in one sphere the same has increased considerably in the other. The serious responsibility of national reconstruction has devolved on his shoulders. He is to direct the growing student along the right path. He is to maintain utmost care in respect of principles and precepts. To him precept is more important than principle. The child today needs the right type of assistance at the right moment to attain his goal. To discharge all these responsibilities the teacher needs to be tactful and a man of character. This makes it amply clear that it is wrong to think that the need for a teacher has been done away with in the new education. At the most it can be conceded that he is not the old dictator and his job is not to infuse knowledge in a child externally but to develop the one the child has within.

School Examinations

Different Types of Examinations

The method and organisation of examinations under the new education have undergone a complete change. The old education was overburdened with essay-type examinations. It would be rather more accurate to say that they formed the basis of the old education. Today a large number of methods are being adopted to assess a child. Those deserving mention are intelligence tests, and achievement tests. These things, however, do not end here; details of a child's day-to-day work are also maintained and on the basis of a collective study of various reports efforts are made to reach a decision in respect of a child's achievement. Any test method is approved of only after putting it to a series of tests in varying circumstances.

Some Characteristics of Old Examinations

To give a more clear picture of the new education it is necessary to hint here at the old system of examination. The old examiner framed only a few but lengthy questions, whereas the new one sets a large number of short questions. The examiner under the old system was considered to be infalliable and the question of examining the examiner never arose. But the new examiner realises that he does not know the entire subject. It is only on account of his experience and study that he is superior to the examinees. But a scrutiny of answer books and marks given therein speak of the tremendous effect on the mental state of the examiner. Not only this much, the awards are affected by the subjective outlook of the examiners also. This indicates the personal weakness of the examiners. In the background of these facts the new education is not prepared to accept that the essay-type examinations and marks given on their basis are a true testomony of a child's ability.

School Records and Report Cards

Under the new education, efforts are nowadays made to keep permanent records of everything in the school. Besides, the marks obtained by a student in examinations, detailed reports of those tests which assess the mental capacity of students are also maintained. Their physical achievements are also not left unrecorded. Now it is the general tendency to maintain records of all the important activities of a student in a school.

Position of the Child

In the foregoing pages it has at various relevant places, been pointed out that our outlook towards the child has changed fundamentally. Under the new education it is the school which exists for the child and not vice versa. It will not be improper to say that in the new education the child is the central figure for the very fact that he is the pivotal point of education. It is around him that every educational activity moves and the teacher and school exist on his account. The new education differs from the old one in as much as that it aims at making the student take the initiative in learning instead of infusing knowledge in him from outside without any regard to his liking and ability. While the old education laid emphasis not on the child but on the teaching of subjects, the new one has shifted the emphasis to the child. The new education's ideal is that all the latent faculties should develop fully and it is difficult to achieve this ideal unless the individual differences and likings of children are taken into consideration and efforts are made to arrange for their education accordingly. The new education prepares students for active participation in the process of learning rather than turning them into passive listeners. The interest of the teacher also lies in bringing out an adequate development of the child and the courses adopted by different schools are but the means to achieve the same objective. The modern school is not only a school but a home and workshop and the teachers are not only teachers but they are also the parents of students. The days of too much of discipline and reading are gone. Under the new education the teachers now agree that the student himself is to make the final choice in respect of subjects. In short, we can say that the new education, so far as its intellectual aspect is concerned, aims at creating a curiosity among children to acquire more and more knowledge and make available for the necessary aids for the same.

New System of Education and India

It is quite relevant to check up at this place if the kind of education described and discussed above is prevalent in India also. India, no doubt, is making some efforts and has also succeeded to some extent in spreading this new education but our educational system as a whole still suffers from various defects. Even today our education is not preparing us to solve our problems through our own activities. Still the practice of listening to the teachers' views patiently and accepting the view points of others without any question is in vogue. The child still does not get an opportunity to express his views on the problems he is to face in life. For example, the socialistic pattern of the society remains merely a slogan of the Government and even to this date has found no place in the school curricula. Teaching in school lays stress on the teaching of the three 'Rs', enforcement of educational discipline, and the adoption of essay-type-examinations. As a result, our schools even today fail to produce an adequate number of persons of free thinking and actions. A great national and social need thus remains unfulfilled. It will not be too much to say that our education after independence has not at all been adequately reformed and that it is not producing the desired effect on us. Some reforms certainly have been introduced, but they are quite inadequate.

Our Duties

Is our duty, under these circumstances, only to remain passive onlookers and not to do the needful? No! certainly not. We are to make determined efforts to bring about such changes in our educational sphere as may fit in with the changed circumstances of the country and prove helpful in creating persons with a capacity to think and do the needful in order to bring the country on par with other advanced countries of the world. We are to model our schools on a new outlook and in a new way so that it may be possible to create a necessary environment for the growth of new ideas. It also calls for a change in the ultimate objective of our discipline and methods of teaching. Teachers are the foundation-stone on whom we can build up the structure of the new educational pattern. In fact, there is no work in the world which does not require human activities. The same applies to the educational sphere as well. It is almost an accepted fact that even the best system of education in the absence of able teachers of character would fail to give the desired result. It is, therefore, a challenge to our Government and to society to arrange, without losing any time, teachers of requisite qualifications in sufficient number along with new schools and new methods of teaching, if they actually intend the country to keep pace with other advanced nations in the world.

It becomes thus amply clear that the new system of education is a revolution against the old one. Efforts have been made to make education psychological to the maximum possible extent. The child has become the central figure in the modern system of education and the position of a teacher has also changed significantly. Changes have taken place in the system of education and in the curricula also. These things give a new look to education.

The big and unwieldy classes, parrot like cramming by students for the sake of examinations, inadequate teaching materials and the unpsychological method of teaching children in their formative age were some flagrant weaknesses of the old system of education. But the new system has brought in its wake great changes. India lacks this sort of education and efforts are, therefore, needed to adopt this system and get its benefit to the maximum. It is to enabling the schools in India (and elsewhere as well) to organise themselves towards these goals that the following chapters are devoted.

Summary

New Outlook in Education: A revolutionary change, uprooting our old educational belief, has in the recent past, taken place in the educational sphere.

New System of Education and School Organisation: The new system of education like the old one retains classes but their ideals and equipment has changed vastly. The schools today recognise a child's individuality and make efforts to provide necessary facilities for its development. Dalton Plan and Montessori System are the conspicuous examples of this approach.

Learning by Living and Doing: The new education emphasises that a child should learn by doing and also by living in accordance with it. The basis of new education is the child and his activities.

Discipline: Under the new education our outlook both in regard to discipline and the manner of discipline has undergone a revolutionary change. We now accept that discipline cannot be imposed upon a child from above. It naturally evolves from within and there is practically no clash between the freedom and discipline of a child. In fact, the child imbibes the true discipline by roaming about in a free environment.

Needs of a Child to be Assessed: The child, after all, is a child and not an adult. The basis for a child's education should, therefore, be the needs of a child and never that of an adult. Naturally, the child has an interest in play and it should, therefore, form the basis of his education.

Studies and Problems: The school is a society in miniature. So children must get an opportunity there to express their views freely on various economic, political and social problems. It helps the child a good deal to understand numerous problems in early ages and facilitates his adjustments with these in life later on.

Curricula and Method of Teaching: Education is a form of training and not telling. The job of a teacher is not to do and say a thing himself but make the child tell and do. Every new method of teaching—Dalton plan, Montessori Projects and the Heurisctic method—accepts self-education as the basis of education. The all-round development of the child is the ultimate aim of education.

Technical Education: Under the new education considerable emphasis is laid on technical education. In the primary classes education is imparted through utility crafts.

Co-curricular Activities and School: Co-curricular activities are expected to occupy a prominent place in various programmes of a new school today. Recreation like reading and arithmetic is a form of art. Extra-curricular activities actually do not remain any more extra but have become co-curricular activities.

Integration and Corelation: Various spheres of life have a basic unity and are interrelated. This fact is not to be overlooked in the course of the education of a child.

Functions of a Teacher: The teacher under the new education is to assume the role of a friend, philosopher and guide. His main function is to help and give sound advice to a child in his efforts to satisfy his curiosity. He is not to infuse anything in the name of knowledge into the child from outside. He is to be the teacher of the child and not of the subject. He is to take the place of parents in the school. To be a competent psychologist is also necessary for him.

School Examinations and Reports: The examination system of school, too, has now undergone great change. Under the new education, various types of tests, besides the essay type-examinations are being adopted with a view to assessing the ability of a child. Elaborate records of all the activities of a child in the school are maintained.

Position of the Child: The child is the pivotal point of every school activity.

India and the New System of Education: Though India is attracted towards the new education, it has not been put successfully into practice. It is, however, hoped that in the near future proper arrangements would be made to derive the maximum benefits from this new outlook of education.

Exercises

1. How has the school organisation been affected by the new system of education?
2. What do you understand by 'learning by doing and living'?
3. Do you agree with the view that discipline in a child evolves from within and is not imposed from without? Support your view-point with logical arguments.
4. 'Child is a child and not an adult'. What do you understand by this? Discuss also in this connection the basis for education of the child.
5. How far have the teaching materials and methods been affected by the new system of education?
6. What is the importance of co-curricular activities in education of the child?
7. Discussing the statement that 'a teacher is a friend, philosopher and guide', point out the requisite qualifications of an ideal teacher.
8. Explain clearly the statement—'A child is the central point of education'.
9. In the light of the speciality of the new system of education, discuss the existing educational system of India. Is our present system of education without an adequate ideal?

Chapter 2

Democracy and Education

The present age is the age of scientific though, due to which man has not only made tremendous progress in mundane life but has also gained so much confidence in his own powers that he wishes to gain complete success by utilising his energies fully in every aspect of life. He has achieved success in the social, political, economic and other fields of life, and is now fully devoting himself to the development of the self and is forging ahead in the intellectual and cultural fields. The goal of man's life today seems to be the advancement of all the necessary means to the development of the human personality. Democracy flourishes due to these ideals. Our country has adopted the democratic system. To protect our independence, it is necessary that we should rivet all our attention on education, because it is through education that we will be able to inculcate noble ideas in the people and protect our democratic set up. In truth, democracy and education are interdependent and as such it is necessary for us to look towards education in order to make the democratic experiment a success.

Democracy is a vast system and it includes all he aspects of life—cultural, political, religious and economic of the individual—but man has accepted it primarily in the political field. That is why even after adopting the democratic system,, intolerance, sectarianism, religious opposition, exploitation and communal riots are still existent and we have failed in eradicating these evils. Hence, it is essential that democratic ideas should penetrate both in the fields of life—individual and group—and each member of the nation takes a vow to behave in the desired way. Only in this way our democratic experiment may be successful.

Practicability of Democracy

In democracy great importance is given to equality, protection of human rights, spirit of brotherhood and freedom. It has been seen that in spite of these high ideals people are doubtful or suspicious of democracy. This is because we have confined democracy to the political field at the neglect of individual and public good. Democracy will be looked at with a jaundiced eye till we rivet our attention on the above mentioned factors—which are the vital force of democracy. In order to dispel the suspicion against democracy we should give it a religious bias for only then will it fully percolate into the public life. So far religious bias—has not been given to it. If we accept the sovereignty of democracy in the various fields of human life then the public will surely be attracted towards it and compelled to repose its trust in it.

In a democracy each individual gets an opportunity to progress according to his intellectual and physical capabilities. Hence the ruler, howsoever capable he might be, cannot exercise any undesirable influence on the ruled. The ruler in spite of being at the helm of affairs discharges his obligations holding himself fully responsible to the individual or the society. There is not much difference between the ruler and the society. This means that there is no possibility of the emergence of the feeling of exploitation at the hands of a ruler even though he may possess special knowledge.

We can utilize the knowledge of a specialist most advantageously only in a democratic set up. This is not at all possible in monarchy because such a system does not provide enough opportunity to the individual to develop his personality.

Ideals of Democracy

By democracy we do not only mean political democracy, but that whose impact is felt in the various aspects of human life. Democracy is a philosophy of life which embodies the unlimited experiences of the human society. In a democracy each individual should be given all facilities required to develop his personality and the social life should be so planned that the individual has the freedom to express his views in regard to the various elements which influence his life. We mention below the main ideals of democracy:

1. *Protection and Sanctity of Personality:* The individual is the wealth of the society. An individual is supreme among the precious possessions of the world and his individuality is always worthy of regard. The idea of the protection and sanctity of a personality is helpful in preserving our rights.
2. *Personal Freedom:* Every one has a right to freedom of speech, of self-expression and unbiased criticism.
3. *Right to Expression of Views:* Every individual should have the right to express his views. Political, social, economic and cultural societies should be established by individuals themselves and there should be such an arrangement that the representatives of the public may be fully able to express their views.
4. *Faith in Human Potentiality:* Democracy reposes great faith in human potentiality and it embraces the ideal of developing all the inherent faculties of human beings. In a democracy man rules over himself and is also ruled over.
5. *Feeling of Liberty and Equality:* Democracy believes that all men of the world are free and equal and also recognises the equality of man's right to the wealth of the world.
6. *Respect for Peace:* In a democracy peace has been assigned great importance. The individual is allowed to develop his personality and each individual is expected to solve the various problems by means of peaceful mutual discussions and exchange of views and to abandon the path of war.
7. *Protection of Minorities:* Democracy believes that in every walk of life the interests of the minorities should always be considered. In a democracy the ruler is chosen by the majority vote. He cannot overlook the welfare of the minorities. There is no room in democracy for communalism, sectarianism, intolerance, feelings of high and low and social bickering.
8. *Feeling of Brotherhood:* In a democracy man respects man completely and believes in doing work through mutual

cooperation. It is only on planning life on the basis of mutual love and regard that democracy will succeed in establishing the utility of the feeling of universal brotherhood.

9. *Feeling of Co-operation and Public Good:* It is essential in a democracy that we should be able to achieve our ends by means of mutual co-operation. When demonic tendencies take over, man become predominant and tries to destroy the spirit of co-operation, it is necessary in a democracy to crush these. If an individual's liberty clashes with the public good and causes hindrance it is desirable to suppress it. Likewise in hours of national calamities the interests of the nation will have to be kept in view and at such a juncture the individual's freedom cannot be given highest importance.
10. *Importance of Environment:* In a democracy such an environment has to be created for each individual that he may be able to develop fully in material, intellectual, cultural and all other fields. Each individual is afforded equal opportunities so that he may develop physically and intellectually according to his own capacity.

Success of Democracy

In a democracy the individual has been given a very significant place. If in society every individual adopts, in an ideal way, the democratic way of thinking, then human society will greatly benefit from democracy. Democracy can be successful only when its principles are given practical application. If we adopt democracy only in its theoretical form and do not conduct ourselves in the required way, then it is quite clear that we have not discharged our obligations fully. If every member of the society practices the principles of democracy in thought, word and deed, then there can be no better pattern of life for human good. The essence of all this is that democracy is a social order and it should exercise its influences on every aspect of human life.

To accept democracy as a way of living it is necessary tha. the individual should not be narrow-minded and be free from conventionalism and traditional narrow views. He must feel completely free to express his views on political, religious, cultural and other aspects of life. If we succeed in awakening such feelings in each individual, then society will certainly benefit from democracy and vice versa because, as has been observed before, democracy is a social set up and it can survive only through the conduct of individuals.

Our Democratic Set up and the Educational Organisation

In the democratic pattern of education all the methods of education should be based on some psychological factors. These methods should be employed in shaping the children as lovers of freedom, independent thinkers, and dutiful and healthy citizens. It is through these that the personalities of children are developed in accordance with their inclinations and abilities. In this system the students and the teachers co-operate with each other. The student tries to achieve his goal by his capacity for thinking through some action. The teacher is only to give some guidance. It is the child who is the prime doer.

In this educational pattern the teacher, the public and the government all have collective responsibility. Education is supposed to extend over the entire field of life from the beginning to the end.

The individual proclivity of the child and his ability as also the good of the society should be kept in view while planning out the educational pattern. The educational pattern should be made child-centred in such a way that the individual while satisfying his private ends may also be able to discharge his social obligations.

In the present day educational organisation the school is regarded as a society in miniature. It is the responsibility of the school to make the students proficient in all those social activities which he will need in his later life. All the subjects should be taught in a correlated manner and the general knowledge of the students should be increased. The entire field should be well controlled and discipline should be related to their inner self and not imposed through punishment and fear.

India has achieved independence after a long period of alien rule and has now adopted a democratic pattern. It is necessary for the protection of our young democracy that every individual of the country moves out of the narrow grooves of traditional thought and develops the feeling of universal brotherhood. Our country has, before it, a number of problems and their solution depends on the citizens, who are still suffering from an inferiority complex. Our democracy will be looked at with an eye of suspicion till the citizens develop the capacity to think independently and to understand the import of personal and public good. For democracy to succeed, education is very necessary. Only through education will the individuals become capable of clear thinking and of working out solutions to their personal problems and learning to keep control over their feeling, and discharging their duties towards society. Democratic education is not much in evidence in our country, for democracy in India has not as yet penetrated into the various fields of life, viz., social, economic and educational, and is confined only to the political sphere. A major portion of the masses in India is still illiterate. So we have to do much in the field of education. If we are able to introduce in the educational system reforms in conformity with the democratic ideals, our democratic experiment will certainly prove successful.

Summary

The principles of democracy should not be applied only to the field of politics, but they must be applied in various other fields also, for example, religious, social, economic and teaching etc. Man has been given a significant place in democracy. In democracy it is believed that only with the development of the human personality, social development is possible. This means that democracy is such a philosophy which influences social, religious, political, economic, educational and all the other fields. If we do not confine democracy only to the political field, and we accept it as a philosophy of life, it is bound to be successful.

The resources of man are limited. Therefore, often some people doubt and misunderstand the practice of democracy. In fact, democracy is a means, a philosophy of life through which personality and social development proceed simultaneously. Our doubt is due to the fact that we have confined it to the political field only. If we accept it as a means of bringing about development in all the fields of human life, our doubt definitely will be removed.

Democracy offers equal opportunity for promotion to every individual according to his capacity and intellect. The main ideals of democracy are the preservation and respect of the personality, freedom of the individual, freedom of speech and expression, belief in man power, liberty and equality, honour of peace, safeguards for minorities, fraternity, co-operation and the idea of collective welfare.

Following the democratic ideology, man can make democracy a success. To follow this ideology, it is necessary that one should not be narrow in one's outlook. Only through education, may these qualities be combined with the human personality and an all-round development made possible. Therefore, a good educational system is necessary for the success of democracy.

In a democracy, the educational system should not be controlled by one person or a group of persons, but the co-operation of teachers, the public and state—all the three—is necessary. The society must create a healthy atmosphere for this.

The prime object of education is the development of personality along with the welfare of society. Educationists have given various new theories of education. They have emphasised that the educational system as a whole should be psychological. In India, democracy is at present in its cradle. We have still to solve so many social, economic, political and cultural problems. For this, it is necessary to produce good citizens through adequate education. Here lies our welfare.

Exercises

1. Write a short essay on the main ideals of democracy.
2. Explain the importance of education in democracy.
3. Outline the educational system in the Indian democracy and point out the new tendencies in the contemporary educational system.

Chapter 3

School and Society

Aspects of Society

The term society may be defined in various ways for it is used in different contexts, but in the present context it implies a group of people who reside at a particular place, from the geographical point of view, and who have common principles, culture and experiences. This group creates within itself some problems for the common good and pursues them, and organises itself into a unit for the achievement of its ideals. Such a group we shall term here as a society.

The question which arises now is how is society organised and by whom? Man has built up a society for the fulfilment of his personal needs, to safeguard his interests, for better protection of the self and to carry out his work harmoniously and peacefully. It is necessary for the society to have mutual accord among its members.

There is no limit to the coverage of society and within its folds there may be two individuals or the entire world. Thus this world itself can be termed as a society. One society may have several units and an individual may be a member of all. Starting from the organisation of a small association we may go on to the whole locality, and the whole town, from the village to the district, from the district to the province, from the province to the whole nation and from the nation to the whole world as a society. Every member of society considers it his duty to help in the achievement of the ideals of the society. Along with the good of the society, the constituent member preserves his individuality. Society is organised in such a way that every member, whether a doctor, a teacher, an artist or a musician may by following the ideals of the society, does his own work.

We have mentioned above that society is organised by individuals to protect their interest and to satisfy their needs. The individual cannot but be influenced by the society once it has been organised. The member of the society has to observe the ideals and the tradition of the society and a defaulter is looked down upon by others. One who conducts himself according to the norms of the society is called a cultured and educated person for he has to improve himself under the influence of the society. The society organises school families, and the state and other social institutions for the education of the individual or its members. All these are helpful in the achievement of the ideals of the society and in the development of the individual. They have a significant place in society.

The Various Units of Society Responsible for Education

The environment exerts a great deal of influence on the development of the child. The child learns much according to the environment in which he finds himself. So it is necessary to keep the children away from an unhealthy environment. The environment should be such that it is conducive to their development in accordance with the ideals of their society. Everyone should try to do his duty towards his child. The various units of the society make arrangements for the education of the children in order to help them develop. Thus indirectly the state also discharges its responsibility towards the education of the child. Both the society and the state are in this manner responsible for the education of the child.

Inter-dependence Between the Society and the Individual

The society and the individual have no existence apart from each other, if one is non-existent the other will find it impossible to subsist. The children are the future of a country. The nature of a society will be determined by its constituent members. If the members of a particular society are selfish and illiterate the society can never be called a good one, nor can it make any progress. Hence the society should for its own progress and protection discharge its obligations in respect of the future citizens. It should provide to the child such an environment that he may develop in a proper way, build up his personality and live as a social being. The development of the individual should not be stemmed by binding him down with bad social traditions, conventions and rules. It is necessary for the society to keep this in view. The society should not go beyond its limits in order to make him a social being.

The Mutual Relationship Between the School and the Society

The school and the family, etc. are the constituent units of the society. These different units need to have mutual co-operation in the manner of the individual and the society. If such a co-operation does not exist, the environment of the child will be vitiated and his personality would remain undeveloped and stunted. According to John Dewey, the school should represent the society. Other educationists also agree with Dewey that there should be a close relationship between the school and the society. But at present such co-operation between our schools and the society is absent. The environment of our society is different from that of our schools. Generally in schools such an environment is built up which is opposed to that of the society.

Thus in our country, the school has not become even an exterior part of our society, when it should have been an integral one. Sometimes so much difference is found between the environment of the school and the society that due to this conflict there exists no harmony between the child's total personality and the atmosphere he is exposed to in his school. Hence co-operation between the school and society is of prime importance. All the arts and crafts and the activities of the society should be included on a small scale in the programme of the school, for then only will the school be able to represent the society.

We now have to see how this gulf between the school and the society can be bridged. The school is an essential organ of the society. It does not have a separate existence from the society because it is an important institution for the development of the society. All the students of the school are the constituents of the society. The school is bound to be affected by their domestic and social problems. The guardians of the students also influence the environment of the school through their various demands and wishes. However, the artificiality of the environment of our schools prevents the school from becoming an integral part or a representative of the society. The reason is that in the schools the children are not taught such subjects which have a relation with their practical life. The schools cannot well equip the students with the ability to fulfil their needs in life. This is the reason why students, after completing their studies, are faced with the problem of unemployment.

Evidently, it is necessary for the school to be close to the society. When the school is close to the society, the individuals will be able to develop self-confidence and self-reliance because they will be equipped by the school with the abilities they require to fulfil their needs. The school should have a close contact with the society and its problems. Therefore, it is necessary for this that the activities in the school are helpful in fulfilling the needs of the society.

It is also necessary for the guardians to be in touch with the school and the teachers. They should take an interest in the activities of the schools because the school is a unit of that very society of which they are members. For this the school should invite the guardians on special occasions and the programme of school work should be explained to them. The teachers should also pay occasional visits to the guardians and should discuss with them the problems and the difficulties of their wards. This will make guardians take an interest in the school and the school will come closer to the society. Some educationists are of the opinion that the school should also be responsible for the cultural progress of the society and for this some programmes should be occasionally arranged in the school. Thus the school will exercise a great influence over the society.

There are two ways of fostering mutual contact between the school and the society:

1. The school may be a centre of social life, and
2. The school may expand itself into the society, i.e., the teachers and the students should enter into the society and influence the society by their education.

According to the first method, the schools should organise social programmes. There was a time when schools had a very important place in our country. The village Mukhia (Head) was usually the teacher or the manager of the school. All the social festivals, functions or festive gatherings were organised by the school. The public had great regard for and faith in the schools and it participated in all its functions. In this way the schools assumed the leadership of the social and cultural life of the people. But the schools of today are different from those. The schools nowadays do not get the full co-operation of the people nor do the people have full faith in the activities of the school and the educational system. To eradicate these defects it is necessary to make the schools the centres of social life.

According to the second method, the teachers and the students of the schools should come into closer contact with the society and its members and explain to them the utility of schools. By this method, the teachers and the students will also get opportunities to pick up the good things of society. On coming into contact with the society, they will understand its needs and problems and will develop the spirit of social service.

We have a democratic government in our country and for its success all the citizens have to be educated. But the majority of our country's population is illiterate and is ignorant of its rights and duties. For the success of democracy it is necessary to acquaint the people with their rights and duties and for this we shall have to turn our attention first of all towards the schools, because it is the schools which can contribute the most towards achieving this ideal.

The students or the future citizens of society, spend that part of their life in schools when they can be easily moulded according to the requirement of the society. During this period a consciousness, regarding their rights and duties may be easily created in them. The school is for the progress and development of society, and thus has a direct connection with it. We have to impress upon the students that it is their duty to help in the work of the school and society. Such ideas may be inculcated in the students only when the programme of work and the curriculum of the school are broad based and are in accordance with the local conditions and needs of the society. When education becomes related to real life, when a feeling of sympathy and regard for the school, society and the country is inculcated in the public and when education is so organised that it is helpful in solving social problems, then alone will democracy be successful and our country prosper.

The Duties of the Society Towards Education

The above discussion gives a clear idea about the close connection between the society and the school. The duty of the society does not end with the establishment of schools. The society is responsible for the all round development of the individual. Its own progress depends on the proper development of the individuals. For the all-round development of the individual, the society will have to work in the form of an educational institution. The family and other social institutions which are the units of society will also have to work in this direction. Thus the society will be able, with the help of other units, to bring about the all round development of the individual. Below, we shall discuss some important activities of the society in this connection.

Along with the mental development of the child it is also incumbent upon the society to provide vocational education to him. This kind of education will infuse in the individual spirit of self-reliance as also of service to others. The children should also be given some training in handicrafts and arts so that they may learn from the very beginning to be self-reliant. In some progressive countries, the society itself makes arrangements for this type of education.

The educated youth today feel it is undignified to do their own work themselves. They look down upon physical labour and attach no importance to it, nor to agriculture. It is necessary to teach the young people the importance of labour so that our educated classes may make plans to solve the economic problems of the country.

Society also has to direct its attention towards the physical development of the individual. Like schools, the society also should make arrangements for the requisite number of gymnasia, 'Akharas' (Stadia), parks, gardens, playgrounds, dispensaries etc. to help the people in their physical development. The society should also direct its attention towards the proper distribution of medical aid, and suitable arrangements for a nourishing diet to help the people remain healthy and immune from disease. For all these, it is the duty of the society to raise necessary funds. Such an arrangement should exist for each child, the young and the old.

The mental development of the child should also be taken into account by the society along with the physical. For this the society shall have to look to the proper mental development of the child from the very beginning so that he may not develop the tendency to accept the views of others without assessing them. It is necessary for the individual to have the capacity for independent thinking and to draw conclusions thereof. To develop in the individual the capacity for free and independent thinking, the society should take the help of the radio, newspapers and magazines, the press, libraries and the theatre. All these are of great importance in education of an individual.

It is the duty of the society to provide education to everyone. At present there is in our country a large percentage of illiterate people. Efforts are being made to educate the men and women under the Social Education and Adult Education Schemes. Various kinds of schools are being established at different places for adult literacy. Literacy under this scheme does not imply only the ability to read and to sign names but it means the diffusion of such knowledge as would enable the adults to understand and observe their rights and duties. They should be acquainted with the needs of day-to-day life.

It is necessary for the progress of society to have persons of good character. For its own existence the society has to direct its attention towards the morality of its members and it should work towards this from the very beginning. The environment of a child should be such as to infuse in him the spirit of humility, co-operation, politeness, patience, liberalism, tolerance and dutifulness. To inculcate these virtues and to eradicate evils like black marketing, dishonesty, etc. it is necessary to have an atmosphere of goodness and morality. These evils cannot be eradicated as long as the society continues to tolerate them. They cannot be rooted out through government legislation. Hence the society should build up a moral environment, so that the individual may himself pick up the various virtues.

It is also necessary for a child to have a sense of beauty and the society should inculcate this in him. This aesthetic sense will enable the child to appreciate public decorum, which will in its course create in him the feeling of public weal. For the development of the aesthetic sense it is necessary that the child has a taste for music, dance, painting and other fine arts. The aesthetic sense means that every action of life is imbued with the spirit of truth, beauty and goodness. It is necessary for the artist that his conduct in life has an element of beauty. If there is a spirit of liberalism, politeness and toleration in his life, then alone will his aesthetic sense be a true one. Aesthetic sense in life will imply the cleanliness of houses, villages, localities, etc. We shall no longer destroy through our bad habits the beautiful objects endowed by nature. There will then be an absence of quarrels and mutual bickering and man will lead his life in a happy atmosphere. The municipal boards can render great assistance in this field.

Religion has an important place in an individual's life because this helps him in deciding his actions and duties and he tries to conduct himself accordingly. Each religion assumes a social aspect also. Hence society owes some duty towards religion too. The social aspect of religion means that, high ideals and principles should be evolved for the public good. For this the individual has to have the spirit of religious tolerance and it is the duty of the society to instil this feeling in him. Everyone should have complete freedom to follow any religion according to his personal belief. In truth, a truly religious man will have in him the spirit of co-operation, social service, public good, universal brotherhood and fellow-feeling. All these feelings should be present in an ideal citizen. The society should establish the sanctity of these ideals and should give complete freedom to each individual to follow his own religion.

Socialisation of the Child

The environment has a great influence on the child. He learns from the very beginning. The child is influenced by each member of the family. When he grows up a little and plays with his friends he learns different types of conduct from the friends. When he goes against the cultural traditions of the society he is checked by members of his family and of society. Hence he has to learn to observe the cultural traditions of the society. This entire process embodies the development of a personality—from the individual point of view—and from the point of view of social ideals this development of the personality is called socialisation. Through socialisation the child learns to conduct himself in accordance with the ideals of the society and to acknowledge the social conventions and also understands the consequences of going against these. Thus he regards himself to be under a kind of social control. The school and the family and other units of society help in various ways in the process of socialisation. Mutual contact leads to the socialisation of the child.

The Need of Co-operation Between the School and Society

The school is a unit of society. So it is necessary for the society to take an interest in the work of the school. In some advanced countries of the West the society takes great interest in the activities of the school and exerts its influence over them, although the system of education is outlined by the government. The child comes under the influence of both the school and the family for his tastes, his activities relating to the home, and his recreation. So he cannot remain unaffected by the atmosphere of the school. Under these circumstances the guardians should not try to mould the children according to their own ideas. The society should co-operate with the school and the school should come nearer to the society and should so organise its working as to be able to get the full co-operation of the society. The inclusion of the science of agriculture and home economics in the curricula of schools will prove very beneficial in this respect.

Besides including the above mentioned subjects, the school should also understand the pulse or attitude of the society. The attitude of the society towards the school is of great importance. So the school should know this. For this the school will have to come nearer to the society. In order to achieve this, the guardians should be invited on particular occasions to see the working of the school. This will develop a feeling of co-operation between the school and the society. It is difficult for the school to arrange for the various means conducive to the development of the child, as it is for the society to provide equal opportunities to all and sundry. From this point of view, mutual co-operation between the two is needed.

Keeping the following points in view, will be very useful in the establishment of a close contact between the school and society:

1. The school should be acquainted with the local needs and it should be its prime duty to fulfil these. This will enable it to get the co-operation of the society.
2. The school should be acquainted with all the institutions of the State and should avail itself of their services.

3. The curriculum of the school should be according to the needs of the society. The society should be the central basis for the curriculum.
4. In the social life much educational benefit may be derived from agriculture, the home, gardens, shops and laboratories. Hence the school should make good use of these means of education.
5. The curriculum should not be rigid and it should be so drawn out that changes may be made according to the needs of the place, circumstances and individuals.
6. Everything cannot be included in the school timetable. So the children should be given a list of such books which may acquaint them with the things left out.
7. The children should be given a chance to draw out the programme of work.
8. The children should get an opportunity of learning through their own experience. It is wrong to try to teach everything always.

It is needless to say that if in the organisation of the school attention is directed towards the above mentioned points, the democracy established in our country may be strengthened.

Summary

Elements of society: By society we mean a group of persons having a common culture and heritage, settled geographically at one place and functioning as an organised unit for the achievement of common goals and ideals.

The society has been formed by a group of persons to safeguard their own interests.

There can be no limit as regards the size of the society. There may be different units in one society. Society has set its own norms.

Society organises various social institutions for the education and development of the man. Both the society and the state are equally responsible for education.

The Interdependence between the Society and the Individual: Children become the citizens of the society in due course. The society will be what its members make it. It should be such as not to check the development of a child's personality. The development of the individual and society is possible through mutual co-operation.

Mutual Co-operation between School and Society: There should be a close co-operation between the various social units.

The school and the society are not different. It is for the school to educate the child. The school curriculum complements the social necessities. Society should take an interest in the functions of the school. There are two methods for the mutual co-operation between school and society:

1. The school to act as the centre of social life.
2. The school should be included in society.

Educational Functions of Society: The society is responsible for the all round development of the individual.

The society should make arrangements for the vocational education of the child. The significance of labour should be explained to the youths.

It should arrange gymnasiums, parks, gardens, hospitals etc., for the physical development of the individual.

An arrangement should also be made for social and adult education.

The society is required to create moral atmosphere so as to make individuals morally strong. For this the society should set high ideals.

It should arouse the aesthetic sense in the child, so that every act of the individual may be good, beautiful and beneficial.

Socialisation of the Child: A child has to adopt the cultural traditions of the society. This process is known as the socialisation of the child.

Necessity of Co-operation between the School and the Society: There should be no element of competition between the school and the society.

It is the solemn duty of the school to be in the constant touch with the local society. The guardians may be invited to visit the school. The school should organise social functions and celebrate important festivals.

Exercises

1. What is the necessity of a close co-operation between the school and society? How can they be complementary to each other?
2. Explain the educational and other functions of the society for the development of the child.
3. How should the schools be organised to strengthen Indian democracy?

Chapter 4

School Organisation for Democracy

Democracy is a great and comprehensive system which includes the political, religious, cultural, economic and other aspects of the life of an individual. In fact, it is a philosophy of life embodying the varied experiences of human society. To the strengthen our democracy we shall have to adopt the democratic way of thinking in our conduct and behaviour. In democracy the individual has to be provided with good opportunities for his all-round development. In order that an individual may live according to the democratic ideals both in principles and conduct, it is necessary that he should be given a suitable education. Education and democracy are inter-dependent. Hence we shall have to admit the responsibility of education in democracy.

Education in Democracy

History bears testimony to the fact that the system of education has always been in accordance with the culture or the social, religious, political and economic order of the different periods of time. With the development of culture, civilisation and social systems, educational systems have undergone various changes.

Man has brought into existence at different times, various institutions to preserve culture. He has also established educational institutions, with the aim that culture may be preserved and man may be given an opportunity to progress. Society is responsible for the preservation of culture. But schools also cannot remain aloof from contemporary culture. Hence their importance has also been realised. Human civilisation is in progress every day and the schools reflect the civilisation of the age, for they are undoubtedly influenced by the problems of the age.

Our country has accepted the democratic system. So the outline of our educational pattern should be determined in accordance with the democratic ideals. In the democratic system the chief aim of education will be the all-round development of the individual. Society should provide equality to each individual and an opportunity to develop fully in a healthy environment. It should curb the individual's evil tendency towards groupism, communalism etc., and provide the opportunity to lead the life of an ideal citizen.

We shall have to reorganise our existing system of education if we are to consider it with the above mentioned ideals in our minds. We shall have to introduce extensive changes in all the fields of education. Our education shall be dressed up anew and shall prove very significant from the point of view of its practical utility when we have changed the courses of study, the school-management and method of education. Such an educational system will contribute to the success of democracy. What will be nature of school-management in a democracy? What will be the basic principles? Issues regarding school, management and its principles are dealt hereafter.

Principles of School Organisation

We have used the word organisation in a comprehensive sense. Organisation includes all aspects, like the ideals of the school, the standard of education, the social usefulness of the school, discipline and control and the system of work in the office, etc. In a democratic system the school organisation serves as a means of achieving the ideals of democratic thought. If the system of organisation becomes an end in itself, then democracy cannot succeed. In this system each individual is taught that he has to develop himself and do his duty to the society. All that this system implies is that the individual should learn to adopt the ideals of democracy both in principles and conduct.

Elements of School Organisation

The following three elements have been regarded as of prime importance in the organisation of the school:-

1. The planning and outlining of each activity of the school.

2. Implementing the plan on the basis of the outline.
3. An assessment of the results of the implemented plan.

If any mistake is made in determining the outline of the school programme, it will not be possible to implement the plan fully. If a mistake is made in assessing the results or in determining the success or failure, the importance of the scheme cannot be correctly evaluated. Hence all the elements mentioned above are interdependent and we should try to bring about a balance among all the three, for then only shall we succeed in achieving our aim.

The Scope of School Organisation

In democratic education emphasis is laid upon the all round development of the individual. Hence, the scope of the organisation of the school is very wide. Primarily, the following aspects are covered by this:-

1. The qualifications of the Headmaster and the assistant masters of the school, their duties and their timetable.
2. The drawing up of the syllabus from the point of view of the social good.
3. Periods of work, chalking out and implementation of plans.
4. Management of co-curricular activities, discipline and control, the school building, furniture in the classrooms, libraries, etc.
5. The scheme of admission, progress and examination.
6. The examining of work pertaining to the income and expenditures in the school.
7. The mutual relationship between the society and the school.

There are many other aspects besides the above mentioned important ones. We shall discuss these in the following pages. The utility of the school depends upon its organisation. Hence, it is our duty to organise the schools in the best possible manner so that democracy is a success.

Basis for the Organisation of the Schools

Every member of society is connected with the school, hence schools have a great importance in democracy. The child learns his responsibility towards society and develops the qualities of good citizenship at school. The school destroys the various social evils and creates a healthy atmosphere.

In a democracy, education is not managed and controlled by one or a few individuals. Co-operation, therefore, plays an important role. If the school does not gain the confidence of the public, it cannot survive in a democracy. Securing this confidence is the real basis of the organisation of the school. The aim of the school should be to make the children learn to be disciplined and self-reliant. The teachers of the school should also seek the co-operation of the guardians.

Responsibility of the Democratic Schools

In democracy schools have a special responsibility and the following points are worth mentioning in this context:-

1. The schools should be helpful in strengthening the democratic trend of thought and putting human civilisation on the road to progress and advancement.
2. The schools should direct attention towards the all-round development of the children and should make them good citizens.
3. They should be able to create in the students the ability to work in the political, social, economic, cultural and other fields of life.
4. They should drive away all narrow-mindedness from the children and make them true lovers of the society and the nation.

The Problem of School Organisation

Formerly, the subjects related to the school were easy and consequently the problem of school organisation also was an easy one. But due to the needs and the various social problems of present-day life, the problem of organisation has become a complicated one. Educationists have analysed this and pointed out the following causes:-

1. The work of the school is not merely to give bookish knowledge but to bring about the physical, mental and spiritual development of the individual.
2. The number of children in schools has increased greatly. The work of the school has increased because of the inclusion of the numerous co-curricular activities and of new subjects in the syllabus.

3. The school is responsible both to the child and the society. The school has to keep in view the good of the society also.
4. In the school syllabi are included industrial, vocational and agricultural subjects involving a lot of practical work. It is necessary to allot subjects to a student in accordance with his taste and inclination. A great care has to be taken in prescribing courses of study after determining the capacities of children through various kinds of mental tests.
5. New educational methods have been evolved. Psychological experiments are being carried out and attention is being directed towards the reform of the examination system. How far should the subsequent educational methods be followed in the changed environment and circumstances? This is the kind of question with which the teachers are faced. These problems have made the work of education very difficult.

Second, education in our country has not yet been wholly reformed and reconstituted. Still, in many cases, the main purpose is supposed to be getting through in an examination. The authorities are displeased with teachers if they do not show good results. But along with this there are some who have devoted themselves to the task of bringing about the all-round development of the child's personality and building character. Hence, under such conditions, the work of the teachers and of management has become very difficult.

The present is a scientific age. Consequently, throughout the world an atmosphere of conflict of ideals and ideas is present. Today it is the duty both of the teacher and the management to walk out of the narrow groves of thought and to realise their responsibility towards the country as also to do their duty towards the society by making ceaseless efforts for the all-round development of the child at school.

Ideal School Organisation

In an ideal school organisation, the child should be provided an environment which is in accordance with his abilities. Efforts should be made to build up his character so that he may be able to contribute towards society. To achieve this ideal a balance should be struck among the aim, method of work and the means. It is necessary to have in the organisation both freedom and discipline. In order to maintain discipline, it is necessary that a scheme should first be chalked out for any project and then its ramifications discussed with those for whom it is framed. After this it should be enforced. Able organisers follow this method and change their set up in accordance with the progress of the time, culture and thought. Nobody should be burdened with unnecessary work and each member should get the facility to freely express his views on the organisation while still conforming to its discipline. It should be borne well in mind that freedom should not degenerate into licence.

In order to make the school organisation good and efficient, it is necessary to fix the system of work according to the circumstances. If the organisers keep in mind (a) the circumstances while enforcing their scheme and fixing the routine of work, (b) remember the principles and ideals to give stability to their programmes and be cordial in providing facilities to persons on the basis of their abilities, then the organisation will certainly be good. School organisation depends on the co-operation of the society. In fact the school is a miniature of society. Hence they will have to cater to the needs of the society and we shall have to base our school organisation on the basic principles of the democratic system. It is our faith that if we bear in mind the above mentioned facts while enforcing our organisational scheme, our schools will verily become centres of education and will be fully equipped to discharge their obligations towards the country.

Summary

Democracy is a popular and ideal form of government. It concerns all the fields of a human life. For the success of democracy, every individual has to follow the democratic ideologies both in theory and practice. Only after providing adequate education to the masses, we shall succeed in achieving the high ideals of democracy.

Education has been the emblem of contemporary cultural and social conditions at all times. This is the reason why the educational system has undergone changes with improvements in the cultural and social conditions. Man has created various institutions to protect his culture. Human civilisation is subject to rapid changes. Therefore, the school organisation is naturally influenced by the problems and changes of our age. Our country changed over to the democratic system of government after attaining Independence. Therefore, the aim of our educational system should be the all-round development of individuals on the ideals of democracy.

School organisation includes the norms of the school, standard of teaching and the social necessity of the school. It is for the school management to provide a befitting atmosphere for the all-round development of the children and to turn them into good citizens of the country. The field of school management is very wide in democracy.

In a democracy school management is not controlled by one person or a chosen few. It requires the co-operation of teachers, the public and the State. This co-operation is the basis of school management. The aim of school management is to make students self-sufficient, to make them capable of running the administration and to make them sincere social workers.

In order to achieve our goal, we should balance the following three elements of school management in the administration of the schools.

Elements of School Management

1. Drawing the outline and planning each project of the school.
2. Implementing the plan according to the outline.
3. Evaluating the implemented plan and discussing its success and failure.

Due to social necessities and various other problems, school management has become complex these days.

The utility of a school depends upon its management. It is our duty to manage the schools in the best manner. Freedom and discipline should be included in the school management.

Exercises

1. Write a critical essay on the elements of democratic education.
2. Explain the main principles of school organisation in a democracy.
3. What are the recent problems of school organisation? How can they be solved?
4. Explain the features of school organisation and draw a scheme of an ideal school organisation for your locality.

Chapter 5

Secondary Education

In a democracy, such as ours, it is a right of the individual to receive at least primary and secondary education. For democracy to succeed, we need able citizens and it is only through good education that good citizens may be produced. To build up able citizens, secondary education may be regarded as playing a significant role because during this period of education the individual is in such a process of development that he may learn a great deal if he is given the necessary opportunity. Before pointing out the aims of secondary education we shall glance over the history of secondary education in our country. This will enable us to understand some of its good and bad features and we shall be able to establish our democratic educational system on a sounder basis.

Development of Secondary Education

The British government started directing its attention in 1813 towards the system of education in India. In 1835, after a due consideration of Macaulay's educational plan, schools were established in India to teach English literature, science and other subjects. Raja Ram Mohan Roy also agreed with this educational pattern. The British government decided later that in government service priority would be given to those who knew English, with the result that education became only a means of acquiring a job and that mentality is visible even today.

In 1854 Wood's Despatch led to the opening of a new chapter in the history of education. In the Provinces, Directors of Education were appointed and it was decided to implement the proposal for the opening of universities. Emphasis was laid on the study and teaching of English language. In the sphere of secondary education English was adopted as the medium of instruction. The mother tongue could not get due recognition, nor was any attention directed towards industrial and vocational education. At that time, the sole aim of education was to secure services in Government offices.

In 1882, it was proposed to the Hunter Commission in regard to the prevailing system of education that vocational education should also be given a place. The Commission planned out two courses of study at the secondary stage, one literary and the other vocational. The recommendations of this Commission were, however, not strictly followed. In the nineteenth century the schools based on private enterprise went on multiplying. Because no attention was paid to vocational education, the problem of unemployment became all the more acute and even educated youths found it difficult to secure jobs.

The Calcutta University Commission of 1917, the Hartog Committee of 1929 and the Sapru Committee, five years later, all placed before the public the significance of vocational education. Similar views were expressed in Abbott-Wood Report in 1936-37, and even in the Sargeant Report published seven years later. That is to say, all the educationists recommended the introduction of vocational education but they could not fully enforce it. Consequently, secondary education remained defective and even today we cannot call it a good one.

We achieved Independence after a very long foreign rule. In the days of this foreign rule the educational system had a number of defects and soon after the achievement of Independence our administrators directed their attention towards educational reforms. The Mudaliar Commission (1952-53) appointed by the Government of India expressed its views on all the aspects of secondary education, its nature, its standard, the problems of teachers and teaching, courses of study etc. In order to raise the standard of education, this Commission recommended that secondary education should be given up to class XI and one year may be added to the degree courses at universities. Some Commissions and Committees were appointed at the provincial levels also. In Uttar Pradesh changes and reforms were made in the syllabus and the courses were divided into literary, scientific, constructive etc., groups in accordance with the commendations of the Acharya Narendra Deo Committee of 1952. The courses in various subjects were also changed a great deal and attention was directed towards vocational education. Still, all the problems of secondary education have not been completely solved, nor has any solution been found as yet for questions pertaining to the reforms and aims of education in our democratic set up. With the help of past experiences and with the study of the educational systems of various countries, we should plan education in our land in such a way as to be made conducive to an all-round development of the individual.

Our democracy is yet in its infant stage. In order to make the democratic experiment a success we shall have to introduce comprehensive changes in our educational pattern, as also shape anew our social, cultural and educational organisations and institutions. The present-day educational system has a number of defects which we shall have to remove. At present, all the emphasis is put on bookish knowledge, the examination system is defective, the courses are not conducive to the full development of the individual, vocational education has not been made easily available to all and the school is not regarded as a miniature of society. The leaders of our nation as also the educationists are trying hard that the above mentioned defects may be done away with and an ideal educational pattern may be adopted so that our democracy may be successful. In democracy it is the birth right of each individual to receive education. We have planned to give free education to children up to the age of 14 years. Hence, it is necessary that our secondary education should be such as would provide full opportunity to children to develop in accordance with their inclinations and abilities. We shall have, therefore, to adopt a healthy system of education after due consideration of the aims and ideals of secondary education.

Aims of Secondary Education

We have adopted the democratic system and consequently it is necessary to give such education to each individual which may enable him to discharge his obligations in regard to the needs and requirements of the society. It is also necessary to establish such social institutions as may help the individual to develop fully and become a healthy citizen. The main aim of education in a democracy should be to qualify the functions and activities of each member of the society for then only will democracy achieve its ends. That is to say, the aim of our secondary education should be to train the individual in such a way that he may not overlook the interest of society while satisfying his personal ends. Each individual should get full opportunity and the necessary conditions required to receive vocational education. To inculcate in an individual all the virtues of good citizenship after bringing about his full development is the main aim of education in a democracy. We shall point out below the aims of secondary education from the point of view of these ideals.

Social Good

The aim of secondary education is not to give bookish knowledge to the individual but to educate him in the virtues pertaining to discipline, self-control, co-operation, decentralisation and social service etc., in such a way that he may become fully aware of his responsibility towards the good of the society. It is the duty of the teachers to inculcate into the students all these virtues by the example of their own character and conduct. It is a duty of the society that it should provide such an atmosphere to each individual that both the teachers and the students may discharge their duties faithfully. The aim of the individual should be to gain knowledge, the requisite acumen for work, to develop the reasoning faculty and acquire practical prudence. By means of these virtues an individual can acquire social prudence and may make his life a success and do good to the nation. Hence, it is necessary for the teacher that he should correlate his subjects to the social good and provide education accordingly. The teacher will have to impart instruction in various subjects for this purpose by taking recourse to the new psychological methods.

There should be such a system in schools that the teachers should be able to impart instruction in social conduct through various practical demonstrations of the playway method. In this way we shall be able to make good and able citizens out of our children by inculcating in them the ideas of discipline, tolerance and co-operation. The aim of secondary education should be to inculcate in the children progressive ideas, to keep them above the considerations of caste, community and social strife so that they become independent thinkers and impartial critics, as also liberal minded persons imbued with the spirit of social service. It is our duty that to achieve the above mentioned virtues and ideals we adopt a well-founded educational system and try to reconstruct society.

Health

Among the ideals of education the consideration of the health and physical fitness of children has a very significant place and it is the duty of our schools to direct their special attention towards the health of children. Although it is the prime duty of the guardians to do the needful for the health of their wards, yet the school should make its own important contribution towards this. The schools should be situated in healthy surroundings and there should be a good arrangement for air and light in the classrooms. A medical examination of the children should be conducted regularly by some competent doctor. There should be a regular provision for midday refreshment in order to provide some nourishment to the students after the mental labour they undergo in the first half of the day. A regular provision should be made for games and sports in the schools timetable and these should be compulsory for all. The timetable for the teaching of different subjects should be chalked out in such a way that the students may not feel tired. That is to say, education in health should find an important place in the scheme of secondary education.

Proper use of Leisure

In man's life both labour and leisure are important. By means of labour we develop ourselves physically and mentally. A proper use of our leisure enables us to chasten our ideas, purify our inner self and set our faculties at rest for some time and experience a kind of mental happiness. It should also be the aim of our education to develop an aesthetic sense in the students. In this way an individual can achieve full physical, mental and spiritual development. Sociology, music, literature and art should also be included in the courses of study. If our children spend their leisure time over these subjects they are bound to make all-round progress.

Livelihood

At present our secondary education is subservient to university education and as such it cannot be regarded as complete in itself. Everyone cannot enjoy the benefits of a university education. Hence, the purpose of secondary education should be to impart instruction to every child according to his inclination in some industrial and vocational subjects also, so that he may be able to earn his livelihood. In the process of secondary education, courses relating to industrial, vocational, commerce and art subjects should be more comprehensive. This would help to solve the problem of earning a livelihood.

Citizenship

It is a great responsibility of education to inculcate in each individual the virtues of good citizenship. Our secondary education is concerned with a child up to the age of 16 or 17 years and this is that period when virtues and good ideas may be inculcated in him. Hence, it is necessary to devote special attention to the inculcation of the feelings of citizenship. The aim of our education is to develop in each child the virtues of citizenship so that he may not become self-centred and may also consider the interests of other people.

We have adopted a democratic system in which persons are elected by the public. Hence, it is necessary that each individual has in him the virtues of healthy citizenship, so that he understands the significance of the vote and is able to distinguish between the true and the untrue and the right or wrong loyalties. It is regrettable point that in our country a majority of the people do not understand even now the significance of voting. Our educational system also is not of such a kind as to make the individual cultivate the virtues of good citizenship. The result is that the nation is getting weaker and a healthy citizenship is not developing. We have so far confined citizenship to the casting of votes. It has not developed in other fields of life. The majority of the people are illiterate and they do not realise the importance of their votes. Hence, our educational system should be such that it makes the individual realise the importance of citizenship in the various walks of life, such as behaviour and conduct towards others, all the aspects of village or town life, and all the functions and activities pertaining to social, economic and cultural life. Consequently, the aim of secondary education should also be to educate the individual in healthy citizenship.

Education is not very wide spread in our country. That is why we have not been able till now to adopt a democratic way as a philosophy of life and are still caught up in the meshes of communalism, groupism, traditionalism and other narrow grooves of thought. What is our responsibility towards the society? To what extent can freedom be stretched? What is citizenship? Towards all such questions we are totally indifferent. That is to say we have not been able so far to cultivate the virtues of citizenship. Hence education should help to remove these defects.

We can inculcate the virtues of good citizenship through school education. The society also owes a duty in this regard. The greatest defect in our organisation is that we regard the school as being solely responsible for the education of the child and we attach no importance to the experiences gained by the child outside the school in the midst of society. The child gains in society both good and bad experiences and often his experiences instead of instilling self-confidence in him or inspiring him towards the good, lead him to frustration and disappointment. Hence for the inculcation of the virtues of good citizenship both the school and society are responsible. The school and the teachers are like lighthouses to dispel the darkness of ignorance and it is incumbent upon the society to co-operate with the teachers.

Power of Leadership

The aim of secondary education is also to give knowledge of the desired subjects in accordance with the taste and inclination of the student, to make him capable of achieving success in the various fields of life, and to create in him the ability for leadership in the vocational, industrial and cultural fields of life.

Summary

It is a fundamental right of every citizen to receive primary and secondary education in a democracy. Every citizen will be conscious towards his rights and duties only through adequate education. We shall have to make material changes in the field of secondary education in order to strengthen our democratic system.

When glancing at the history of secondary education, we infer that education till this time has been a means of securing employment. The general trend was towards the study and teaching of the languages and literatures, and no adequate attention was paid towards industrial and vocational subjects. The Calcutta University Commission, Hartog Committee and Sapru Committee placed the significance of vocational and industrial education before the public, but it could not be implemented. Consequently, the educational system remained defective and educated youths continued to be unemployed.

Our national leaders paid special attention after attaining freedom, towards improvement in education. The Mudaliar Commission gave valuable suggestions pertaining to the problems of the secondary education, curriculum and school management. Some recommendations of the Acharya Narendra Deo Committee were enforced in Uttar Pradesh. The reorganisation of the secondary education is engaging the attention of the Government of India. It is necessary in a democratic system that an individual is given a type of education which can result in the all-round development of his personality. We give below the aim of the secondary education:-

Social Benevolence: Only bookish knowledge should not be taken as sufficient for an individual. All-round development of the individual should be the first concern. The aims of our education should be to arouse the sense of discipline, devotion to duty, co-operation, self-control, and social service. It is the responsibility of society to create such an atmosphere in which individuals may automatically learn these virtues.

Health: It should be one of the purposes of secondary education to arrange for health education. It is the joint responsibility of the teacher and the society to pay constant attention towards the health of the children.

Utilization of Leisure: We can utilize our leisure time in the study of sociology, music, literature and fine arts. Education should aim at arousing the aesthetic sense of the individual.

Livelihood: The aim of secondary education should also be to secure some means of livelihood after having attained agricultural and vocational or industrial education according to the student's ability and capacity.

Citizenship: Secondary education is limited to the children of 16 or 17 years of age. The aim of our educational system should be to produce good citizens. They should earn their livelihood with co-operation and self-control, should do their duties in a disciplined manner and should have a sense of right and wrong. It means that equal opportunities should be given to every individual and the virtues of citizenship should be cultivated in every individual in a healthy atmosphere.

It is also the duty of the society to help schools in achieving these targets. These targets cannot be achieved by the efforts of the schools alone.

Exercises

1. Trace the development of secondary education in India.
2. Explain some of the main objectives of secondary education in our country.
3. Explaining the ideals of secondary education in democratic conditions, describe the defects in our education system. Show how they can be removed.

Chapter 6

The Principal

The position of a principal[1] in the school is like that of the Commander-in-Chief in any army. He is life-blood of the school. His personality, ideals and thougths affect all the individuals and all the activities of the school. On his policy depends the social prestige of the school.

In our country the duties and responsibilities of a principal are very important and also comprehensive because educational expansion is still in its infant stage and various traditions and evil practices like casteism and provincialism are prevalent. The principal or the headmaster has to eradicate all these evils with the help of his associates so that high ideals may be placed before the students. the principal is the leader of the school and the guide of the teachers and the students. Hence, he is expected to have certain qualities which we shall mention below.

Qualities of Principal or a Headmaster

1. *High Character:* the principal should bear such a moral character which inspires the teachers and students. In the absence of a good character he will not be able to place good ideals before others.
2. *Politeness or Culture:* The conduct, behaviour and general aspects of the principal should be extremely polite and

1. The head of a secondary school is generally known as the Principal. But at certain places he is also known as a Headmaster.

polished and capable of inspiring confidence and commanding respect from others.

3. *Optimism:* The principal should be optimistic, otherwise, he will damp the spirits of the students and teachers at every step, He should have an interest in life and faith in human power. His way of thinking should be ideal so that the others may follow it and realise their objectives in life. He should also have implicit faith in his profession, that is, in teaching. If he is not optimistic, he will infect his colleagues also.
4. *Capacity of instilling Inspiration:* The principal should be capable of instilling inspiration in others. He should be an active leader and should be such guide to the teachers and students that their dormant powers may be developed. He should infuse high ideals in others.
5. *Health:* Good health is the key to success in life. To be a torch bearer to others it is necessary that the principal exudes cheer and is radiant with high spirits. This comes only with good health.
6. *Ideals:* The principal should be a man of high ideals, for then only will he be able to make the teachers and the students love and pursue high ideals.
7. *Learning:* It is necessary for him to be a master of his subject as also ahead of his colleagues in general knowledge. To succeed as a principal it is necessary that he should command respect from his colleagues for his learning. Hence, he should possess a personal library with a good collection of books on education. He should also read magazines dealing with researches in the field of education so that he may be acquainted with the latest advancements.
8. *Interest in Mankind:* The principal has to come into contact with teachers, students and guardians of different tastes. Hence, he should have an interest in solving the problems of all these, else his influence will not be very widespread.
9. *Administrative Capacity:* The principal should be a good administrator. The progress of the school depends to a great extent on his management of the affairs. The principal should

know how to secure the best services of the students, the teachers, the clerical and other staff of the school.

10. *Professional Knowledge:* The principal should have a good knowledge of literature pertaining to education as also of the Education Code and the various Rules and Regulations of the Education Department.
11. *Efficiency in Work:* It is natural for a school to be faced with different situations and circumstances and the principal should have the ability to take the right step. It was thought that the principal was a horrible creature who inflicted heavy punishments on simple matters. But, now under the democratic system, he is regarded as a kind hearted, just and sympathetic individual. He now treats the students, the staff of the school and the guardians with love and regard. He takes interest in all the activities of the students and fully considers their representations. His aim is to prepare students not only for examination but for life.
12. *No Haste in Introducing Reforms:* The principal should not show undue haste in introducing any reform. Before launching upon any scheme of reform he should understand its ins and outs and, as far as possible, he should consult the teachers, students and guardians.

Duties and Responsibilities of the Principal

The principal has varied duties and responsibilities. The progress of the school depends upon him and he owes a duty towards all the workers of the schools, the students, the teachers and the guardians. That is to say he has to see that the school work is carried on efficiently. We mention below some of the main duties and responsibilities of the principal.

1. *As a Teacher:* The principal has multifarious work to do and as such he cannot devote more than two or two and a half hours to teaching in a day. But, it is necessary for him to do at least this much. It is necessary for him to know each and every student in order to run the school properly. He should daily teach at least one lower class, one middle and one

higher class. This will bring him in touch with students at different levels.

2. *General Inspection:* The principal should see that various class registers are properly maintained. It is necessary to maintain a daily account in the cash book. This is maintained by the clerk, but he principal has to endorse each item and as such the ultimate responsibilility devolves upon him. There is an Attendance Register for each class. This register also has columns pertaining to the statement of school fees. After collecting the dues, the amount is handed over to the office and finally deposited in bank. The principal should see that no laxity is shown in this respect.

   The statement of Teachers' Provident Fund should be entered in the Registers soon after the disbursement of salaries and the account of each teacher should be properly entered in separate Pass Books. The Scholar's Register is an important document of the school. In it is recorded the date of birth, date of entry and the date of promotions of each student. The principal should be extra-cautious in preparing this. There is also a Stock-Register in the school, detailing the articles purchased, that is, their prices, number, name of the person who purchased it and the number of the Bills etc. Of late, some schools have started maintaining a cumulative record of students. This records the tendencies of the students. With the help of this record guidance is provided from time to time. The principal should pay special attention towards this statement.

   Besides the above-mentioned registers, there are Registers for Hostels, Caution-money, Results, Scholarships, Library, Attendance of Teachers, Games Fund, Log-Book, Visitors' Book and others in the office of the principal. All the papers are signed by the principal and consequently it is entirely his responsibility in regard to these.

3. *Supervision on Teaching:* The principal should see that the teaching work in the school goes on well. The students and teachers should go to their respective classes as soon as the bell rings. The principal should also occasionally go to

classes while teaching is going on, not as a critic but as a friend and collaborator. He should not criticise any teacher in any class before the students. If he has to make any suggestions, he should make these to the teacher in his own office.

The principal should also periodically inspect the written work done by the students. This will acquaint him with the work and the teaching method of the teacher. He should give instructions to the teacher so that all the written work with the requisite details may reach him in time. The principal should inspect all or most of the copies and see whether the mistakes have been marked in red and necessary instructions have been given to students. There should be a separate note book for each teacher in which he should express his opinion in regard to the written work, e.g., 'good work', 'much attention has not been given to the mistakes of a particular students' etc.

In order to improve the method of teaching ideal lessons should be occasionally planned and the principal should also take part in these. The principal should also keep a check over the teachers in regard to private tuitions, else many will devote most of their time to this. It would be best not to permit the teacher to undertake private tuitions, but this is not possible till the salaries of the teachers are increased considerably.

4. *Examination:* The principal has to do a great deal in regard with the various examinations in the school. He should see that the questions set in the papers are suitable and they cover all the aspects of the prescribed course. He should also see that time, prescribed marks and optional questions are also printed.

5. *Progress of the School:* The principal is chiefly responsible for the progress of the school and as such he should see that no hindrance is caused to the students in their physical, mental and material progress due to any mismanagemnt in the school. He should see that there always exists a moral atmosphere in the school.

6. *Text-books:* The principal should see that such a text-book is selected out of the approved ones which will be most suitable for the students. He should counsult the teachers in this regard. He should not select a text-book under the pressure of any author or publisher. In the selection of text-books he should be guided by the following considerations:
   1. Has the book been written in accordance with the prescribed course?
   2. Is it good from the point of view of printing and language?
   3. Is its paper and lay out good?
   4. Does it include all the suitable maps and illustrative figures?
   5. Has the matter been presented coherently?
   6. Is the style—such as—will develop in the students the power of self-thinking?
   7. Are the facts given in the book correct?
   8. Are the given questions and exercies appropriate?
   9. Is the price of the bok reasonable?
   10. Does the subject of the book co-relate itself with others?
7. *Hostels:* A superintendent for hostels is always appointed but the principal also has to see that there is no hindrance in the fulfilment of the ideals of the hostels. Hence he should make a periodical inspection of the hostels at different hours of the dya or night, so that he may acquint himself with all the aspects of life in a hostel. The rooms in the hostel, dining halls, corridors, bathrooms, lavatories, drains, and the surroundings should be inspected by him and necessary instructions given.
8. *Guardians:* The principal should maintain good relations with guardians. They should be invited to the school from time to time so that they may see how the work goes on in the school on the occasions of social functions and otherwise. A get-togehter of guardians and teachers should also be organised sometimes, at which the principal should explian the general policies of the school and invite suggestions for improvements in the school.

Whenever the guardians visit the school they should be treated well by the principal. By establishig good contacts with the guardians, the various difficulties pertaining to students can easily be resolved.

9. *The Tone of the School:* If is difficult for the school to fix its tone or its definite policy and several years are spent over it. The tone of the school should influence the students and teachers in such a manner that they may become imbued with a sense of duty and their all-round development may be brought about. The principal has a duty in this regard also. In the school with a good tone the conduct of the students is more or less flawless, they do not cause any harm to anybody and the fundation of their ideal character is laid during their school life.
10. *General Administration:* The principal should also look after the co-curricular activites in the school. He should pay full attention to the sports and games for the students as also educational activites like monitorial, dramatic and literacy associatios, etc. He should himself occasionally take part in these and encourage the teachers of the school to do so.

He/She should reach the school at least ten minutes before the scheduled time for the school work and he should take a round of the school when the work starts so that he may know how the work is going on. After this he can attend to the 'Dak' in his office and also to the visitors. As far as possible he sould daily inspect each class though he may just have peep at some classes. He should try to bring round the lethargic and indisciplined students. He should have a sympathetic word for the students who come in late and the teachers and know the reason for their unpunctuality. He should also inspect the work of the office daily.

Our Society and the Principal

The position of the schools of our country is not very satisfactory for they are faced with economic and social problems. Hence the responsibility of the principal becomes very onerous. Numerous weaknesses have crept into our society due to the lack of education. It is the moral responsibilty of every principal to understand the weaknesses pertianing to his own surroundings and to awaken the teachers and the students with ideas on how to remove these. He should take advantage of the various opportunities associated with social work, and then only will he be able to do well for the society. Our society today is infected with evils like communlaism, provincialism, casteism, 'purdah'* system, child marriage, dirty politics, immorality, dishonesty, indiscipline, physical violence an uncultured behaviour. It is the prime duty of the principal and the teachers to attract the attention of the students towards these. The principal will have to take the lead in this because in the absence of instructions from him the teachers of the school will hesitate in taking any steps within their power.

The principal should not think that his position is superior to that of other teachers and as such some work is derogatory for him. His function is not only to criticise the teachers or to issue instructions to them. He should regard himself as a teacher and should help other assistants in their work. Then only will he be successful in removing, with their co-operaion the evils widespread in society. The principal should bear in mind that he has to educate not only the students but the whole society and he should instil this spirit in other teachers also. Today our country is in dire need of such principals who can devote themselves heart and soul to the discharging of the above mentioned responsibilities and obligations.

Summary

The principal is the head of the institution and the guide of the students and teachers.

He should be a man of morals. He should be very polite in his dealings. He should be an optimist and influential. He should possess sound health. He must be a scholar. He should have an interest in human beings. He must be a good administrator. He must have professional knowledge. He should not hurry to effect reforms without weighing the pros and cons.

Class-room teaching is neccessary for him. The inspection of registers and the supervision of teaching work must be done by him. An examination of the written work of the students is also very important. The principal is responsible for the progress of the school.

---

* Veil

He should take care in the selection of text books. He should also inspect the hostels. He should be polite to the guardians. A good tone, custom or convention should be established in the school. He should supervise activites supplementary to the curriculum.

The principal should make efforts to remove the evils prevalent in society.

Exercises

1. What should be the qualities of a headmaster or principal and why?
2. What are the duties and responsibilities of a principal or headmaster? What should he do to get co-operation from students, teachers and guardians?
3. Which registers of the school require the special attention of the principal and why?
4. What are the factors that should be taken into consideration by the principal in the selection of text-books?

Chapter 7

Teachers and the Distribution of Their Work

Education today is supposed to be child-centred. Yet the place of the teacher in the education of the child cannot be overlooked because he remains with the student as his guide and the success of education depends mostly on his power of guidance and his method.

Qualifications

Character: The child regards the teacher as his ideal in everything and tries to copy him. Hence the teacher should be a man of very high character so that he may not place any wrong ideal before the child. If the teacher is a man of character he will make an indelible impression over the children. Hence the teacher should be a bundle of virtues like hardwork, dutifulness, service, benevolence, truthfulness and tidiness.

Affection for Children: The teacher should love the children. If he has no regard and affection for children, he should not become a teacher.

Training: The teacher should be trained because during training issues pertaining to the science of teaching are taught. He is taught child psychology and educational psychology. He cannot do his job well without a knowledge of a these subjects.

Dutifulness: The teacher should always remain mindful of his duties. If he neglects his duty, he will cause harm to the students and will not do all that is needful for the development of their personality.

Ability in the subject: The teacher should be a master of his subject, else he will not be able to remove all the doubts raised by the students. The students ask various questions in the classes and if the teacher is not able to answer these, he will be laughed at by the students. Hence the teacher should cultivate the habit of self-study.

Patience: Virtues are gradually and slowly cultivated by the students. Hence the teacher should not show unnecessary haste in his work. If a child is not able to easily grasp a topic, the teacher should not become impatient but should have faith in his ultimate success.

Interest in co-curricular Activities: The teacher should have an interest in other subjects besides his own as also in other co-curricular activities, for then only will be he able to contribute towards the full development of the child.

Love for Humour: The work of a teacher is a difficult one. So he should have the capacity to remain cheerful in the midst of difficulties. This quality of the teacher will greatly impress the students and they will also learn to be cheerful against all odds.

Health: Health is the root of all virtues. If the health of the teacher is good, all the desirable qualities will automatically develop in him. On coming into contact with teachers having good health, the students will get an impetus to build up their own health. The healthy teacher will take part in the various activities of the school and will, by his co-operation, help in the development of good qualities in the students.

Pleasing Personality: The personality of the teacher should be such that the students may be attracted towards him by his behaviour, nature and qualities and may grow desirous of learning good things through contact with him.

Optimism: The optimistic teacher makes the students also optimistic and the pessimistic teacher takes the students unwillingly towards pessimism. The optimistic teacher keeps faith in the progress of the students and remains prepared to fight against all ordeals. He succeeds in inculcating all these tendencies in the students.

Originality: A teacher with this quality can offer original solutions to a problem and thus encourage the students towards original thinking.

Quick Decisions: During the work at school several occasions arise when immediate decisions are called for. Hence a teacher should have the capacity of making quick decisions, else the students will be adversely affected.

Self-respect: The sense of self-respect carries the individual forward. If one does not possess this he is likely to develop a flaw in his character at the least temptation. If the teacher possesses this virtue, he will instil it into the students also.

Sharp Intelligence: There are students of different calibre in a class and the difficulties with which they are faced are also of varied nature. Only the teacher who has a sharp intellectual faculty can understand the individual differences and can evolve solutions for them.

Selection of a Teacher

We can well understand on the basis of the above discussion, the qualities which are needed in a teacher. Hence, while selecting a teacher for appointment, it should be ascertained whether the teacher is capable one or not. The state of affairs in our schools on this score is very unsatisfactory. In our country the private schools far outnumber the government schools. In fact the number of the government schools is almost negligible in comparison with that of the private ones. It is often found in some private schools that the teachers are selected not on the basis of their qualifications but on that of recommendation. Consequently, a large number of incompetent teachers are found in some private schools. Such teachers cannot fulfil their obligation.

It is also seen that the headmaster's or the principals's opinion is very often not listened to and the majority in the Managing Committee has the last word. This state of affairs is very regrettable. The headmaster or the principal has to work with the teachers and as such his opinion in this regard should carry weight.

Making the Teaching Profession More Attractive

Due to trivial reasons the teaching profession has today ceased to be attractive, and only those who have failed to achieve success elsewhere opt for this profession. Today the teachers do not enjoy that respect which they did in the past and consequently they have developed an inferiority complex.

Most of the teachers of private schools in many parts of our country feel constantly afraid lest they should be served a notice terminating their services any time. This feeling of insecurity keeps them depressed and they cannot work wholeheartedly.

If we wish to raise the standard of the teaching profession we will have to remove the above mentioned defects because unless this is done it will be difficult to find teachers with the aforesaid qualifications. In order to make the teaching profession more attractive the Mudaliar Commission* has made some recommendations. We shall mention below some of its important suggestions.

Suggestions for the Betterment of the Teacher-Community

1. Uniform principles should be laid down for the appointment of teachers in all kinds of schools.
2. It is necessary to have a selection committee for the appointment of teachers in all private schools and those run by the local boards. The headmaster should be part of this committee.
3. The probation period for trained teacher should be of one year.
4. Trained graduates for all subjects should be appointed in high schools, while teachers with higher qualifications should be selected for higher secondary schools.
5. Teachers doing the same kind of work should be placed in the same pay scale and the same category.
6. In order to set the minds of the teachers free from worry for the future, provision should be made for pension, provident fund, insurance, etc.
7. Committees should be set up to give a hearing to the appeals made by the teachers in regard to their dismissal or termination of service.
8. The age of the retirement of teachers who are physically sound should be fixed at 60 in consultation with the Director of Education.
9. Free education should be given to the children of the teachers up to the level of the school.
10. With the help of the co-operative societies residences for teachers should be built near about the school.

---

* Report of the Secondary Education Commission, 1952-53, pp. 174-76.

11. Teachers who want to go out of station during holidays or to participate in some conference or seminar, should be given travel concessions.
12. Free medical treatment should be given to ailing teachers.
13. There should be uniform rules for leave in all the schools.
14. The practice of private tuition should be abolished.
15. The salary of the teachers should be raised to such an extent that it attracts competent and able men to the teaching profession. The salary of the headmaster also should be high so that good and able men may come to the profession.

Training Colleges have an important role in making a teacher efficient. Hence the Mudaliar Commission also hinted at the responsibility of the training colleges in this regard. Apart from their regular training courses, these colleges should organise refresher courses, conferences and seminars. The efficiency of a teacher may be improved a great deal by these means. If the teaching profession becomes attractive, able persons will join the training colleges and thus the number of able and competent teachers will increase. The practice of charging fees in training colleges should be abolished and good arrangements should be made for the residence of teacher-students. If the above suggestions are implemented, the teacher community will undoubtedly make a tremendous progress.

Distribution of Work Amongst Teachers

While distributing responsibilities amongst the teachers the headmaster or the principal should bear certain aspects in mind. The principal should not think that some individuals are totally incapable and also that everyone cannot be good at everything. We are mentioning below those things which a principal should bear in mind while distributing work.

1. *Individual Allocations:* The principal should try to allot work to the teachers according to their tastes. Some teachers are greatly interested in games and sports, while others in work pertaining to literary assemblies etc. Hence, individual tastes should be considered in the allotment of work, else the teacher will not be able to put in his best.

2. *Individual ability:* Individual abilities should be carefully considered while allotting the work. In our schools there prevails the practice of allotting ninth and tenth classes to graduates, seventh and eighth classes to under-graduates, and other lower classes to matriculates. The qualifications of a teacher are solely assesse by the examination passed by him, but it should also be seen whether a teacher has the ability to teach a particular subject or not. Classes and subjects to be taught should be allotted on the basis of the ability of the teacher. It is quite possible that some Intermediate and High School passed teachers of experience may be able to teach higher classes. Such a teacher should be given higher classes. The principle that the junior teacher should always be given junior classes and the senior higher ones, should not be blindly followed.

The Ideas and Temperament of the Teacher: Besides individual tendency and ability, the ideas, shortcomings and temperament of the teachers should also be taken into account while allotting work. A teacher should be given a class after the due consideration of all these factors.

Class-Master or Specialist Teacher: One method of the distribution of work is that a single teacher is asked to teach all the subjects to a class. This is called a class-master system. The other one is that in which different subjects are taught by different teachers. This is called the specialist system. We shall discuss below the merits and demerits of these systems:

Merits of the Class-Master System: In this system the teacher comes into closer contact with the students and can thus impress the students with his personality all the more. Another theory is that when a teacher teaches all the subjects in a class he can co-ordinate his lessons and thus correlate the different subjects. This will lead to a proper co-ordination of the knowledge of the students. The outlook of the teacher teaching all the subjects also becomes broad because then he does not keep himself tied down to the narrow limits of the particular subject. The broad outlook of the teacher helps to broaden the horizon of the students also. Due to this method the timetable of the school is easily prepared and the work also goes on smoothly.

Defect of the Class-Master System: It may be argued against this method that one single teacher cannot do full justice to all the subjects because no one can be a master of all subjects. He cannot also have the knowledge of the method of teaching of all those subjects. It is also said that the students feel bored with the same teacher teaching all the subjects and because of the same method of teaching the pleasure of reading decreases.

Merits of the Specialist System: When a teacher teaches the same subject to different classes he masters the principles of teaching that subject. Being thoroughly at home in that subject, he teaches it well and makes it very attractive to the students. The specialist system affords to the teacher the opportunity of deep study and research in the subject. It needs no specific clarification that his knowledge and erudition make a good impression on the students. In this specialist system the students come into contact with different teachers and derive benefits out of the contact with different personalities. In this way their mental horizon and their ideas become very broad. In higher classes a single teacher cannot teach all the subjects satisfactorily. Hence it appears necessary to adopt the specialist system.

Defect of the Specialist System: The great defect of this system is that the teacher remains confined to his own subject only and he finds it difficult to bring about a co-ordination with other subjects. In this system the teacher gives greater importance to his own subjects and tends to neglect the work in regard to other subjects. Hence, this system is not suitable for lower classes. In this system the attention of the teacher is riveted not on the child but on his own subject. So there is no contact of personalities.

From the above discussion we arrive at the conclusion that for lower classes (up to seventh or eighth) the class-master system should be adopted as far as possible, because at this stage individual contact and co-ordination of subjects is necessary. One teacher is fully responsible for the whole class and he looks after all the children. This is very important for lower classes. From the ninth class, the students have, under the prevailing system of education, some freedom in selecting subjects of their own choice. Hence the specialist system can be adopted from this stage.

The headmaster or the principal should keep the following facts in mind while allotting work to the teachers:

1. All the teachers should be allowed to express their opinion in regard to the distribution of work so that the scheme of work may be chalked out in such a way that the teacher may take it to be his own and may give his full co-operation. The headmaster or the principal should have full confidence in the abilities of the teacher. Nobody else knows anything. After the distribution of the work, each teacher should be given freedom to work in his sphere. This is the demand of democratic education and with the conceding of this demand, democratic feelings will be instilled in all.
2. In distributing the work all teachers should be given equal consideration. Such a situation in which the load of work is too much on some teachers and too little on others should be avoided, because this leads to discontentment among the teachers.
3. In the distribution of work, all the requisite facilities should be provided to all the teachers.
4. After the distribution of work, the principal should inspect the work and keep a record of each teacher's work in separate books.
5. Meetings of teachers should be convened occasionally in order to discuss the system of distribution of work. A plan which is made in consultation with the majority of teachers will definitely be the best.

The teachers besides teaching have to complete some other jobs also namely, maintaining attendance and marks, realising monthly dues, and keeping a diary, etc. In this way the teachers are burdened with work and because of this they should be given the greatest possible help, encouragement and advice. If along with this, necessary facilities are also provided, their teaching efficiency will certainly improve. How splendid would it be if the authorities concerned relieve the teachers from such clerical work as the maintaining of registers, and with the time thus saved from this mechanical labour they try to increase their teaching efficiency.

Summary

The teacher is the ideal for the child. Therefore, he must have various qualities. He should bear an exemplary character. He should have affection and respect for children. Apart from these qualities, he should have devotion to duty, ability to teach his subject, patience, a sense of humour, attractive personality, optimism, novelty, capacity for research work, and self-prestige.

Selection: At the time of selection, the comparative qualities of the candidates should be the main consideration. The opinion of the principal should be the deciding factor.

To Make the Profession Attractive: The profession of a teacher is no more an attractive one. It is necessary to provide various facilities to the teachers in order to make the profession more attractive. Increase in salaries, free education to their children, arrangement for pension and insurance, formation of autonomous committees to redress their grievances, etc., are some of the facilities, which should be extended to teachers.

Distribution of Work: In the distribution of the work, the principal or the headmasters should take into consideration the personal likings, qualifications, ideas and temperament of the teacher. As far as possible, class-teacher system should be adopted in lower classes and specialization system in the higher classes.

All the teachers should be consulted in the distribution of work, which should, as far as possible, be equal on all the teachers. Our teachers are overloaded with unnecessary work at times. They should be given the necessary facilities.

Exercises

1. What are the qualities necessary for a teacher?
2. What should be done to improve the conditions of our teachers?
3. What are the factors to be taken into consideration in the distribution of the teaching work?

Chapter 8

Admission and Classification of Students

Admission and classification of students imply the same thing because in a broad sense the question of their admission involves in itself their classification. We shall discuss here in brief the question of the admission of children and thereafter that of their classification.

Admission of Students

The question of admission of students comes before the principal of any school as the foremost consideration. In our country the guardians always try to get their wards admitted in the highest possible classes but the principal should always admit children to different classes strictly in accordance with their individual capacities so that all the students of the same class may study in a harmonious way. To do this the principal will have to consider the child's mental capacity, his knowledge and health.

Education develops the inherent capacities of the child and develops his personality to the highest point. In any country the children are its hopes and its wealth and the progress of the country depends upon them. Hence it is the duty of the country and the society to protect them as well as to equip them fully. The proper development of the personality of the student depends on the proper methods of suitable education. It is from this point of view that the Government Education Department has laid down certain rules relating to the admission and the education of children.

Unlike other countries, India has a very small number of nurseries for children of four or five years. Most of the children in our country, after reading at home till the age of four or five, join either Basic or Primary schools.

The Education Code mentions a few rules regarding the admission of students. The child cannot be admitted in the school without the consent of the headmaster or the principal and the guardian of the student. The satisfaction of the principal in regard to the age of the child is necessary. The principal can even ask the guardian to produce evidence of the age of the child. According to section 175 of the Uttar Pradesh Education Code, the child at the time of admission should be around 5 years old. Section 93 (A) of the Education Code lays down the ages of the children for admission to respective classes as follows:-

For the third class the maximum age is 12 years.

Similarly	for class	4 - 13	years
	for class	5 - 14	years
	for class	6 - 15	years
	for class	7 - 16	years
	for class	8 - 17	years
	for class	9 - 18	years
	for class	10 - 19	years

A student who wishes to be admitted into an institution has to submit a copy of the Admission Register or a School Leaving Certificate of the institution previously attended by him.

In the question of admission of students we have to consider the number of students in each class. The number of students in each class is closely related with the development of the child. This development implies his social development which is possible only if the number of students in each class is such that proper attention can be paid to the individual differences of students. The lower the class the smaller should be the number of students because there is greater need to pay special attention towards the small children. The teacher has to keep his eye on each and every activity of the children. Hence, the number of students in a class should be fixed in such a way that all the qualities of the class teacher may be exploited and the individual differences of students may be attended to. Then only the development of the child will proceed on the right lines.

Various experiments have been tried in foreign countries in regard to the fixing of the number of students in each class, and the conclusion that has been drawn is that there should not be more than forty-five students in any class. According to section 96(B) of the Uttar Pradesh Education Code, the number of students in each class has been fixed as follows:-

33 in Primary classes
35 Middle classes
40 Ninth and Tenth classes
50 Intermediate classes

But this rule is followed no where. Now in each class there are 50 students or even more.

The child should be first allowed to sit in a class and if he proves suitable for the same he should be allowed to continue, else he should be put into another class. The criterion for the progress and development of the child should not be merely getting through in an examination because his real progress lies in the all-round development.

In order to give consideration to the individual differences it will be better if each child is placed under the supervision of a single teacher. In this way only the teacher will be able to scrutinise each and every activity of the child and will be of great help in his development. It is not possible to have a separate teacher for each child because this scheme involves a lot of expenditure and also because so many teachers are not easily available. The number of students in a class should be such that the greatest possible attention may be paid to the individual differences of students and in addition to this the distribution of classes should be made from the point of view of the similarities among the students.

Classification of Students

The classification of students should be made in such a way that there may be similarity among the students in a class as far as possible. It should be better if the following facts are borne in mind while the students are being classified:-

1. Intelligence.
2. The results of the previous examinations.

3. Interest.
4. Sex.
5. Physical fitness.

1. Intelligence: By intelligence we mean the intellectual capacity of the student which is hereditary in him. Some intellectual capacity and emotions come to the students as an inheritance at birth. These may be estimated by means of mental testing. We can also find by this means the intelligence quotient of each child and thus students with a similar intelligence quotient may be placed in the same class.

Besides intelligence testing, achievement test and performance test also help us a great deal in the classification of students and we should take their help. In our country these are not generally used, because these have not been planned from the viewpoint of our students.

2. Result of Previous Examinations: When classifying students the previous records of their achievements in examinations should also be considered. The student should not be admitted all at once. He should be allowed first to sit in a class and if he proves to possess abilities similar to those of the other students in the class he should be permitted to continue, else he should be transferred to another class. In the classification of the students, use can be made of the reports of the teachers as also of the results of the monthly, half-yearly and annual examinations.

3. Interest: The individual interest of the student also has a great importance in the classification. In fact, one has to have a taste for a particular subject in order to study it. To teach to the student a subject in which he is not interested is to ask him to do the impossible. For this it is very necessary that the subject should be made attractive to the student. The interest of the student develops in the school. Students of similar taste should be put in the same class.

4. Sex: There are some natural differences between man and woman. These are indicated from the very beginning by the process of the development of boys and girls. Boys and girls may be taught together in the same class of the same school, till the age of eleven. But after this the physical and mental development of the girls is more rapid than that of the boys who lag far behind. Under such conditions it will not be proper to teach them in the same class. This is the reason why in higher secondary schools boys and girls do not read together. At the age of eighteen the development of the girl goes on very slowly for some years. The growth of the boy does not stop and his physical development goes on in the same way. At this stage, the boy gains in physical strength. After this age, the boys and girls may be taught together. Thus in the classification of students the consideration of sex is also important.

5. Physical Fitness: Before making any classification, the children should be physically examined and should be classified accordingly. To a great extent physical health determines the mental prowess of an individual. The physically weak student cannot keep pace with the physically fit one. The aim of education is not only to bring about the mental development of the child. In fact, the teachers have to pay attention also to the health of children. In order that a student may work satisfactorily with other children in the class it is necessary to consider the health of the children while classifying them.

Along with health it is also necessary to consider the age and height of the children. Various tastes and powers develop in a child according to his physical development. Hence, students of the same age group should be put in one class, because then only will they be able to work in co-operation with one another. The education of children should be according to their processes of development and tastes and capacities.

When classifying the students, their height also has to be considered. It will not be good to make a tall boy sit in the midst of short statured ones and vice-versa. Such students will regard themselves as different from others and will not mix with them. This will create in them a feeling of inferiority.

A classification made on the above mentioned lines will prove good and it will be easier to consider the individual differences of most of the children. Along with the classification of the children the consideration of their individual differences depends much on the ability of the teacher. The teacher should try to know more about the child. He should sort out such students who can progress along with the other children of the class and thereafter apply to them the necessary tests and then try to remove their difficulties. If these students do not fit in with the class, they should be transferred to another class. It is not proper to promote the children to higher classes only on the basis of one examination. The promotion to another class should be based on the work during the year. The health and physical development of the child should also be fully considered.

Summary

In a wide context, the admission and classification of students are identical problems.

Admission of Students: The principal should admit students according to their qualifications. They should be admitted to various classes according to their intelligence, learning capability and health.

The highest development of a child's personality depends upon his proper education. Some rules and regulations have been prescribed in the Education Code regarding the admission of students. The Principal should satisfy himself in respect of student's date of birth. The minimum age for admission to a basic school should be 5 years. The maximum ages for admission to various classes have been detailed out in the Education Code. The maximum number of students admitted to a primary class should be 33, to a middle class 35, to IX and X classes 40 and to an Intermediate class 50.

Classification of Students: It will be advisable to consider the following factors in the classification of students:-

1. *Intelligence:-* It is necessary to take into account the child's intelligence. It can be ascertained through intelligence testing.

2. *Records of Examinations:-* At first the students should be allowed to sit in a class for some days. If he proves worthy of that class, only then he should be allowed to remain in that class. The quarterly, half-yearly and yearly examination results and annual progress reports may also help in the classification.

3. *Interest:-* Interest plays a very important role in the process of learning. The student having the same interests should be kept in one class.

4. *Sex:-* It is necessary to consider the sex in the above classification.

5. *Physical Health:-* A physical check up should be prescribed for students. The performance of a student also depends on the physical force. It is also necessary to pay due attention towards the child's age and height, otherwise an inferiority complex will creep in into the

child's personality. The student of lower age or short stature keeps himself away from the company of others. This habit casts adverse effect on his development.

Exercises

1. What are the rules regarding the admission of students as detailed in the Education Code? What is their importance in your view?
2. What are the factors to be taken into account in the classification of students? What can be the consequences of their contravention?

Chapter 9

Timetable

The students spend quite a long time at school where they do different kinds of work. At school they not only read in the classrooms but besides this they also take part in games and sports, etc. All the work is carried out systematically by means of a timetable so that while making the best use of their time they may work in co-operation and gain varied experience. Hence, it is necessary to have in the school a proper division of time. The successful working of a school depends on a suitable timetable.

Need for the Timetable

It is difficult to carry out the work of the school without a proper timetable. In its absence the headmaster or the principal cannot know what subjects are being taught to different classes at a particular time or what work is being done or even which teacher is teaching which subject. Hence, for the proper management of the school and to carry out all the work properly it is necessary to have a scheme or table of work and all the work should be done in accordance with it. In this way there will be no danger of any kind of mismanagement of the school work and the headmaster or the principal will be in a position to know what work is being done by the students of a particular class at a particular time. The timetable will help him in carrying out the work of the school efficiently. He will also be able to make arrangements for another teacher when any one is absent.

The school should have two kinds of timetables one pertaining to the teachers and the other to various classes. The first one will indicate the subjects and periods of the teachers and the second will deal with the work of the different classes.

The scheme of timetable will deal not only with the subjects of study of the student but with his work in the school including games, sports and other co-curricular activities. The proper utilisation of time, smooth working and the success of the work of the school depends largely on a suitable timetable.

The Importance of Timetable and its Uses

With the help of a suitable timetable the teachers and the students retain interest in their work and they do not find their work of teaching and reading cumbersome. By working according to a fixed timetable efficiency is gained and the good habit of working in a systematic manner is formed. This also trains the teachers and the students to make proper use of their time.

Due to the timetable the students know the work they have to do within the prescribed time limit. In this way they become clear in regard to their objectives and they do not have to waste their time in schools.

The timetable also helps in maintaining discipline among the students. The timetable should be drawn out in such a way that the students do not waste their time in wandering about but remain busy in their work. Indiscipline is rampant among students of those schools which do not have a good timescheme and thus due to remaining idle they are led into thinking of undesirable things. Hence the timetable has a great bearing on the discipline in the school. If the time of the students is properly utilised, they will be well-disciplined.

General Principles of Timetable Construction

We have mentioned above the need and the importance of the timetable. We shall discuss below those general principles which should be borne in mind while drawing out the timetable.

1. The ideal thing will be to allow the students to choose the subjects they like to read in different periods, as is done in many Western countries. But due to our particular circumstances, it is difficult, and impossible to do this. The reason for this is the paucity of funds in the schools, the

shortage of teachers and the lack of proper accommodation. Besides, we do not have sufficient number of subjects which the students may choose from. Students select only subjects of a particular group and have to read them according to the timetable of the schools. Under such circumstances, the interests of the students should be considered while drawing the timetable so that the students may get sufficient time to read the subjects of their choice. The timetable will have to be prepared with great care.

2. The aptitudes of the students in regard to subjects may be found out in two ways. The first method is that the teachers may draw out a tentative list of the subjects for which the students have an aptitude and then give them due place in the timetable. The second method of finding out the aptitude of the students is asking them to name the subjects of their choice. It is evident that the second method will be more suitable. In this way, the timetable drawn out in accordance with the taste of the students will be more suitable, but in our country no attention is paid in this direction. In many schools timetables are drawn out beforehand and in some schools the students have to study according to the timetable of the previous years. It is generally seen that in higher classes more than one subject are taught in a period. So a student cannot read more than one subject of his choice at a time.
3. It is also necessary to keep the courses in view while drawing the timetable. The period fixed for various subjects during the week should be in conformity with the syllabus. All the subjects should find a place in the timetable and the number of period for the teaching of any subject during the week should be fixed according to the syllabus.
4. Close contact between teachers and students is of great importance. The teacher may be of use to the student only when he has the necessary information about the student. Unless the teachers establish a close contact with the students it will be difficult for them to pay attention to their individual differences. The teachers in our country regard it as a sign of their superiority to remain serious and aloof from the students.

This attitude is not proper and hence the timetable should be drawn in such a way that the teachers and the students may come into as close a contact as possible. For this purpose, occasionally such activities should be organised in the schools which may bring the teachers and the students into contact even outside the classroom so that they may get an opportunity of understanding each other. This will also help in maintaining discipline among the students.

5. While drawing up the timetable the headmaster or the principal should not consider the aptitudes of the students only but should also pay sufficient attention to the taste of the teachers. Hence, the subjects to be taught should be allotted according to the abilities of the teachers. If a teacher is given a subject in which he is least interested, he will not take any interest in teaching it and the students will not be able to derive full benefit from his abilities. Thus most of the time of the students will be wasted.
6. All the teachers of the school do not have similar or equal abilities. There are some who can work more than others but the principal has to allot equal work in the timetable to all the teachers and also has to consider their abilities and potentialities. While allotting a subject to any teacher it should be borne in mind that an equal amount of labour is not needed in teaching all the subjects. There are some subjects like English and Mathematics in which the teachers have to work harder, while in history and civics they have to work comparatively less. Hence, while drawing up the timetable it should be kept in view that the observance of the timetable is not burdensome to the teacher.
7. The timetable should not relate only to the courses of study but to all the activities of the school. In our schools at present, attention is given to the prescribed courses and to imparting bookish knowledge. This hampers the all-round development of the child. Hence, the timetable should be drawn in such a way that no child should remain aloof from any programme in the school, that is, from activities pertaining to the playing-field, library and courses.

8. As has been indicated above the principal while drawing up the timetable should bear in mind that the timetable should be helpful in instructing the students in efficient working, observance of principle, proper use of time and in the strengthening of determination. If the timetable aims at these, the school will be able to achieve its ideals, for the timetable is a means to this end.
9. The timetable should not be such that the child does not understand it easily. If the children have to go to different classrooms in various periods, much time is wasted in this way. Special attention should be paid in this respect to children of lower classes.
10. We have mentioned above the need of keeping in mind the courses while drawing up the timetable. The time required for covering the prescribed portion of the course in a particular class should be equitably distributed for the whole year. The work relating to the prescribed subjects can be fixed by the teachers for each month, week or even day for various classes. Its greatest advantage will be that all the subjects will be given the requisite time. This will also include the teaching work of the teachers for each week and day. But at present there is a lot of confusion in our schools in this matter, so much so that, most of the teachers leave their homes without knowing what they will have to teach that day. The diary which is given to the teachers is just in name and mostly the teachers fill up the diary in one day. If the teaching work of the teacher is fixed, the time of the students will not be wasted. This will also enable the principal to know which teacher needs more time for teaching his subject.
11. In the timetable each subject should be given due place. Along with this, as mentioned earlier, requisite time should also be given to games, exercises, literary get-togethers and other educative activities. It is very difficult to give necessary time to each subject in lower or higher classes, because for different subjects in each class a different duration of time cannot be fixed. But it is possible to have the later periods of shorter duration than the earlier ones.

Aspects Relating to Fatigue

We have mentioned above a few principles relating to the framing of the timetable. We shall discuss below some such aspects which, if considered well, will not make students tired.

There are some days in the week when the students are less inclined to study than on other days. Hence, such days should also be considered in the timetable. The school opens, barring Sunday, for fix days in the week. From Saturday the students begin to think about the Sunday holiday, and they wish on Saturday to finish quickly, so that they may enjoy one day's holiday. Similarly on Mondays the students do not come in a proper frame of mind to study because the hang-over of the previous day's holiday continues. Thus both Mondays and Saturdays are not regarded as good days for hard study. On both these days the students are inclined to be indolent or have the holiday mood. From the point of view of teaching the remaining four days i.e. Tuesday, Wednesday, Thursday and Friday are regarded as good days. Hence, it is quite natural for the students to be devoted to their work on these days as it is to be indifferent on Mondays and Saturdays. The teachers should remember this because this will help them in fixing the work for the whole week. It will be proper if the teachers do not teach difficult portions of the lesson on Saturdays. Thus, if a teacher has to teach Mathematics on Monday, he should take up geometry for it is comparatively easier. Similarly it will be better not to teach Sanskrit grammar on these days. It is necessary to follow this method, in order to make the students retain their interest in the subjects.

The Place of Various Subjects and the Sequence of Periods

Some subjects are more difficult than others. Therefore such arrangements should be made for the teaching of these subjects which help the students in reading them. For such subjects the best hour or period of the day when the students are fresh in mind, should be fixed, Mathematics and Language are such subjects. If difficult subjects are taught in continuous periods, the students feel tired and they cannot devote full attention to such subjects. Consequently, due to lack of interest these subjects become difficult. As such it is necessary that difficult subjects should not be taught one after another.

Usually it is not proper to have the same kind of work in two periods, for example, it is not good to make the students do written work for two or three periods because written work can thus become distasteful. Hence, it will be more interesting as well as psychologically proper to have oral work after written work. It is also necessary along with this to give some rest in between so that they may refreshen their energies. In the last period when the students feel tired after the day's work, subjects entailing brain work should not be taught. It will be better if games, physical exercises and other similar activities are arranged in these periods.

Just as Monday is not regarded as a good day for hard work, so also it is not possible for the students to set himself to hard work soon after coming to school. Hence, it will be better to create an atmosphere of study by means of prayers etc. After two or three hours of work the students begin to experience lethargy. When the school starts working at 10 o'clock the students become lethargic at about midday. It is necessary to give the students some recess at this time, for after this the students will again apply themselves to hard work. The second and third periods, as also the one after the recess, are such when the students can devote themselves easily to any subject. Hence, difficult subjects like Mathematics and Languages should be taught in such periods. What is suitable for the students will be so for the teachers also. They should not be given either difficult subjects or a single difficult subject to teach in one period after another in succession.

Fatigue, the Period and the Age of Children

The capacity to do any work or the amount of interest taken in it depends on the age of the children. Small children cannot concentrate on any subject for a long time. Hence the teacher should take care not to make the students do one kind of work for such a long time that they may become tired. Although children differ from one another in their capacity for work, yet usually children between 6 and 10 years of age can rivet their attention on a subject for twenty minutes, those of 12 years for twenty-five minutes, of 14 years for half an hour and those of a higher age group for forty-five minutes or so. The concentration of the mind depends to a large extent on the will of the student. It will be improper, for the student, to teach him a subject for more than the requisite time. Change of subject is a very helpful in removing fatigue. While teaching, written and oral work should be taught alternately to get best results. This plan depends upon the teacher. When he finds the children tired, he should bring about a change in the work expected from the children, in the teaching of a particular subject, so that the muscles which are not being used and are lying idle may become active and the others which were being used may relax a little.

Surroundings, Classrooms and the Weather

Besides the above there are some other things also which tire the students. First of all there is the location of the school and the classrooms. If the school is situated at such a place where the atmosphere is not peaceful or its construction is not very suitable, it is natural for the children to get tired soon. The proper accommodation in the classroom, fresh air and proper light, all these also are related to the physical and mental fatigue of the children. Apart from this, if the weather is not good and the rooms are very hot, the children will soon get tired. Hence in the school timetable it should also be considered that the load of work should be less in summers and more in winter. In this, the situation and the construction of the classroom are of great importance.

The Work in the Beginning and in the End

The principal should bear in mind that the time for the working of the school may be conducive to the atmosphere during the whole day and can also take the mind of the children to the required level. Hence, it is necessary to have the children do some such work in the beginning as may be conducive to the necessary atmosphere and therefore no distasteful work should be given in the beginning. In the beginning, prayers and some such work which may instil enthusiasm in them, should be done. Similarly, the children carry home the impression left on their minds in the last periods in the school. If some interesting work is done in the last period the children carry home happy recollections and impressions. Thus an interest in school will be created in them. Hence it will be better if in the last periods games, music and literary activities are fixed.

Timetable should be Flexible

The timetable should not be made in such a way that no change in it may be possible. The timetable should be helpful in successfully carrying out the work of the school. It is only a means for the fulfilment of the ideals of the school and it will be wrong to regard it as an end in itself. Hence the timetable should be such as to permit changes. On occasions there may arise such situations when a change may be necessary.

Some system of education like the Project Method and the Dalton Plan have objected against the use of timetable. According to these the children in the schools should not be compelled to conform to any fixed timetable. The child should have complete freedom of work in the school and he should be allowed to work according to his own free will because he gains experience out of the work done by himself. But due to the conditions obtaining in our country, the Project Method or the Dalton Plan cannot be enforced.

Timetable cannot be Flawless

It is extremely difficult to have a timetable which is completely free from defects. It is impossible to fix different periods of work strictly in accordance with the individual capacities of each child. It is the opinion of the advocates of the Dalton Plan, Project Method and Playway system that by means of the timetable the students are robbed of their freedom and they do not remain free to work according to their own will. The children are tied down by difficult rules and regulations in the school. Some subjects require less time whereas some others more. This fact is not considered in the framing of the timetable. Sufficient time is not given to all the subjects and the children cannot study all the subjects with equal care and interest and without feeling tired because the reading of other subjects produce fatigue. The timetable fixes the work for each day and because of rigidity and inflexibility in the timetable they begin to find it monotonous. It is difficult to give due consideration to all the individual peculiarities of students in the timetable. The children do not get the opportunity to work together or solve problems or learn from their personal experiences. In this way it is quite natural to find such defects in the timetable. Periods after the interval are considered good. The work of the same nature should not be given to children for a long time. But this does not imply that the timetable serves no useful purpose. If the timetable is made after due consideration of the aspects mentioned earlier, it will prove very useful. We should remember that under the present circumstances the work of the school cannot be carried out without a timetable.

Summary

The affairs of a school can be conducted in an organised way through a timetable and the students may make a maximum utilisation of their time.

The Necessity of a Timetable:- The timetable is necessary for the proper management of the affairs of a school. Through this, the principal knows the work of every class and every teacher. The timetable is concerned with all the activities of the students.

The Significance of Timetable and its Uses:- The work according to a fixed schedule brings efficiency and skill. The good habit of working regularly is cultivated. It results in the saving and proper utilisation of the time. The children stick to the target. It helps to maintain discipline and order.

Important Points in Preparing the Timetable:- Arrangements may be made for the study of subjects at the proper time according to the student's interests. The subjects of their interest should be elicited from them. Attention should also be paid towards the syllabus. Facilities and opportunities should be offered to establish close relationship between teachers and students. The interests of the teachers should also find a place in the timetable. The load of work should be equal on all the teachers. Only textbooks should not be their concern. The timetable should be so prepared as to let them teach the students efficiency in work, regularity, proper utilisation of time and firmness. The timetable should be intelligible to the students. Each year's programme should be fixed in the case of the teachers. Every subject should get sufficient time according to necessity.

Key Points About Fatigue:- Consideration for week days: Saturdays and Mondays are not suitable for teaching, like other days of the week.

The place of various subjects and their turns should be well-determined. Such periods should be allotted to tough subjects, when the mind of the child is not tired.

The power of working or concentrating the attention is subject to the age of the child.

Timetable should be flexible:- The teacher should work according to the schedule of the timetable.

Nowadays the Project Method, Dalton Plan and Playway Method are not in favour of the timetable.

There are some inherent defects in the timetable prepared in our schools.

Exercises

1. What is the necessity of timetable for schools? What are its advantages?
2. What points should be taken into account, while preparing the timetable?
3. What factors are responsible for making children tired and what do you suggest to remove them?
4. Point out the merits and demerits of a timetable.

Chapter 10

Curriculum According to the Ideals and Needs

The proper organisation of the curriculum is necessary for the success of education. The curriculum should not be such that it does not allow any change when there is a need for it. It should be in conformity with the economic, social and political conditions of the country. The curriculum helps in the realisation of the desired goals. The ancient Spartans had organised such courses which were conducive to the development of the children as powerful soldiers because at that time they needed to defend their empire. The Athenians did not have a programme like that of the Spartans because they had different ideals. They wished to bring about the full development of the human personality by means of education. They did not aim only at giving military training to the boys. Hence, their courses of studies were different from those of the Spartans. The curriculum in Athens included various fine arts and religious subjects. Thus the curriculum is drawn out from the viewpoint of the needs and requirements of society and only that curriculum may be deemed suitable which fulfils the ideals of education as also the needs of the society. The progress of any country depends to a large extent on the courses of studies.

In ancient India Gurukuls were established to educate the children. The students resided in them and obtained education. At that time there were various castes and classes of people who educated their children in accordance with their vocations. At that time, education had a religious ideal as also a quest of the truth which transcended the visible world. Hence the curriculum was organised accordingly. During the medieval period the Muslims wanted the propagate their religion and with this end in view they established Maktabs etc. The British tried to consolidate their empire in India and to secure some assistance in administrative work through the courses of studies they organised these from this point of view.

The curriculum is organised in accordance with the conditions of the time and place. The courses of studies now-a-days should be organised according to the needs of our independent country. We wish to make advancement like other big nations in every field of life. The conditions in our country are now quite different. There is no religious fanaticism as in the past. With the progress of science man is getting involved all the more in materialism. Hence, religious and moral education is also needed today. These objectives may be achieved through a well-organised curriculum. Hence it will not be good to show indifference in the least towards the courses of studies.

Factors for Organising the Curriculum

Realising the importance of the syllabi the Education Departments in the various States in our country have taken upon themselves the work of drawing out the courses of studies. The teachers try to cover the prescribed course within the time fixed, but this does not in any way belittle their importance because the success of the courses depends largely on its being well organised in various classes. It is the duty of the principal to organise these courses in such a way that the all-round development of the students may be possible and the aim of education may also be fulfilled. For this it is necessary that useful subjects may be selected from the point of view of the students and these subjects should be such as may conduce to the physical, intellectual and moral development of the children, to the sharpening of their reasoning faculties, to the harnessing and organising of their imaginative faculty and their ideas, and thus to the building up of their character and thereby helping in the progress of the country.

It is necessary to keep in view certain things in order to implement at any place the prescribed courses in a well organised manner. First of all the curriculum of a school should be such as may fulfil the requirements of the place and may be in accordance with the circumstances obtaining there. It is necessary for the courses, to have a local bias, for example, it is necessary to teach agricultural subjects in the schools of a place which is primarily agricultural.

In the organisation of the courses both the physical and mental development of the child should be considered. It should be the all-round development of the child.

It is also necessary for the success of the curriculum that the school has a sufficient numbers of teachers, who maybe capable of teaching the various subjects.

The curriculum should be such as not to be contrary to the climatic and atmospheric conditions of the place. Apart from this sufficient time should be allotted for the completion of the courses.

For the successful implementation of the curriculum the school should have all the necessary equipment relating to its various courses. Then alone will it be possible to implement the curriculum well.

It should be borne in mind while drawing out the syllabus that the subjects of studies are meant for the children and not the children for the subjects. Hence, the subject and method of teaching should be to the benefit of the students. Subjects relating to the culture of the child, to his social and mental equipment and his general good, should be incorporated in the syllabus. Besides these, instruction in economics, mechanical training, and vocational guidance etc. should also be given. The syllabus should be such that all the necessary subjects pertaining to human life may be included in it.

Apart from the subjects of the syllabus the aspect of teaching them is not less important. The function of the teacher is to give the student a real understanding and knowledge of the subjects and along with this to help develop his imaginative faculty so that he may comprehend the subject in the desired way.

We shall now mention those principles of selection of subjects which should be borne in mind while organising the curriculum. There should be a criterion for assessing the value, and making a selection of various subjects for a curriculum. Only those subjects should be included which satisfy this criterion.

Principles of Organisation of Curriculum

The curriculum should be related to real life. For the co-operation between the school and society it is necessary that the school should fulfil the requirements of the society and this is possible only when the curriculum of the school is closely related with real life. At present the curriculum of secondary schools is defective. Even after completing his secondary education, the child is not fully educated and he is incapable of eking out his existence easily. The aim of the secondary school is not only to prepare students for universities. The education at this level should be such that the child may learn all that is necessary for his daily life, because a number of students discontinue their studies after this. Along with this, a knowledge of Language, Science and Mathematics should be given at this level in such a way that the students may experience no difficulty in the university.

Teaching of Mother-Tongue

Teaching of mother-tongue is of great importance and attention should be directed towards it from the primary stage. All the subjects should be taught through this. The deeper the child's knowledge of the mother-tongue the greater will be his capacity of self-expression and of concentration of thought. Students who do not have a good knowledge of the mother-tongue are usually not good at other subjects. Along with the mother-tongue, subjects like Arithmetic, Social Science, that is, History, Geography, and Civics, General Science and Music, etc. are not of less importance in the syllabus for primary schools. These subjects should be taught in greater detail in secondary schools. It will be good to impart instruction in some foreign language at the secondary stage. English language may be easily taught at this stage.

The Curriculum should be Comprehensive

The curriculum should be drawn out from the point of view of its need and utility. Since the requirement of individuals differ, the curriculum cannot be drawn out on any universal principle. The form of the curriculum should be very comprehensive in order that subjects of all kinds be included in it and the children may get education of their tastes and be successful in the campaign of life. According to some, instruction in the 3 Rs. should be included in the primary education of the children and after this at the secondary stage instruction should be given, from the point of view of the needs of life. Some people are totally averse to vocational instruction in schools, but it is good to give such instruction in the last years of the primary and secondary schools.

The Curriculum should Synthesise the Requirements of the Child and the Society

Along with the requirements of the life of the child, the requirements of the society should also be given a consideration in the curriculum, because from birth the child becomes a member of the society and owes a responsibility towards it. Education does not imply the imparting of instruction in some particular subjects only. In fact, it should be related to the whole life of the child. It should be borne in mind while drawing up the curriculum that both the child and the society are the main adjuncts of the curriculum. Hence, on one hand the child's tastes, inclinations and individual differences have to be considered, and on other his environment, that is, the society, because the child has to do his duty towards society. Hence, there should be a complete synthesis between the requirements of both the child and the society in the curriculum.

Independence of the School

The school should have complete freedom in the organisation of the courses. The government should only lay down some general principles so that no school in the country may go against it. While teaching, the teacher should have complete freedom. It is wrong to draw out one uniform syllabus for all the schools, because the capacities and the requirements of all the children are not alike. When given freedom, the responsibility of the teachers will increase and to discharge these responsibilities new trained teachers will be needed. Besides, for the success of the teachers and of the school, necessary changes will have to be made in the social and economic set-up.

The teachers should not, on getting this freedom, forget their duty. Some people have doubts that as a result of this freedom the teachers will teach only from those books which will be easily available and then they will not discharge their duty in regard to the teaching in the school. There is a danger of neglect of such duty but this can be due to two reasons: (a) lack of necessary facilities and (b) dearth of good teachers. After overcoming both these difficulties, the educational organisation may be successful. For example, such difficulties had cropped up in the educational organisation in USA, but after removing them the educational system has proved a great success.

When the teacher becomes responsible for organising the courses, he will have to pay special attention to certain things. These are as follows:

Consideration of the Child's Aptitude, Capacity and Needs: It is necessary for the expected development of the child that proper attention is given to his different aptitudes, capacity and needs. Hence the aim of the courses should be pre-determined. The teacher should start the education of each child from the stage at which the child is. Thus the child will be educated in a psychological manner. It is very necessary to know about the disposition, capacity and requirements of the child. For this, intelligence testing and aptitude testing will be of great help.

Importance of Textbooks and educational Aids: Textbooks and educational aids have a particular importance in the curriculum. If these materials are not available, the success of the syllabus will become doubtful. Hence, these should be sought out before organising the courses. The children are instructed by means of education and for this certain equipment is required. Without the necessary implements, maps and drawings, the teaching of Science, Geography and History will be useless. Hence, for successful teaching the above mentioned aids should be available. The courses should be organised from the point of view of the available materials and efforts should be made by the schools to increase them. The teachers should not rest content only with the available materials.

Curriculum only Means: It will be a blunder to regard the syllabus as an end in itself, for, it is only a means for the fulfilment of the aims of education. It is attempted to bring about by means of the curriculum the development of some desired capacity in the children and to enable them to understand the various aspects of culture. Thus a regular development is brought about. That is to say, the aim of the curriculum is not only to give the students some acquaintance with certain subjects but to create by it such an ability in the children that they may contribute towards the development of civilisation. For this it is necessary that the child is taught in an interesting way, because the thing in which the child feels interested is easily learnt by him.

We may state in the following way the above mentioned principles of the organisation of courses:

1. The curriculum should be suitable to the social and economic conditions of the country.
2. In the curriculum attention should be given towards the all-round development of the child, for the curriculum is for the children and not vice versa.
3. The curriculum should be flexible so that necessary changes may be made from time to time.
4. There should be a synthesis in the curriculum of the interests of the individual and the society.
5. It should be progressive.
6. It should relate to the entire environment of the child and only books should not form its basis.
7. The curriculum should be life-centred.
8. It should help to solve the problem of the earning of livelihood.
9. Particular attention should be paid to the teaching of the mother-tongue.
10. The various subjects of the curriculum should be interrelated.

Demand for the Reorganisation of Syllabus

At present there is an all-round demand for the reorganisation of the curriculum. There are several reasons for this. Due to various scientific inventions as also due to the democratic way of thinking in the country, the value of life has undergone a great change, and this change is fast developing. Consequently, we wish that our educational pattern should be in keeping with these changed conditions. For this it is necessary that various social activities should find a place in the schools, that is, the schools should come closer to society. This will enable the students to acquire efficiency in social work with the help of the school. It is evident that we shall have to make a great change in the curriculum in keeping with the changed outlook.

There has been an increase in the variety of vocations in the country, although there is still a demand to increase these further.

Consequently, greater accent is being given on vocational education in the curriculum.

With the help of various psychological investigations the aptitudes of the children are being found out. A demand is being made to widen the scope of the curriculum in keeping with these.

With a view to reforming the prevalent curriculum of schools in the country, the Kothari Commission Government of India (1964-66) has put forth several suggestions. Their value can be realized only after they are implemented. The readers may themselves assess the utility of these recommendations on the basis of the discussion in the foregoing pages.

Summary

The curriculum are organised on the basis of national needs, contemporary conditions and objectives of education. Now our country is passing through a transitional period. Therefore, the curricula are to be prepared accordingly.

The State Education Department is responsible for preparation of curricula, but it does not undermine the importance of teachers. The curriculum should be so designed as to develop the children both physically and mentally, and by providing good shape to their imaginations and ideas, by building up their character the society may progress.

It is necessary to pay attention to some important factors while considering the organisation for the curriculum in a well-organised manner. The duty of teacher is not only to teach the child various subjects but his power of imagination is also to be developed.

The Relation of Curriculum with Life: To meet the needs of the society the relation of the curriculum with practical life is very necessary.

The Teaching of Mother-Tongue: For the centralisation of ideas due emphasis should be given to the teaching of the mother-tongue. Along with the mother-tongue, Arithematic, Social Science, General Science, Music and other subjects should also be included in the curriculum. The constructive power of the child should be developed. The curriculum should be comprehensive so that the children of various talents may receive education according to their taste.

In the curriculum there should be a co-ordination of the needs of the child as well as the society.

When allowing an institution to organise its own curriculum freely, the responsibility of the teacher increases. He should pay attention to the taste, capacity and needs of the child, while organising the curriculum.

The availability of the textbooks and appliances as prescribed in the curriculum is very necessary.

The curriculum should be treated as a means and not an end. The demand for the improvement of the curriculum is increasing nowadays.

Exercises

1. Discuss some main factors of curriculum organisation.
2. Discuss the curriculum of the Junior High School of your State.
3. Discuss the merits and demerits of the present curriculum of the High Schools and frame an ideal curriculum for classes IX and X.

Chapter 11

Co-Curricular Activities: Games & Exercises within School Hours*

Before Independence the educational system of India had the sole aim of producing loyal servants for the continuance of the British Rule in the country. The education of those days was a mechanical means of turning out office workers mainly. The courses of study were also in keeping with the ideals of education of that time. After the achievement of independence the evolution of the democratic system of education led to tremendous changes in the ideals of education. Under the new educational ideal the schools have been imbued with form of a society in miniature and thereby given the responsibility of bringing about the all-round development of the future citizens of the country. The aim of education is no more mere imparting of bookish knowledge but to make the youth good citizens by bringing about their mental, physical and social development. That is why it has become necessary to accord a proper place to the various co-curricular activities in the educational set-up.

These co-curricular activities are based on the spirit of co-operation and have social import. Co-curricular activities can be divided into two categories. The first constitutes those which greatly influence the physical development of the child, while developing in him the social spirit and in the second category are those which have a great bearing upon mental development. In the first are included games, sports, physical exercises, N.C.C., N.S.S. Training and Scouting and those activities of the monitorial guides which relate to physical development. The second includes the literary meets in the school,

---

* Towards the close of the Book in chapters No. 29, 30 & 31, we will discuss the importance of other types of Co-curricular activities that may be organised after the general school timetable meant for teaching various subjects.

students' committees etc., which while bringing the school closer to society, conduce to the mental development of the children.

Utility of Co-curricular Activities

In the co-curricular activities the students participate on a community basis which gives them an experience of community life and develops in them the virtues of good citizenship. Along with the inculcation of the spirit of dutifulness, self-reliance, leadership, independent thinking, self-control, tolerance and the ability to discharge their responsibilities, a tone of discipline is also created in them. Through these activities the physical and mental development of the children is brought about in a proper manner and they learn the lesson of utilising their leisure. These help a great deal in establishing the system of synthesis and the standard of the school is raised. These activities establish a close bond among the school, the children and the society.

Arrangements for Co-Curricular Activities

Several difficulties crop up on the carrying out of these co-curricular activities in the school due to economic stringency, absence of proper supervision or the indifference of some students towards these. Thus, this is becoming problem for schools, but considering their utility it is not only necessary to make them feasible but almost compulsory. We shall first try to consider below the activities of the first category in which may be included games, drills, physical exercises and scheme for military education.

Provision for Various Games

Like other subjects, co-curricular activities also have great importance. These activities may prove very beneficial with the help of proper supervision and guidance. Hence, it behoves the principal or the headmaster to appoint such a teacher for supervising games and sports, who himself is a good sportsman. It is not necessary while making this selection to give any consideration to the question of seniority or pay scale. There should be a regular period for games in the timetable and it should be treated at par with other subjects.

In rural schools, land for a good playground is easily available but in the towns the schools do not usually have this facility. Two hours in the afternoon should be fixed for games. For some classes in the school the first and for the rest the second period may be allotted to games. The students should be divided into various categories according to the kind of games to be played. In this division class or ability should not be considered, but the capacity of skill in games should be taken into account. There are some games which require lesser space while others require more. From this point of view there should be in the school one small and one big field. It should also be borne in mind that while one group of children is utilising the big field, another group should play such games which may require the small one. Thus there would be an interchange of fields and players and all the students will get an opportunity to participate in different games.

Considering the quality of the games all the students should be given an opportunity to participate in the compulsory games. Thus, in volleyball the lesson of co-operation is taught but sufficient physical exercise is not provided. On the contrary, in football and hockey physical exercise is provided though very few children are involved. In like manner games like cricket, basketball, kabaddi, etc., have different places of importance in accordance with their capacity for developing in the students the spirit of co-operation or cultivating their taste, sharpening their intellect and providing physical exercise uniformly. Considering these things, students should be provided equal opportunities to participate in these games. For this purpose a time-table for games should be prepared in the same way as for other subjects, keeping in view the availability of playgrounds and their dimensions.

Provision for Game Materials

The principal should select from amongst the members of the staff a teacher to look after the games and the other related subjects in the school. This teacher should classify the students into different groups, with an elected captain, from the point of view of tastes, skills in games and the need of different games for the development of children. The captain should be held responsible for the sports and games, as well as, the materials for his particular group. This will help to develop in the students the spirit of leadership and constructive thinking and the games also will go on in regular manner.

If the finances of the school do not permit the provision of separate game materials for each group, then two groups may be combined. The principal should distribute the annual games fund of the school among the various groups and intimate the captains of each group the amount put at their disposal. All the expenses during the year will have to be met out of the allotted funds. Games material should be purchased from the stores or in its absence from co-operative stores or by the games superintendent. In this way, the students will regard the material as their own. The captain should draw up a list of the members of his group and depute, by turns, one member to be in charge of the equipment everyday. In this way everyone will realise their responsibility.

Co-Operation of Teachers in Games

It is generally seen that during the game period the teachers stand aloof and watch the students playing and anxiously wait for the period to be over. This makes a bad impression on the students and they also grow indifferent towards games. The teachers should play with the group, whether it constitutes big or small children. The teachers should, for this purpose, be acquainted with rules and methods of the games. The teachers also have to act as the referee and hence it is necessary for them to be thoroughly acquainted with the rules. If the games are not played in accordance with the rules, then neither will the full pleasure be derived from them nor will the students gain full benefit. Hence, it is necessary for the teachers to pay particular attention towards this.

Utility of Indian Games

Nowadays the games played in schools are mostly English in origin. Besides these, there are some Indian games which neither need much material nor space. Of these Kabaddi is the most useful. It is a very popular game of India and practically all the children are acquainted with it. In order to increase its utility the rule of stopping the breath may be broken and a time limit for the game may be fixed. The teacher should make the children play different games from time to time, so that their interest in games may go on increasing.

Organising Matches

Matches should be organised in order to sharpen the interest and enthusiasm of the students and also to give them an idea of their skill. These matches may be played among the various teams of the school or those of other schools. In accordance with the number of students, three, or even more groups may be made for the purpose of games and matches may be played amongst these. At least once a year, either on the day of the annual function of the school or on some other occasion, the students should be provided with an opportunity to demonstrate their proficiency in games, physical exercises and other co-curricular activities. There should be a competition between the junior and senior teams. By awarding prizes to all the winning teams the students may be given additional impetus. First, one junior team should play against another junior team and senior teams should play against one another. Then in the end the winning junior team should play against the winning senior team. No kind of consideration should be shown on the ground of 'junior' and 'senior'. On such functions various kinds of games, physical feats, eassy and elocution contests should be organised. Such annual meets should be organised either at the end of one term or at the end of the year.

Providing Equal Opportunities

It is usually seen in schools that with a view to constituting a best team attention is directed only towards some particular students and the remaining students are not given the opportunity to play even though they are interested in them. This has a bad effect on the children, As far as possible all the children should be given full and equal opportunities. Such a situation arises only when the teacher with a view to playing matches against another institution or participating in state competitions, selects only one team and concentrates his attention only on those 11 students. The responsibility of the school does not end with the training of these 11 students, for it has to bring about the all-round development of all. It the majority of students are denied the opportunity for games, it implies that they are deprived of the following benefits and training from games:

1. Through games the child cultivates the spirit of co-operation, honesty, fair play and corporate life.
2. Through games the full mental and physical development of the children is brought about.

3. Through games children learn the lesson of discharging their responsibilities and by coming close to social life, they successfully plan out the work in their future life.
4. The creative spirit is developed in the students and they get lessons in the proper utilisation of leisure. Hence, the arrangement for games should be such that all the students may benefit.

Scope of Games

Since all the students do not get equal opportunities to play games and there is country-wide illiteracy even today in our country, the spectators far outnumber the actual players. The spectators do have a taste for games but they could not get the opportunities required to play games. We have forgotten our old exercises and games in such a way that if we see their demonstration nowadays we dub them unhesitatingly, as magic performances. A necessary part of education in the ancient Indian educational institutions, monasteries, and Gurukuls, was imparting of instruction in exercises, games, sports and military training. We need to revive this practice. The schools are the best means for popularising them. Through primary schools we may come very close to the rural populace. Besides instructing the children in games, we may create interest in their guardians also by organising special functions and inviting them to these. Indian games as well as cheap Western games may be easily arranged for in rural areas, for there is no paucity of space. Football, volleyball and kabaddi are games which may be easily arranged for them. The schools should occasionally organise matches with these village teams and thus give them encouragement and create in them an interest in and sympathy for the schools.

Girl Guides and scouts may help a grèat deal in this regard. First the small children will be influenced by these activities and thereafter even grown-ups will start taking an interest in these. Hence, our primary and secondary schools should direct special attention towards these because they are in a large number in the rural areas and they can be more successful in affecting the rural populace.

Training in Discipline Through Games

Real pleasure may be derived from any game only when it is played in a proper way and according to the rules. Nearly all the students wish to derive the greatest pleasure from games and this is the reason why they themselves learn the lesson of discipline. As an illustration of their spirit of discipline it is noteworthy that as soon as they hear the whistle of the referee their hands and feet stop automatically at once and they wait for instructions. In this way, while playing, the spirit of discipline is infused in them automatically. Hence, it is for the teacher to be alert and dutiful in the playground and to pay as much attention towards the students and the inculcation of the spirit of discipline as they do while imparting instruction in other subjects in various classes.

Drill and Physical Exercises

Besides the games, it is necessary to have a provision for drill and physical exercises in schools. Exercises help in the development of the body and even the lost mental power may be regained through them. There are different kinds of exercises for each part of the human body and a due observance of these may make the exercises very beneficial. It must be borne in mind that exercise should be done in a regular and proper manner, else there may be a possibility of harm instead of benefit. In regard to the importance and utility of exercise it will be proper to mention that by means of regular and proper exercise even bodily incapacities and deformities may be removed. Today, many physical ailments are treated through exercises and yoga.

Things to be Considered When Exercising

If the exercise is not done properly there will be a danger of harm. Hence, first of all, the students have to be free from disease, for it is possible that the exercise may have an adverse effect on a student suffering from some disease. Therefore, before instructing a student in some exercise, it is better to get him medically examined. The students should be made to do such an exercise as may help remove the bad effects of sitting in one place for long hours and those organs of the child may develop which need development. Small children should not be allowed to exercise for more than twenty minutes. In the beginning such exercises should be taught which may be easy and may involve less exertion and then gradually the more difficult ones may be practiced. It is necessary to have different exercises for children of different age-groups.

Provision for Exercises

The students of the school should be divided into different groups according to their age and height and no consideration should be given to classes. Periods for exercise may be fixed in accordance with the availability of material and the number of students. One captain should be selected out of each group. The teachers should gain necessary knowledge about the exercises through books and should give necessary instruction to the captains of the various groups. Thus the work will be carried on under the guidance of captains and the teacher will be able to make a proper inspection of the work of the various groups. While inspecting the work the teacher should see whether the students are practicing the exercises correctly. It is necessary to give practical demonstrations of some feats in order to explain them to the students. The teachers should obtain all the necessary information from the staff members who have received physical training and acquaint the captains of each group with all the particulars. In this way all the students will get an opportunity to exercise and proper guidance and inspection will be possible. The physical instructor will also be able to inspect the various groups and will also be able to acquaint them with the proper exercises.

Drills

In schools drills are of importance only to the extent that they are able to remove fatigue, feebleness and incapacities. Military drill is very harmful for young children. In this case also the students should be divided into groups and should be given practice together if a big field is available, otherwise by turns. Besides the drill master, other teachers should also take part in the drills so that the drill master may be able to inspect and guide the various groups.

Games, exercise and drill are such co-curricular activities which greatly influence the physical development of students. There are some such co-curricular activities which contribute greatly to mental development. Among these the following ones are more important: 1. Student Bodies; 2. Co-operative Societies; 3. Scouting and Girl-Guides; 4. Red Cross Societies; 5. Literary Associations; 6. Junior National Committees; 7. Functions of School; 8. Magazines; 9. Dramas; 10. Picnics; 11. Gardening; 12. Habits; 13. Lectures etc.

Summary

Utility of co-curricular activities: Co-curricular activities are based on co-operation, a spirit of dutifulness, self-reliance, leadership, independent thinking, self-control, tolerance and a sense of discipline are inculcated through them. Physical and mental development is also accelerated through these activities.

Provision for Various Games: A teacher should be made incharge of co-curricular activities. All the students should be encouraged to participate in them. Co-operation of other teachers is also very necessary. Indian games should also be given a due place. Matches should also be organised. Opportunities should be provided to all.

Drills and Physical Exercises: Definite periods should be fixed for these.

Exercise

1. **Discuss the place of co-curricular activities in the education of children.**
2. **How will you organise co-curricular activities in your school? What types of activities will you include in your plan and why?**

Chapter 12

Self-Government and Students' Union

Self-government

In the foregoing pages we have emphasised that in a democracy the function of the school is not only to impart information but to bring about an all-round development of the child; to inculcate in him a sense of social responsibility, to make him worthy of understanding the philosophy of life, of democracy, and to develop his natural capacity for leadership. Hence, it is necessary that the students should know the rules of the school and realise their responsibility towards discipline. They should regard the school as a miniature form of society and by living a disciplined corporate life they should acquire the virtues of social life. Self-discipline is of great importance in the present set-up. It is only through this that the ability to follow rules and the capacity to reason are inculcated in the students. If our students realise the importance of self-government and work in the school on the basis of mutual co-operation they will be fully equipped for social life. Self-government develops in children the virtues of good citizenship and they realise their responsibility towards their rights and duties.

Advantages of Self-government

1. *Sense of Responsibility towards Government:* Self-government develops in the child a spirit of self-control. By working freely he realises his responsibility. He understands the scope of his rights and duties. Hence, he also comes to realise his responsibility towards the government.

2. *Spirit of Co-operation:* Through self-government the student realises the significance of co-operation. Self-government is the chief means of infusing the spirit of co-operation.
3. *Development of Virtues of Social Life:* Through self-government the students take part in all the activities of the school, such as, athletic competitions and other co-curricular activities and thereby acquire the virtues of social life and become used to working in an organised set-up.
4. *Strengthening of Ties between Students and Teachers:* Through self-government the teachers simply give instructions and the students help in all the work. Hence, the students and the teachers become fully acquainted with the personality of each other. The students should be given an opportunity for self-government in order to inculcate in them the feeling of citizenship and strengthen the relations between the teachers and the students.
5. *Love for Educational System:* In an atmosphere of self-government the student community itself takes part in the work of the school. Hence the students wish to get success in every field, and they achieve it; working under the instructions of the teachers. Consequently a love for the school is naturally created in them and they begin to have a high regard for the educational set-up.
6. *Efficiency in Work:* Efficiency cannot be created in the child only through oral instruction, it is obtained through practice. Through self-government the student himself does everything and rectifies the errors and acquires complete efficiency. By oral instruction we can only give theoretical knowledge. Hence self-government is a good source of developing practical efficiency.
7. *Development of the Spirit of Leadership:* In the democratic set-up we need in all spheres of life such men who may have a sense of duty and an ability to make decisions. In the system of self-government each student is given an opportunity to work and through practice, the capacity for social leadership is also created in him.

Establishing Self-government

1. It is necessary for the establishment of self-government that both the students and the teachers should realise its significance. If even one party fails to realise this significance, establishing a self-government will become difficult.
2. In the system of self-government the students usually cannot discharge their duties well in the beginning. In cases of such difficulties the teachers and the principal may, by giving correct advice, remove these difficulties.
3. People believe that the students do not possess mature minds, hence they should not be allowed to govern themselves. But experience has shown that if a good student is given an office or the responsibility of a work/he proves himself worthy of the trust. The teacher should, of course, give instructions as a guide.
4. Through elections even an inefficient person may get an important office. Hence, as far as possible the period between elections should be reduced. If the students are explained the significance of elections before holding one, the defects may be minimised. In the system of self-government the students should be told about the aims of students' unions, their rights and duties and they should be given complete freedom of work.

For self-government to work successfully, we should remember the following things:

1. The work should be done through mutual co-operation among the principal, the teacher and the students. Self-government maybe successful only after a realisation of the significance of co-operation.
2. Students should be vested with rights gradually and the scope of self-government should be fixed. After due consultation between students and teachers, the constitution of each society should be approved.
3. The election of office-bearers should be conducted properly and it will be better to have in each society a teacher to advise the students when necessary.

4. The election should be conducted under the supervision of a teacher and it should be so arranged that each student may be able to cast his vote for the person of his choice without any kind of coercion.
5. All the meetings of the various committees should be held in the college and the income and expenditure should be thoroughly checked. Unnecessary pomp should never be encouraged.
6. Everyone should be given an equal opportunity in the committee and no single student should be entrusted with many offices.
7. The principal should supervise all the activities of the council and should treat the teachers and the students sympathetically.
8. For the success of the system of self-government different committees should be formed for different functions. We shall discuss here some of these.

Discipline Committee: The aim of the discipline committee should be to foster discipline in the school. With its help it will be easy to maintain discipline.

Literary Council: The aim of this council should be to awaken and inculcate in the students literary tastes. Under its auspices Kavi-Sammelans, Mushairas, Elocution contests, *Antyakshari* contests may be arranged.

Cultural Committee: The work of this committee should go along with that of the Literary council and functions like musical evenings should be arranged under its auspices.

In like manner, the sports committee and the students' aid committee etc., will be of great help.

If we are able to impress upon the students the significance of self-government, and to develop in them the virtues of good citizenship, then self-government will prove very useful for the school. The entire atmosphere of the school as also all the activities should be shot through by the spirit of self-government, for then alone shall we achieve our aim.

Students' Council

The old school of thought did not allow any opportunity to the students to take up responsibilities but according to the new educational ideas, the school should see that the students work in the various areas of the school curriculum themselves, by forming different committees. They should share with their teachers the burden of work in the school by forming committees for discipline, literary activities, cultural functions and sports etc. Even now in many schools no provisions has been made for students' committees. In such schools committees should be established and the students should be gradually given the right to be responsible. The student council may, by forming different committees, do many things in school. The aim of producing ideal citizens for our democratic set-up may be achieved through student councils.

Summary

The aim of our school is to effect an all-sided development of the children. To attain this goal, it is necessary that the students should realise their responsibility towards the school as far as in maintenance of discipline by self-government is concerned. Self-government has been given an important place in the modern educational theories. This provides in the students the sense of obeying the rules and regulations, and the qualities of a good citizen develops in them. They also become familiar with their rights and duties. Self-government is therefore very useful for students.

Main Features of Self-government System:

1. There should be co-operation between the principal, teachers and the students.
2. The constitution of the self-government should be drawn with the consent of the students and the powers should then be transferred to the students gradually.
3. In every society organised by the students the presence of a teacher is very necessary, and only the deserving candidates should be elected as their office-bearers.
4. Freedom of election should be allowed to the students.

5. Income and expenditure should be audited.
6. Every student should be provided with an equal opportunity to work in the government according to his ability and taste and in no case a student should be given many offices.
7. The principal should supervise the working of the student council.
8. Proctorial boards, literary societies, cultural societies, games federation, constructive work, societies etc., should be established in the schools.

Exercises

1. Discuss the importance of self-government in schools.
2. What are the obstacles in the way of establishing a self-government system in a school? How can these obstacles be done way with?
3. What is the importance of the students' union? How can an ideal students' union be formed?

Chapter 13

Religious Education

Various problems crop up in regard to religious instructions in schools. Religious instructions cannot be imparted in government schools in secular State. Children of different religious sects go to school. So it is not proper to impart instruction in any particular religion to all the children. Hence, it is worth considering what type of religious instruction should be provided in schools where children from various religious groups come to study.

Religious and Moral Instruction

In some schools moral instruction is imparted in place of religious education. Efforts have been made to remove the difficulties in regard to the provision of moral instruction to children of different religious groups. To provide moral instruction is the demand of the time and each school should meet this demand. However, the problem is very difficult and great care is to be taken in this regard.

Moral instruction incorporates in itself the basic elements of all religions. Hence, the importance of religious education will have to be recognised. Moral instruction can succeed if it is based on religious principles. It should adopt the basic and broad elements of all religions instead of the tenets of any particular religion.

A person who receives moral instruction based on any religion finds a meaning and significance in his life. In moments of distress he listens to the voice of his soul and fulfils his obligations. Moral instruction based on religion develops man's knowledge of the self and adds to the reformation of his soul.

It is religion which makes morality a vital and inspiring force. An individual chalks out his path of duty on the basis of the holy instructions and invaluable teachings of saints. Religious thinkers for these provide him with an inspiration. Religiousness directs one's sense of duty to the correct path, as also chastens it due to which the moral sense is sublimated. In other words, it is due to religion only that morality may remain a vital force.

Religious Education and Instructions in Schools

It is evident from the above discussion that in our life religion is of great significance. Hence, religious education has to be provided in our schools. We should instruct the children in the ideals and duties based on the basic principles of religion in order to help them develop spiritually, intellectually and physically. In schools where there are children of only one religious group provisions may be made to instruct them in that particular religion. But schools with students of different religious groups may arrange for religious discourses by inviting experts on various religions. Now the question arises whether religious education should be given to each and every child in the school? It is the opinion of some that religious instruction should not be a compulsory subject in the school and no student should be compelled to receive religious instruction. The teachers should be tolerant in this respect. But if the basic elements of different religions are presented before the students in complete and comprehensive manner, they will certainly feel interested in them and will automatically be driven towards religious instruction. It should, however, be remembered that it is not within the capacity of everybody to impart religious instruction. This may be done only by persons having moral integrity, and sense of truthfulness, duty and tolerance. Such a person should be put in charge of religious instruction in schools.

Time for Religious Instruction

No agreement has been reached about the time for imparting religious instruction. In some schools it is imparted at the commencement of the daily schedule, in others at the end of the school work, and in a few during the working hours. After the day's work the student feels tired and it is in the fitness of things to give him leave or to arrange games etc., for him. It is not a good time for religious instruction. A fair number of teachers will be required to impart religious instruction during the working hours and this is not possible. So it is best to hold such meetings collectively for the students at the commencement of the daily work and for this a man of good character and religious inclinations should be selected.

Prayer

In religious instruction prayer to God should be given primary importance. To pray—various religious texts should be used. In schools with students of different religious affiliations the form of the prayer should be such as to be acceptable to all, whereas in those which have students of only one particular group the prayer may be based on that particular religion. Prayer will enable the student to gain a divine power which will bring success to him in his life. Besides the prayer, occasional discourses by an expert on a particular religion will be very useful. The students listening to his discourse will chalk out their own path of duty and gain moral stimulus. Students should also be given practice in silent prayer. This should not be confined simply to remaining silent, but the students should be made to practice the controlling and disciplining of their organs of perception. Thus, they will be able to cultivate concentration and mediations.

Prayer-House

It will be good if every school has separate room for prayer. In the schools there are students of different religious affiliations. So books of various religions should be kept in the prayer-room so that students may study them. If there are students of one religious group, texts, of that religion only may be made available.

Study of Religious Books

Every school should give its student the opportunity to study various religious scriptures. The students will, according to their own taste, study the different religious scriptures. This will enlarge their knowledge. Students should also be occasionally given an occasion to express their own views on some particular religious topic. While doing this they should not criticise any religion, but should discuss them from the point of view of practical utility. Occasional lectures by teachers will also be very useful.

Practical Application of Religious Instructions

We have so far expressed our views about the form and principles of religious education but this education will achieve its ends only when the students make a practical use of it in their daily life. Bare theoretical instruction will be of no use. We also have to see whether or not our students work in their daily life according to these principles, whether their behaviour is in keeping with these principles or whether on being faced with some practical problem they behave according to the religious teachings. For this we should put before the students some problems connected with their own life and full opportunity should be given to them to think independently on this problem. They should be guided to find the basic factors of the problem and be directed to study their causes themselves. They should analyse the causes and find out whether these are individual or general, and also the aspect of the moral character of the individual or the group and the circumstances which have created the problem.

After analysing the problem from the aspect of the individual, the group, character, and circumstance the students should examine the problem from the point of view of religion. Religion is an indispensable part of human life. Hence, the study of any problem from the religious point of view is very necessary. It is necessary for the students to find out what the religious texts say about the problem of the particular individual. In this way the students will accept religion as an essential aspect of life and will also come to know the main cause of the problem as also the moral defects which have led to it.

After an examination of any individual or group problem from the religious view point, the students will themselves determine their duty. They will know fully what they should do individually or collectively in order to solve the problem. The teachers should give guidance to the students and examine the work done by them. This is the best way of giving practical instruction in religion. If our schools direct their attention towards the imparting of such practical religious instructions based on the broad principles of religion, our students will certainly profit much. The utility of religious education will also be proved. The aim of our religious education should be to help the students develop their character and have a spirit of righteousness, duty, generosity and tolerance.

Summary

There are different views regarding imparting of religious education in schools. In Government schools the teaching of any particular religion is not possible. In private schools or in the institutions in which the students of only one religion study there is the facility of teaching of a particular religion. In the institutions where the students of various religions study, there may arise many problems in religious teaching.

Religious and Moral Education: In some institutions moral education is imparted in place of religious education. In moral education the fundamentals of every religion are included. So the significance of our religious education is to be admitted. The popular form of religion is included in moral education. Man is a social animal. Therefore, it is natural that the moral of an individual should be infused with religious thoughts. A moral education with no basis of religion will not be effective.

Religious Education and Teacher of Religion in Schools:* Religiousness in life has an important place. Therefore we should manage to impart religious education based on the fundamentals of various religions. Religious education should not be prescribed as compulsory subject, yet it should be taught in such an interesting manner that children may, of their own accord, be attracted towards it. The person who is to be entrusted with the teaching of religion must been a lover of morality, truth, duty and sympathy.

Prayer: In religious education, first of all, a prayer based on various religious books should be sung before beginning the routine of the school. The prayer of some particular religion may be sung in the schools in which the students of any particular religion study. In the schools, in which the students of various religions study, such a prayer should be sung which may be accepted by all. At times the lectures of some learned persons after the prayer will be useful.

Prayer-Hall and Study of Religious Books: In the schools there should be Prayer-Hall in which the students may study the books of their respective religions and may also practice mass prayer.

The Implementation of Religious Education: The religious education will be fruitful, only if the students practice it in their life. Sometimes problems pertaining to the life of the students should be placed and discussed before them, thus the religious education would be exercised in a right way. The children will independently scrutinize the basic causes of the same and they will also wish to know if it is an individual or social problem.

Exercises

1. Write a short essay on the significance of religious education in schools.
2. What do you mean by moral education? What is the importance of religious education in it?
3. Throw light on the importance of prayer in religious education.
4. How can religious education be implemented in practical life?

Chapter 14

Examinations in Schools

At present in our schools all the teaching is done from the point of view of examinations. The ability of the students is adjudged from the results of the examination. Even employment is given on the basis of examination results. Hence, every school aims at producing the largest number of successful candidates at examinations. Under these circumstances it is natural for the present day examination system to be defective. We shall discuss below the needs, nature, aims, merits and demerits of this system.

The Need for Examinations

It will be wrong to think that examinations are harmful. If the examinations are well-organised there is a greater possibility that they will facilitate the work of teaching. In schools the students should be developed in such a way that they may pass their days happily. Our forefathers had to face various kinds of problems and they gained varied experiences. The aim of the school is also to acquaint the students with these experiences. Various experiences are presented before the students in the form of various subjects. The span of human life is not so long as to enable one to learn everything through personal experience. Hence, these experiences are handed over to the students in the school in the shape of a legacy from ancestors. By means of examinations the knowledge gained by students from their own experiences is tested. The students are given further instruction in experiences of life according to the knowledge acquired by them. But the examination should be such that they may achieve the desired aim.

Examinations should enable us to get an idea of the ability of the student in acquiring wisdom through experiences as also the measure of success achieved by the teacher in his work of teaching. Only the bookish knowledge of the student is not to be tested through examinations but the mental capacities are also to be assessed.

Antiquity of Examinations

The history of examinations is very old. In the ancient period various examinations used to be held to testing the intelligence and the knowledge acquired by students. Among the Aryans suitable examinations used to be held for boys of different age groups. The child in ancient India had to go to the forest and live away from his relatives. He himself had to cater to all his needs. Thus his capacity for self-dependence was tested. We read in the Mahabharata stories about Guru-Dronacharya instructing his pupil in archery by requiring him to aim at the eye of a bird sitting on a tree. Due to his concentration Arjun alone amongst all the five Pandavas, succeeded in this test.

The ancient examinations were individual, practical and oral. The teacher examined each student separately. The students were not asked to assemble at one place and answer a few sets of questions, as is the case today. Another feature of the ancient system of examination was that the student had to give proofs and examples in support of his statements and answers. The student had to argue out his viewpoint. We find in ancient Indian history a number of instances of literary discussions among the scholars.

The Gurukulas had different kinds of examinations, viz., testing of comprehension, intelligence, personality, skill in arts and crafts and of the knowledge of religious texts and others. These examinations were held either at the time of entering or leaving a Gurukula. When a student fully qualified in these tests he was permitted to enter or leave the Gurukula.

The Functions of Examinations

The function of examinations is varied as is their aim. We shall discuss a few in brief:

1. That which is meant to be tested through the examination-questions should be tested in a real, complete and detailed manner.

2. The examination should be such as to enable one to assess the depth of the intelligence of the student.
3. A proper idea of the student's measure of success, his acquired knowledge and his progress may be gained through the examination.
4. The examination should also enable one to find out the ability of the child to make a practical use of the acquired knowledge.
5. The examination should not relate itself only to the newly acquired knowledge of the child, but also to his potentialities for future acquisition of knowledge and for understanding new subjects.
6. The examination should also enable one to find out the proclivities of the student.
7. The examination should provide to the student a stimulus for gaining knowledge in future. It should not aim only at disclosing the weakness of the students and thereby dishearten him.
8. It should develop the thinking capacity of the student.
9. It may enable the student to solve the problems and riddles of his life.
10. The examination should give an idea of the student's capacity for work.
11. The student's power of retention of memory should be thoroughly tested by means of examination.
12. The examination should help the teacher in his teaching and be such that the teacher may find out the real knowledge of the student and may teach him accordingly. Through this the teacher may also find out the suitable method of teaching.

The Present System of Examination

In most of the schools two examinations are held every year, in some three are held. These are called Terminal, Half-yearly and Annual examination. The pass mark for each student is 33 per cent of the aggregates. We shall discuss below the merits and demerits of the present day examination system.

Demerits of the Current Examination System: At present the essay type of examination is prevalent. There are 10 or 11 questions in a paper out of which the students have to answer 5 or 6 in the three hours. The main defect of such a system are as follows:

1. This does not take a real test of the student's knowledge. This system creates in the students the spirit of rivalry against one another.
2. The students resort to unfair means to get through the examination. At the time of examination the students are not trusted and teachers are appointed to invigilate in the examination rooms. It has been seen that a student who fails in all the subjects at a High School examination passes in first division next year through unfair means or through getting himself impersonated by some other person who can do better in the examination. To adopt unfair means in examinations, guardians try hard to get the examination centres of their wards changed to more favourable places to succeed in adopting unfair means. Thus the current system of essay type examination has been reduced to a mockery.
3. The questions in the examination paper do not relate to the whole course but only to a few items. Hence, the students try to guess the questions likely to appear in the paper. If the expected questions are asked they secure good marks by answering only a few questions and if it happens otherwise all that they have studied goes futile.
4. All the questions in the paper carry equal marks. This is not fair because all the questions are not of the same standard. Some questions involve harder work and more time while others less. Hence, marks should be distributed according to the difficulties involved.
5. Such examinations only test the writing capacity of students and neglect several other things. A student who has a good power of expression will answer questions in language and history etc., in such a way that he will secure more marks than one who lacks this power although he may be better than the former in mathematics, physics and other subjects.
6. The marks secured by the students do not depend so much on his ability as on the whim of the teacher. If the answers of a student are examined by different examiners, different marks

are awarded. Not only this, even the same examiner awards different marks to the same answer at different time.

7. If the expected questions are asked and the mood of the examiner is also favourable then the examinee will secure more marks.
8. The answers to the questions do not conform to any particular method or type. Some student emphasises one point and another one a different point, one student attaches greater importance to reasons and argument while another to information. Thus in answering question the different mental processes are not harmonised.
9. There is no fixed criterion for the award of marks by examiners. He awards marks on the total impression. The reaction of the examiner to the answer, the handwriting of the student and the easy style and language largely determine the award of marks.

The Merit of the Present Examination System: Inspite of the above mentioned defects the present system of examination has some good features. This system makes the students think about some question or problem and also learn the method of presenting his ideas in a systematic way in a coherent manner.

Various Kind of Examinations

Considering the above mentioned defects of the examination system it is necessary to remove them. The United States and other Western countries have adopted quite different systems, viz., intelligence tests, achievement tests, memory tests, performance tests, etc. Due to paucity of funds these tests have not been introduced in our country which is still faced with the problem of literacy. Some of the defects of the examination system may be removed through these tests but these methods cannot be regarded as perfect. In these tests the award of marks does not depend upon the mood and whim of the examiner. Besides, the answer book of the student may be examined by different examiners. Yet he will secure the same marks as awarded by any examiner. These tests assess only those things for which they are meant and not other abilities. In these the students do not have any option to leave certain questions. It is very difficult to set questions for these tests.

The reason for the evolution of these tests is the defective examination system of the present day. But it has to be remembered that these tests are not useful for subjects like literature and language. They are, however, useful for subjects like history, and geography.

Reform of the Current Examination System

We have mentioned above that due to financial and other circumstances new systems of examinations are not being adopted in our country. We have to improve the system gradually.

We shall first consider some of the main recommendations for reforms as made by the Mudaliar Commission and the Second Narendra Deo Committee (1952-53).

Recommendations of the Mudaliar Commission[1]: The Mudaliar Commission appointed by the Government of India has made the following recommendations with a view to reforming the system of examination:

1. The number of external examiners should be reduced. The scope of the individual whim of the examiner in the essay type examination should be narrowed down. For this the available tests should be made use of. The method of questions in the essay type examination should be changed.
2. The school should maintain a complete record of each student in order to understand thoroughly the development of the child and to chalk out the future of each student. The record should contain an account of the periodic work of the student and his progress in various fields and subjects.
3. In the annual assessment, the results of the internal examinations and the general record of each student should be well considered.
4. In the records of the schools and those of internal external examinations symbols should be used in place of marks.
5. There should be only one general examination at the end of secondary education.

---

1. The Report of Secondary Education Commission, October 1952, June 1953, pp. 153-54.

6. On the certificates awarded to the students the school record and the results of the internal examinations should be mentioned alongwith the results in each subject at the general examination.
7. The system of compartmental examination should be adopted.

Recommendations of the Second Narendra Deo Committee[1]:

1. Examinations cannot make a true assessment of the achievements of the students and do not test their abilities and skill.
2. Hence, other methods of examinations should be evolved. Intelligence tests should be introduced because these are more reliable. The intelligence test, however, cannot take the place of the existing examinations.
3. According to the subject there should be both written and oral examinations. In the preparation of the annual examination results, the record of work done under the supervision of the teacher should be well-considered.

Keeping in mind the above recommendations we make below some suggestions for modifications in the existing system of examination:

1. The examination should be held in a natural or everyday environment in order that the students may not consider it as anything different from the daily routine.
2. The examination should be a part of the process of the daily instruction. This will prevent the emergence in the child of the spirit of rivalry with others. He should not burn the midnight oil over his lesson at the cost of his health, in preparation for the examination, because the examination will be a part of daily routine. In order to remove the fear complex from the student's mind the teacher should ask the students to write all the he knows without any fear.
3. The teacher should pay special attention to the framing of question papers, because by means of question papers some of the defects of the existing examination system may be removed.

---

1. Report of Secondary Education Reorganisation Committee, U.P., 1953.

(i) First of all something should be asked from each aspect of the course. This will have the advantage of checking the students from making guesses about the examination question.

(ii) The teacher should not aim at framing a difficult paper. It is unpsychological to hunt for difficult questions and put them in the question paper. This will give no encouragement to the students, rather it will discourage them. Questions should be such that the largest number of students write as much as they can.

(iii) Some of the questions must be according to the higher ability as expected in the students.

(iv) It is not good to set the question paper at one stretch, because in this way only those questions are framed which come easily to the mind.

(v) Questions may be such as to assess the thinking capacity of the students. The students should have a freedom to express their own ideas.

Examinations which are conducted by the teachers in the schools are called home or internal examinations. Some examinations are conducted by the Education Department or the State or Central Board. These are called Public Examinations. Examiners for both types of examinations should bear in mind the above suggestions because the nature of the question papers determines the method of teaching, i.e., instruction is imparted from the point of view of the question papers. The teachers teach according to the nature of question papers so that the students may pass the examinations with good marks. If the question papers are framed with care, the teachers will also have to take more care. Hence the examiner should know the art of examining students. The examiner should bear in mind the following:

1. The language of the question should be easy and clear and it should admit one answer only.
2. The question paper should cover the entire course.
3. The answer to the questions should not involve only the facts of the books but should call upon the students to express their own independent ideas and thereby show their own intelligence and knowledge.

4. The questions should help develop the mental capacity of the students.
5. The question paper should not have any evil effect on the method of teaching.
6. The examiner should know all about the courses and the subject, for then only will he be able to frame a good paper. The teacher should draw out probable questions while teaching the subject and make use of these while framing the question paper. The teachers for home examinations can frame out questions while teaching the subject but the examiners for Public Examinations should read all the prescribed books and then set the paper.

It will be better if teachers themselves are appointed examiners, because they will be able to give suitable questions in the paper. It is generally found that the examiners for Public Examinations are mostly university and college teachers who have not much concern with the courses of those classes. The reason for this is that these teachers have a pull with the Education Department. Some are of the opinion that there will be a danger of leakage of question papers, if the teachers of schools are appointed examiners, because they will not be able to maintain secrecy in the matter. But it is wrong to think this. If the teachers are entrusted with a responsibility they will leave no stone unturned do to it honestly.

The importance of examining the scripts is quite difficult. In fact, it is more difficult to examine a script than to set question papers. To remove these difficulties some suggestions are being given below:

Some opine that such questions should be set in the paper that may be answered in a few words only and these answers will indicate a sure measure of the students' knowledge. If the capacity for writing is to be tested not more than 20 per cent of the marks should be allotted for this. Thus there should not be only a few questions but a number of them. The questions in this system of examination will be like those of the Intelligence-test and the method of awarding marks also will be of an identical nature. But some others are of the view that the students should have an ability to express their own view by synchronising the various aspects of his study of language, literature and other subjects and this power cannot be developed by setting questions in the above mentioned manner. Hence, it is not good to set questions in this way.

It is obvious that there are two views about the setting of question papers. It will be better to frame the question paper in a way that will incorporate the good features of both the views. So the papers should be set in such a way that the testing of a student's capacity may not be neglected nor other aspects be sacrificed for this sake. Along with this we should remember that the awarding of marks should not depend on the whim of the examiner and the students should not be able to guess the questions. For this it is necessary to have a sufficient number of different types of questions in the paper which may involve an answer ranging from three or four words to three or four pages.

About the examining of answer books, some people are of the opinion that the examiners themselves should first think out a model answer and main headings and then award marks accordingly. Some examiners award marks on the basis of the ideas of the students. If the examination is conducted in a natural environment the students will not be afraid of it. The examination will help the teachers in their work and they will also have an idea about their success in their work. The examinations make the students learn their lessons. Thus examinations also work as an inspiration for students for these help develop the knowledge of the students and out of emulation they try to learn more than others. Hence, examination is a necessity and the ways of reforming it should not be ignored.

Summary

In these days much significance is attached to examinations. Keeping in view the utility of the examination it may be said that it is very necessary.

Defects of the Current Examination System: The knowledge of the student is not rightly tested by the modern system of examinations. The atmosphere of the examination remains artificial. The student is not relied upon. The question paper does not cover the whole of the curriculum. All the questions are allotted equal marks. Only the power of writing is tested in these examinations. The marks obtained on the answer books more or less depend upon the whim of the examiners.

A weaker student obtains more marks than a brilliant one. The answer of the questions are of different types and there is no standard of marking the answers. The setting up of the question paper is taken to be an easy job.

Various Kinds of the Tests: On account of the defects in the modern examination system, intelligence tests, achievement tests, memory tests and performance tests have been devised. The tests have, to some extent, removed the defects of the modern examinations.

Reforms in Modern System of Examination: The examination should be conducted in a natural atmosphere. The examination must be a part of the curriculum.

The examiner should be well-acquainted with the curriculum. It will be better if only the school teachers are appointed as examiners.

The question of examining the answer books is difficult. The question paper should be set up in such a manner that it does not ignore the writing power of the student. The marks obtained by the students should not be affected by the whim of the examiners and the student may not guess the important questions. For it the question paper must consist of enough and different types of questions.

Exercises

1. Discuss the merits and demerits of the modern system of examinations.
2. What are the main functions and aims of the examinations?
3. How can the modern system of examination be reformed? Give concrete suggestions.

Chapter 15

Discipline in School

Importance of Discipline

An opinion may be formed about a school by observing the discipline among its students. It is necessary for every school to enforce certain rules of conduct to ensure discipline. Conversely, discipline is essential if rules are to be implemented. If the students and the teachers of a school are not disciplined, it will be difficult for the school to realise the goals of education—namely all-round development. To inculcate the virtues, desirable in a good citizen, discipline is absolutely essential.

Forms of Indiscipline in School

1. *Reaching the School Late:* There can be many reasons for unpunctuality. It is possible that due to some domestic circumstances a student gets late or other students might be teasing him while he is on the way to school. Hence, before punishing the student on this score the principal or the teacher should find out the cause.
2. *Talking in the Class:* The reason for this may either be an uninteresting method of teaching or the large number of students in the class. In order to make teaching interesting the teacher should try to get the co-operation of the students along with other useful methods. Students who are found talking may be seated separately.

3. *Destroying the School Property:* The students should be punished for this and some fines should be realised from them as far as possible. If the student can repair the articles he should be required to do so.
4. *Neglecting Homework:* There may be several reasons for not doing the homework. It is possible that the amount of homework in the various subjects becomes so much that the student cannot do it, or due to family circumstances he is unable to complete it or his negligence may be responsible for it. In fact, the real cause should be found out before giving any punishment.
5. *Bullying the Younger Students:* It will be good in this case to make the offender apologise.
6. *Telling Lies:* The students often tell lies for fear of punishment. Hence, they should be treated with love and sympathy.
7. *Disrespectful Behaviour Towards the Teacher:* First of all the cause for this should be found out. The principal may make the student apologise for his misconduct and warn him not to repeat it in the future. If the offence is repeated the offender may be given corporal punishment.
8. *Truancy:* Some student run away from the school. This may be due to disinterestedness in studies. Hence, the individual difficulties of the student should be attended to. It should also be found out how the student passes his time after running away from the school.
9. *Stealing Things:* Some students steal pencils, books, pens and other articles from their classmates. The reason for this habit may be an excessive fondness for that particular article, self-conceit, exhibition-complex or the feeling of revenge. Hence, the real cause should first be found out. If excessive fondness is responsible for this, those articles should be provided to the student. If exhibition-complex is responsible other means should be provided for the expression of this complex. The student should be treated with love in order to cure him of the feeling of revenge.
10. *Copying at Examinations:* Some students have the habit of copying at examinations. For this the school should raise its moral standard and instil in the students the spirit of morality.

The students should be strictly warned when caught for the first time, but one who does this repeatedly should be turned out from the examination hall.

Principles of Discipline

In a democratic society discipline should be self-imposed, otherwise it will assume the form of an external imposition. For the inculcation of the habit of self-discipline we may keep the following in mind:

1. The basis of discipline should be mutual love between the teacher and the student. There should be no element of fear, because discipline based on fear does not serve its ends. The students should obey the teacher out of a feeling of reverence and not out of fear. On the basis of respect alone mutual confidence may be created between the teachers and the students. This spirit of mutual confidence is the true and permanent foundation of self-discipline.
2. The student remains in the school for about 6 or 7 hours and the remaining time is spent either at home or in society. Evidently, the responsibility of inculcating discipline in the students does not fall only on the school. The guardians and the society also have a responsibility in this respect. Hence, the co-operation of the guardians should be elicited for the establishment of discipline. Through discussions with guardians, the problems and difficulties of the students should be found out. If the co-operation of those persons who are closely related with the students, is available, it will not be difficult to discipline the students.
3. Discipline should not be enforced on the basis of punishment. Punishment should be given only when it is unavoidable.
4. It is one of the demands of a democratic set-up that each individual should have control over himself. Only he who can influence others, knows how to exercise control over himself. The students should be made responsible for the establishment of discipline amongst themselves, because in this way they will exercise control over themselves and will exert a good influence

over others. Hence, the principal should give an opportunity to the students to control themselves.

5. Discipline should be regarded as indispensable for the collective life of the school. Its significance should be well-explained to the students. This means that breach of discipline should not be regarded as a revolt against the teacher but an attack on the collective life of the school. If a regard for the collective life in the school is created in the students, they will themselves understand the significance of maintaining discipline.
6. In the interest of discipline it is necessary to provide in the school the necessary facilities for study and teaching. In this connection the following things should be taken into account:

   Classroom: There should be sufficient and comfortable chairs and desks for the students.

   The School: The necessary means for the physical, mental and moral development of the students should be available in the school. The standard of teaching in the school should be of a high order.

   The Principal and the Teachers: The principal and teachers should be efficient when discharging their various responsibilities.

   The Home: The environment of the home should be peaceful. The people at home should take an interest in the education of the student and should not place any hindrance in his studies.
7. It is necessary in the interest of discipline to make the student understand that discipline does not consist only of observing the rules and regulations of the school, but it also includes the observance of the laws of society, that is, discipline is not confined to the school only but is related to the whole-life.
8. Since discipline is related to the whole-life, attention should necessarily be paid to the following:
   (i) Observing rules to maintain one's health and to avoid evil habits.
   (ii) To make constant efforts towards mental development.
   (iii) Inculcation in the student of the democratic virtues of dutifulness, and co-operation and the ability to discharge obligations and responsibilities.

(iv) To become liberal-minded.

(v) To avoid ill will against anybody and to be always imbued with the spirit of tolerance, love and justice towards others.

Such an atmosphere should be built up in the school that the above mentioned virtues may be automatically developed in the students.

Democracy and Discipline

The above discussion indicates the basis on which discipline should be built into a democratic society. In a totalitarian set-up discipline is enforced between the master and the dependent. In a democracy, free individuals have to learn to discipline themselves. There is no room for any misgiving in this sphere. The essential elements of discipline in a democracy are enumerated below:

1. A compromise between individual rights and those of others.
2. A regard for others' personalities.
3. Tolerance, love and justice for others.
4. Devotion to the nation and society.
5. Sacrifice of self-interest for social good.

If we place before the students the above ideals from the very beginning and inspire them to live up to the same, they will become disciplined and contribute towards the strengthening of the democratic set-up in our country.

Means for the Inculcation of Discipline

We have indicated that in order to make the students disciplined, we should create the suitable atmosphere in the school. Mere theoretical discussions and speeches will not suffice. Hence the organisation of school, its ideals and all its activities and programmes should be based on democratic principles. It is obvious that the best means of discipline is the maintenance of the necessary atmosphere and for this we have to give our attention to positive measures. Under very special circumstances some negative measure may be necessary.

Positive Measures

1. Pupil's self-government
2. Parent-teacher co-operation
3. Moral instruction

4. Desirable tone and tradition of the school
5. Provision of necessary facilities for studies in the school
6. Organised games and sports
7. Co-curricular activities in the school
8. Due recognition of the merits of the various students
9. Corporate life of the school

Negative Measures

The negative measures include various types of punishment which we shall discuss in a separate chapter.

Causes of Indiscipline in our Schools

At present indiscipline in our educational institutions is a serious problem. It extends from the secondary schools to the universities. In society itself we find several manifestations of indiscipline and it is the wonder that these have serious repercussions on the educational institutions as well. The following may be some of the important causes of indiscipline in our schools:

1. *Lack of leadership in Teachers:* Today teachers do not enjoy that respect in society which they did in the past. Consequently, students also do not show due respect to their teachers. Some teachers get involved in the cesspool of politics and self-interest, and lose their ideals and they do not show any interest in the development of the students. Very often these teachers excite the students and use them as tools for the realisation of their selfish ends. Due to the practice of private tuitions the prestige of the teacher in society has gone down. Their miserable economic conditions add to this. Due to all these reasons, the teachers have lost originality in thinking. As a result, they are incapable of giving guidance to students in the various situations of life. So it is no wonder to find indiscipline among the students.
2. *The Current Education System:* The current system of education is being criticised at all times. Hence, the students have begun to feel that the education which is being given to them is not good. As a result they have no regard for this education. They consider it merely as a means of getting some employment. The prime aim of the present day educational system has become the

securing of a good division at annual examinations and the students do not desist from adopting any means to achieve this objective. This is also a cause of indiscipline.

3. *Lack of a Sustaining Ideal in the Students:* At present the condition of our society is pitiable. Many people, because of their self-interest, have started attaching greater importance to the ends rather that to the means to achieve them. The social values are undergoing rapid changes, as such the individual errs in fixing his moral standard. This has shaken the very foundation of our society. Today the individual is not sure about the security of his life and property. The control exercised by the government is slack because it is caught up in the meshes of political maneuverings. Those who have some pull somewhere are happy and those who cannot pull wires are pushed behind in this six penny race. Therefore, there is a lack of a healthy ideal among the students. Hence indiscipline is increasing among them.
4. *Economic Difficulties:* Our economic conditions has deteriorated to a deplorable degree. The population has increased, unemployment is a national problem. The students are always haunted by the fear that their future is dark. So they cannot chalk out their path of duty and on occasions they behave in an indisciplined manner.

From the above discussions we may conclude that the responsibility for indiscipline does not rest only with the school, but also with the home, the society and the government. Hence for its eradication the co-operation of all the concerned is necessary. On the basis of the causes mentioned above, some suggestions are given below to solve the problem of indiscipline:

Suggestions for Rooting out Indiscipline

1. In order to create in the teachers a spirit of leadership, their living standard should be raised. Their emoluments will have to be sufficiently increased. They will have to be provided with the required facilities so that they are not compelled to undertake private tuitions. This will afford opportunities to them for self-development and their moral strength will be increased. It will

develop in them the power of leadership and they will be able to give correct guidance to the students.

2. In order to develop contact between the teachers and the taught the number of students in a class should be within reasonable limits.
3. Vocational education should be included in the educational set-up so that the students may get education according to their particular tastes and aptitudes.
4. Lack of funds should not cause any hindrance in the path of the higher education of any student.
5. Each individual should be given an equitable opportunity in the scheme of education according to his individual merits and demands.
6. Efforts should be made to minimise the defects of the current educational system through constructive suggestions and mere theorising should be avoided. Merely theoretical criticism creates distrust in the students.
7. Such ideals should be inculcated in the students as may create in them the spirit of tolerance, love, fair-play and self-sacrifice for the good society.
8. Such conditions should be created that the students may get full opportunities for their physical, mental and moral development.

Summary

Discipline connotes various meaning. It is indispensable to carry on the moral working of the school.

Forms of Indiscipline: The following are some of the examples of indiscipline in the school:

To come late to school, To talk at the time of teaching, To harm the school property, To tease younger students, To tell a lie, To misbehave with a teacher, To run away from school, To steal things and copy in examinations.

Measures for Maintaining Discipline: Affection between the teacher and students, The co-operation of guardians, Judicious punishment, Self-control, Love for social life, Sufficient facilities for studying and teaching in the school, Observation of norms of behaviour.

Democracy and Discipline: In a democratic set-up the individual himself is the base of discipline. To serve others, to value love, justice, sacrifice of self-interest for the sake of society is the real basis of discipline in a democracy.

Exercises

1. What is the importance of discipline in a school organisation? What should be done to maintain discipline in a school?
2. What are the common forms of indiscipline in our schools? What will you do to remove them?
3. What are the causes of growing indiscipline in our school? Suggest some measures for ensuring better discipline in schools.

Chapter 16

Rewards and Punishments

Discipline has been given a very significant place in modern educational thought. To run a school in a satisfactory manner, disciplined students are essential. The importance of rewards and punishment has been recognised to maintain discipline in schools. We shall understand both these factors in this chapter.

Rewards

There are different ways of giving rewards in our schools today. On securing a high position in some field, a student is rewarded with some plaything or a trophy, a medal, books or certificates. To appreciate the students for the good work done and to encourage them in this habit, rewards are given. Rewarding students is important due to the following factors:

1. The spirit of competition is awakened in the students and they get an incentive to work satisfactorily and systematically.
2. The tendency to discharge duties readily and to imbibe good habits is created in the students.

There has been some criticism of the system of giving rewards. The basis of their argument is that nature has not gifted everyone with equal or similar intelligence and physical powers. He who has a sharp intelligence and good physical power will get the reward. Hence, a reward does not attach importance to the labour of an individual. It is also said that students who do not get rewards become lazy and their progress is checked. Keeping this criticism in view we may now think about the aims and occasions for rewards.

Some people are of the view that rewards should be given collectively and only in particular circumstances should these be given individually. The moral aspect of the child should be given greater consideration in the award of rewards. The rewards which are based on the day to day work and on the conduct of the student, have a special importance. Rewards given on the basis of some particular performance (standing first in the class, securing good position in games and sports or participation in Scout and Red Cross activities, etc.) are indicative of the achievement of the student only in one particular field. Hence, these cannot be regarded as very significant. The hardworking and painstaking students must be rewarded. While rewarding them it should be clearly pointed out to them that they have been given the reward for their good qualities. This will inspire other students to become hardworking.

Punishment

An institution, society or association is influenced by contemporary thought. Our country has adopted a democratic set-up. Hence the influence of democratic thought is evident in the political, cultural, educational and other fields of our life. In the past, corporal punishment was regarded as very effective and it was considered necessary for maintaining discipline. In a democracy great importance is attached to the personality of the individual, who is given due freedom and opportunity to develop himself. This aim cannot be achieved if punishment is given in order to get a thing done by the student. Punishment destroys in the children the spirit of love, courage and also the power of discussion. Their health is impaired, several mental complexes arise and their physical, mental and spiritual development is stemmed. Thus punishment defeats the purpose of education.

To abolish the system of punishment from our schools, society has to become perfect. But this is not possible. There are sure to be some undesirable elements in us. Hence punishment cannot be totally banned. In some situations punishment may create a conducive atmosphere to fulfil the purposes of education. There are several types of punishments. We are mentioning some of these below:

1. *Corporal Punishment:* At present corporal punishment is given to student in schools. Boxing the ear mildly, slapping, or caning are some of the forms of punishment given in schools. Corporal punishment should be avoided. When all other forms of punishment have failed, only then should corporal punishment be given. While giving corporal punishment the following things may be kept in mind:
   (i) Corporal punishment should be given only for a very serious misconduct or offence, viz., disrespectful behaviour towards the teacher, disobedience, agitation, serious charges relating to character etc.
   (ii) The principal of the school alone should give corporal punishment. The assistant teachers should not be given this right.
   (iii) When any serious charge against any student is proved only then should corporal punishment be given. It should not be given when there is any doubt regarding the offence.
   (iv) Small children should not be given corporal punishment.
   (v) While inflicting corporal punishment, the health of the child should be taken into consideration.
2. Scolding: It proves very effective when employed properly. One has to be very careful while scolding. Abusive language should not be used.
3. Insult: Insulting the student is a very bad punishment. If a teacher makes a student in the class stand on the chair or makes a few unsavoury remarks against him, this will have greater and more lasting effect on him than corporal punishment. Hence, great care should be taken in this respect. The success of the scolding given depends on the personality of the teacher.
4. Fines: If the student has committed such an offence which has caused economic loss to the school or his class-fellows, fines may be imposed in order to compensate the loss. However, the imposing of fines is not very good.
5. Detaining the Student after School Hours: This is not good from the psychological point of view. The student begins to feel tired after 4 or 5 hours of work in the school and he is not inclined to read after that. Sometimes the evil effect of this go so far that the

students develop a dislike for the studies and also for the teacher concerned. If any student has not done his homework, or has left out a portion of it, he should be advised to complete it so that he may learn to be systematic. A psychological approach should be made so that the student may do his work the next day and may become regular in his work.

6. Social Boycott: If any offence of a student is condemned collectively by the students, he is likely to give up his bad habit.
7. Apologising: If any student has committed a serious offence, he may be asked to tender an apology. It will be better if he apologises to the teacher and principal.
8. Removal from a Post of Responsibility: If a student does not discharge his responsibilities or if he has done something wrong while holding a responsible post, he should be removed from that office (viz., presidentship, monitorship or secretaryship of the class or some association).
9. Reducing Marks: It is seen in some schools that some marks are awarded for good work and some marks are deducted when the student misbehaves. If marks have been fixed for some work the awards should be made separately for the work concerned. It is not desirable to deduct marks from answer-books for any other wrong committed by the student elsewhere.

Some Rules for Punishment

Punishment maintains discipline in schools. Hence, punishment should not be given out of a feeling of revenge or retaliation. The following principles should be borne in mind while awarding punishment:

1. The main job of the school is to give education. Hence punishment should be resorted to under very special circumstances.
2. Punishment should be given only when sufficient proof is available. There should be no feeling of revenge when punishing a student.
3. If the offending student is tackled independently on a psychological basis, it will be far better. In this way the student will not commit the offence a second time.
4. Polite language should be used while warning the student.

5. Rousseau has accepted the principle of the punishment of natural consequences, but it is not proper to use it everywhere, nor can it be implemented everywhere.
6. The personality of the student should not be insulted, but only his bad habits should be discouraged.
7. Expulsion from the school should be resorted to only under very special circumstances and for serious offences.
8. Only common punishments should be employed and while awarding the punishment nothing should be said against the student's family, his background or his parents.
9. Before awarding the punishment the parents of the student should also be informed for it is possible that the student may be brought round through a warning.
10. Such a punishment should be given as may be acceptable to society. It should not be that heavy punishment is given for minor offences or light punishment for serious ones.
11. Corporal punishment should be resorted to for very serious offences. It should not hurt the student unduly. It should not be resorted to out of a feeling of revenge. No punishment should be against the rules of the Education Department.

Punishment has been introduced with a view to maintaining discipline in the school. In order that the students may be completely disciplined and there may be no increase in indiscipline, many remedial measures may be adopted. We mention below some of the main methods:

1. A complete meaningful contact should be maintained with the students' parents or guardians and they should be regularly informed about the conduct, work and behaviour of the students.
2. A close contact should be established with the students and they should be treated sympathetically.
3. Each moment of the student's life should be considered as useful and he should be kept busy all the time.
4. A study of the student's nature, proclivity and work should be made and he should be entrusted with responsible work suited to his ability.

5. Attention should be directed towards the individual behaviour of each student and the cause behind each breach of conduct should be explored.

Punishment has been regarded as means for maintaining discipline in schools. We should not consider it as an end in itself. If in our school it is employed as a means and other remedial measures are also adopted, we shall surely be successful in achieving the ideals of education.

Summary

Discipline occupies an important place in human life. Our Education Department has also accepted the necessity of punishment and reward to strengthen discipline in schools.

Reward: In our schools students are rewarded for standing first or for securing an honoured position in any competition or for showing an ability in games, examination or any other work.

Punishment: The aim of the school should be an all-sided development and maintenance of discipline with love. In school management punishment and threat should have no place. Punishment mars the development of a person, reason is destroyed and various mental diseases come up. Even then the necessity of punishment is felt in practice. Our society is surrounded by an unhealthy atmosphere. Our children are also affected by society, therefore, some punishment in the schools is necessary at times.

The Principle of Punishment: Punishment should not be given with the idea of revenge. It is only a means by which we maintain discipline in schools. Punishment should be awarded keeping in view the following points:

1. It should only be given when it is badly needed.
2. Punishment should not be given if persuasion can help the child.
3. Abusive language should not be used when warning a child.
4. The personality of the students should not be hurt.
5. Expulsion from the school should be resorted to only for a serious offence.
6. A punishment which may be acceptable to society, should be awarded. Full co-operation should be extended to the guardians

and before awarding punishment the students must be warned once.

7. Corporal punishment should only be given for serious charges.
8. The punishment should not be given against the rules and regulations of the Education Department.
9. Punishment should be given only on finding definite reasons.

Exercises

1. What is the importance of discipline in schools? How far are reward and punishment helpful in maintaining discipline?
2. Which reward should be treated as an ideal one? Discuss its importance in a school.
3. Explain the necessity of punishment in schools and discuss its various kinds.
4. Which kind of rewards or punishments are popular in our schools? Discuss their merits and demerits.

Chapter 17

The School Building and Equipment

Sufficient attention should be given to the school building. At present much attention is not paid to the school building and a school is opened wherever some space is available. The teachers are not consulted in this matter. This has a bad effect on our children. We should keep many aspects in mind when raising a school building.

Site

The site of the school should be chosen after great consideration. It should be neither far off from the inhabited areas nor very close to them. It should be close to a main road, in a free atmosphere, so that the students do not face any difficulty when attending school. There should neither be a sugar factory or a cloth mill or any other kind of workshop near it. The site of the school should be completely peaceful and open so that the students, may get fresh air and light and may escape the attacks of common diseases. The site should be such that good play-grounds may be carved out and a small garden may also be raised. The site should be so expansive that changes may be made according to needs and buildings may be expanded. If there is an arrangement within the campus of the school for the residential quarters of the teaching staff, it will be very good. Many schools are opened in the beginning up to class eight but later on these grow into High schools, Intermediate and Degree Colleges. In some schools only a few subjects are taught in the beginning, but afterwards some more subjects are introduced. Hence from the very beginning the site of the school should be such as to allow expansion. The need for a hostel is felt when students come from long distances. Therefore from the very beginning, such a site should be chosen that a hostel may be constructed when a need is felt for it.

The site for the school building should have a high plinth because in low lying tracts of land rain water stagnates and becomes a breeding ground for mosquitoes. Hence the site should be neither be too high nor too low. There should be no drains and pools nearby. It should have very healthy surroundings and should be even.

The ground of the site should not be affected by insects of any kind. If the ground is not good there is a possibility of great harm to the school building.

There should be an arrangement for well water on the site for school. If the town has a water-works department there will be no need for wells. In order to keep the place safe and secure it is necessary to have a boundary wall all-round and trees may also be planted.

For primary schools 5 acres, for pre-secondary and secondary schools 10 acres of land may be sufficient. This will be a good arrangement for the towns, but schools providing instruction in agriculture will need at least 10 acres of land in addition to the above.

Building

The building of the school should be impressive. Buildings which resemble the English letters T, E, L, H and U of the alphabet look very beautiful. The 'E type' of building is regarded as the best, while the double E and double H type is considered to be good. In the E type building the Hall is the centre and air and light can easily reach all the rooms. It will be good if the building faces south and the corridor runs inside the building in all the four directions. There should be a good arrangement for windows and ventilators. A single storeyed building is desirable. The height of the building should be 16 or 17 feet and the rooms should be 22 or 25 feet long and wide, and each one should be independent. Windows and ventilators should be in sufficient number. The windows should be 3 1/2 or 4 feet or 1 1/4 metres to 1 1/2 metres high from the ground. The long and short of it is that the building of the school should be the best possible from the point of view of utility, health, grandeur and environment. When necessary it should be repaired and whitewashed.

The following rooms are necessary in a school building:

1. A separate room for each class.
2. A separate room for each subject.
3. Two rooms for science classes, and one for practical work and the other for lectures.
4. Big rooms for Library and Reading.
5. Hall for general assembly.
6. Gymnasium hall.
7. Room for the principal.
8. Big room for the office of the principal.
9. Room for the staff.
10. Special rooms for geography, painting, book-binding, etc.
11. Separate rooms for commerce, etc.

Besides, there should be one or more rooms to store school materials. In each room there should be a wall, studded almirah and the best possible arrangement for light. If the light comes from the left side it will be excellent.

In the school it is necessary to have for the boys a big playground, the number of which will depend on that of the boys.

The hostel should be separate from the school building and its affairs should be managed by an experienced teacher.

Desks and Chairs

In the schools various types of furniture is also required. In primary schools students squat on mats. For written work a desk is often used. The students are also made to write placing their exercise notebooks on their knees. In secondary schools desks and wooden chairs are used. In this context it will be sufficient to observe that the desks should not be very long ones. For each student there should be one chair and a desk so that he may do his work freely. The chairs and desks should be so arranged in the classroom that the teacher may be able to go to any student easily. The size of the chairs and desks should be according to the respective age of the student. The table of the teacher should be placed high so that he may be able to look at all the students.

We shall describe below the size and shape of the above mentioned chairs and desks in a school.

1. All the desks, chairs and benches in the classroom should not be of one size. They should be of different sizes and shapes according to the age and height of the students. For small children there should be small tables and chairs and for older children bigger ones.
2. The benches should have a back rest. This makes sitting convenient and the students do not feel tired quickly.
3. The benches should be placed at right angles to the wall so that sufficient light may fall on the table.
4. The desks should provide 18 inches of space for each student and there should be so much space in between the rows that there may be no difficulty in movement in the class.
5. The chairs and tables should be so placed that the knees of the students form right angles and the feet may rest on the ground. The knees of the student and the inner edge of the table should be in one straight line. If the chairs and desks are made from this point of view the students will sit straight and their spine will not be adversely affected.
6. The surface of the table should curve inwards at an angle of 150-degree.

Blackboard

Two kinds of blackboards are used in our schools: (a) Wall-studded and (b) Wooden blackboards. From the point of view of teaching the wooden blackboards are more useful. These can be used even when classes are taken outside of the classroom. These can also be adjusted according to the light and both the sides can be utilised. All the students cannot read all that is written on the wall blackboard, because the effect of light on it is unchangeable and the portion written at the bottom cannot be easily read. It can of course be used in Art classes but in other classes its use is not convenient.

Cupboards

In every classroom of the school building there should be many wall-cupboards which are useful and do not occupy much place. To store maps, globe etc., open shelves will be all right. To hang maps and charts and other useful articles a string fixed to nails at 7 1/2 ft. or

2 metres height may be used. In science rooms there should be a number of cupboards.

We shall now consider each room which is needed in a school.

Hall

The size of the hall should be in proportion to the number of students and the area occupied by the school building. If the number of students is big, a larger hall will be required. For our primary schools in which generally 400-500 students read, a hall 100 x 50 ft. will be sufficient. The hall should not be in any case smaller than 63 x 60 ft. Debates, *Antyakshari* competitions, meeting of the students council, lectures by literary and other important personalities, annual prize distribution, cultural shows, kavi sammelan, mushaira and dramatic shows etc., are arranged in the hall. The hall should be kept clean and tidy and tastefully decorated.

Art Room

An art room is very necessary. It should be sufficiently big and there should be a proper arrangement for air and light. Light should always come from the north and skylights should also be well provided. There should be a good blackboard, good charts, cupboards to keep necessary materials and a big table for the teacher. In the art room students generally sit in a semicircular form. Hence desks and stools should be provided for them. In this room there should be a separate table to display the exhibits and the charts made by the students can be displayed on the walls.

Science Room

To impart proper instruction in science and for practical work there should be in the school a room 30 × 42 ft. in size and another of 25 × 30 ft. for lecture purposes. Along with this, there should be another adjoining room to keep materials for practical experiments. In the practical room there should be a big table for the teacher. To ensure that all the students may easily watch the experiments, students' desks and stools should be placed as in a lecture theatre. There should be a good provision for light in this room. A good blackboard will also be needed. Water taps are also needed in this room. If the school is electrified it will be fine. In place of electric appliances spirit lamps may also be used. In the practical room a big table should be provided for the students.

In order to enhance the importance of the science room it is necessary to provide photographs of famous scientists and other charts exhibiting great experiments. Cupboards for equipment used in practicals are required. First-aid materials should also be kept in readiness.

Geography Room

This is the age of science and in a scientific age great emphasis is laid on instruction in geography. A geography room will be of added advantage to the school. The geography room does not need many windows. The walls can be utilised for maps. Adjoining the geography room, there should be a good arrangement for a sun-dial, weather-vane, rain gauge, charts, blackboards, globe, projection screens, compass etc. In this room tables, not desks should be provided. There should also be space to keep a projector and cupboards for maps etc. Greater emphasis should be put on practical teaching in geography.

Language Room

In the language room facts about the famous writers, poets and others should be chronologically presented on charts. Photographs of famous literary figures should be displayed. The best extracts should be copied out and displayed.

In like manner rooms for history, mathematics, english, etc. should be completely decorated. Besides these, there should be other rooms also in the school. We have mentioned these earlier.

Each school should provide a games room for students so that they may enjoy themselves in their leisure time. There should be a separate room for the students to take their afternoon refreshments. For the teaching staff there should be a well-furnished room and one for the guardians. This is the age of democracy and in a democracy the teachers will have to come into close contact with the guardians. Hence there is a need for such a room in which the principal, the teachers and the guardians may meet together and discuss the problems of the students and the needs and requirements of the school.

If we construct the school buildings according to the above mentioned principles, our students will be healthy, amenable to discipline and true servants of society.

Summary

At the time of planning a school building, first of all we should pay attention to the place where it is to be built.

Site: The school should be neither very far not very near a city. It should be situated in a healthy environment. There should be proper arrangement for playgrounds and gardens. If in its vicinity, arrangements for a hostel and residential quarters for the teachers are made, it will be better. The place of the schools should be so spacious that an extension in the building may be possible if needed.

Building: Buildings where 'E' shaped are best. Buildings in shape of T, L and H are also built. There should be a good arrangement of windows and ventilators. The building which is single storeyed is best. There should be separate rooms for the teaching of various subjects.

Desks and Chairs: Single seated desks and chairs are more suitable. The desks and the chairs should be big and small according to the age and height of the students.

Blackboard: The wall blackboards and wooden blackboards are used in a school. The blackboards made of wood are more useful.

Cupboards: Wall cupboards are more suited as they save space.

In addition to these a room for students, a games-room, a separate room for guardians, a refreshment room where students may take mid-day meal and one teachers' room should also be provided in the school building.

Exercises

1. Discuss the importance of the site for a school building. What place would be suitable for a school building?
2. What are the special rooms required in a school? What are the uses of keeping separate rooms for various subjects? Describe the equipment required in a room to teach any one of the subjects.

3. What is the importance of furniture in a school building? Explain if the same kind of furniture will be required in the rooms for teaching science, art, geography and language. If not why?
4. What type of building will be suitable for a school? What will be the main consideration in building the rooms of a school? Explain.

Chapter 18

Hostel

In a school the spirit of corporate living, unity and self-reliance is inculcated in the students and they are made to develop their personalities in such a way that they may live happily without harming others. The hostel should not be regarded merely as a living place for the students. The hostel should help realise the ideals of the school and provide an opportunity to the students to develop the spirit of corporate living. The hostel should be so arranged that the student may get an opportunity to put into practice in the hostel the ideals he is taught in the school.

An ideal hostel helps to maintain discipline and teaches the students the lesson of co-operation and self-reliance. It is necessary for the achievement of the aims of the hostel that it should be well-organised and managed. The personality of the hostel superintendent exerts a great influence over the inmates of the hostel and as also on its organisation. Just as a teacher in the school is put in charge of the school library and his teaching load is not reduced, similarly a teacher is put in charge of a hostel without having his teaching work reduced. Under this plan the ideals of the hostel cannot be achieved because such a superintendent of the hostel does not take sufficient interest in the activities of the hostel. In fact the hostel superintendent should be a person who can devote all his time to managing the hostel.

The Need and Utility of a Hostel

All the students of a school do not come from one place or locality, but from different places. The students carry with them the influence of their environments. Students who come from long distance make private arrangements for their residence near about the school. On such students their guardians have no control. The students of middle and secondary stages need to be under the control of their guardians. In a hostel proper control may be had over the students and a suitable environment created for their physical and mental development. We shall discuss below the utility of a hostel life.

1. First of all, as we have already mentioned, the spirit of co-operation is inculcated in the students in a hostel. In the hostel there should be a system of self-government and it should be organised in such a way that the students may learn to be self-reliant.
2. In the hostel a student lives as a member of one family. He treats others with love and sympathy and develops the virtues necessary for living in society. He gets an opportunity to become an ideal social being, and he comes to realise that only his individual inclinations and convenience are not to be always considered.
3. By creating a proper environment in the hostel the students may be made to feel at home and may be treated with love.
4. This helps in disciplining students. There is no possibility of the student's becoming indolent, rude and indisciplined, because the students try to observe the regulations of the hostel.
5. In the hostels the students do not remain narrow-minded. There they may be provided facilities for games and studies according to their individual tastes and inclinations. This may broaden their outlook.
6. The student realises his responsibility in each sphere and learns to adjust his expenditure with his parental help. The hostel superintendent should take care that the student does not spend his money uselessly, but it does not mean that the student should be made to feel dependent upon others. In fact, the students should feel complete freedom in the hostel, for then only their proper development will be brought about.

7. There should be complete democracy in a hostel and there should be no caste distinctions. The poor and the rich should be treated alike.

Hostel Superintendent and His Responsibilities

The proper organisation and management of the hostel depends to a large extent on the personality of the superintendent who should be very efficient in his work. He should have in him the virtues of an ideal teacher as well as those of good parents and guardian. Along with this he should have a good organising capacity. It will be better if an able and experienced teacher is appointed to this post, but he should have less teaching work and should be provided other facilities. The creation of a proper atmosphere, for the desired development of the students depends solely on the ability, skill, patience and sympathetic treatment of the hostel superintendent.

The hostel superintendent should treat the students with paternal affection and sympathy. Like a father he should keep an eye an all the activities of the students and consider the propriety and impropriety of each act. He has to see that the student does not do anything which may prove harmful to him. He should also see to the expenditure incurred by the student so that he may not spend unnecessarily. The hostel superintendent should pay attention to the following things:

1. He should try to make the student an ideal citizen of democracy having a sense of duty. This training may be given in the hostels. The superintendent should try to manage the affairs of the hostel with the help of students. This will inculcate in them the spirit of self-reliance and they will learn to work jointly with others. He should not be dictatorial in his attitude. For the management of the hostel affairs he should form several committees of students. These committees may also be formed by holding elections. There may thus be committees for cleanliness, entertainment and games, discipline, mess management, etc.
2. The hostel superintendent should always try to make the atmosphere of the hostel suitable, clean and beneficial.

3. He should see that no student violates the rules and regulations of the hostel and works for his own physical and mental development.
4. An important duty of the hostel superintendent is that he should try to come into contact with the parents and guardians of the students living in the hostel and he should never let go of any opportunity which comes his way. In this way he will be able to know something about the economic condition of the guardians and this knowledge may be useful for the proper development of the students as also for the proper management of the hostel.
5. The hostel superintendent has to look to the all-round development of the student. For this he should fix the hours for games, studies, bedtime and wake-up time, etc.
6. The hostel superintendent should keep the guardians informed about the progress of the students. For this he should know the address and other necessary particulars.
7. He should try to remove the feelings of caste-distinction, rich and poor and high and low among the students and he should see that all are treated properly without any distinction.
8. He has to remember that hostel life should not become so expensive that an average individual may find it difficult to put his ward in the hostel.
9. The hostel superintendent should see that the atmosphere of the school does not prevail in the hostel also. He must create a different atmosphere so that the student may feel quite at home.
10. The above facts do not imply that the students should be deprived of their liberty and be placed under strict control. Life in the hostel should be like that in a family and the superintendent like the guardian. He has to see that the development of the student is on the right lines. He should inspect each aspect of administration so that he may contribute to the good of the students.

Messing and Its Supervision

The development of one's body depends on meals. Therefore, such meals should be provided as may be conducive to physical development. It is needless to say that this is the duty of the hostel superintendent. Physical and mental development are correlated. The students should be provided with such meals which may contain all the vitamins, carbohydrates, fat and protein. For this the superintendent should know which foods contain these vitamins, carbohydrates, fats, etc., and in what degree. The superintendent has not only to see to this but also that the meals are prepared in such a way that the food value of the articles are not destroyed. Water is also a necessity along with food. Arrangements for pure drinking water should be made in the hostel.

Method of Living of the Students

Some good servants should also be employed in the hostel to maintain cleanliness. These servants should be men of good character and temperament and should have the capacity to discharge their duties well. The superintendent should entrust each one of these servants with the responsibility of taking a particular job at a fixed time. The superintendent has to pay special attention towards the cleanliness of the hostel because uncleanliness is the main cause of all diseases. Regular inspections of the entire hostel are a must. These should be regularly cleaned everyday. He should see that the students do occasionally hang out their clothes in the sun. The superintendent should also see that the students do not keep their rooms in a disorderly manner. He should check to the cleanliness of the kitchen and the dinning hall. For all this it will be better that he solicit the co-operation of the students.

Ailments and Regulations

There should be a small dispensary for the school and the hostel. The hostel should be occasionally disinfected in order to prevent the spread of infectious diseases. The students should be inoculated and other precautionary measures should be adopted to keep them safe and sound. Each hostel should have two or three separate rooms in which the students suffering from infectious diseases may be lodged. Medicines which may be given to the inmates by way of first-aid should be stored in the hostel. The superintendent should, with the help of students and other teachers and principal, frame out certain general rules for good health and other desirable habits which should be observed by each inmate of the hostel. These rules should be few and only the essential ones rigidly followed by the students. The hostel must have some rules regarding the method of living of the students. Thus there will come into existence in the hostel a system or tradition which will be greatly helpful towards a peaceful, healthy and happy life. Besides, the superintendent should also see that there is a proper arrangement for the studies of the students and for fresh air and light. The windows in the rooms should be kept open in the night so that fresh air may enter the rooms.

Health and Games

Games should be an essential part of the method of living in a hostel. Mental and physical development are interdependent and the development of the different aspects of a student's personality are inter-related. During games the various muscles come into operation and the lungs work with greater rapidity. Thus the flow of blood is increased and the lungs get more fresh air. All this affects the health of the students. Therefore, games are very necessary for health. Games bring into operation the various organs of the body and the mental faculty gets a rest and are reinvigorated. In this way it may be said that games and physical work help in studies, because through these activities, mental fatigue is driven away. Through games other such virtues are created in the students which are very useful for their future life and to make them ideal citizens. Through games the spirit of co-operation, singleness of purpose, self-reliance, dutifulness, honesty, etc., are learnt. Through games they learn to face reality, because they have to put up with both success and defeat. They learn to obey their leader. In this way games help in the maintenance of discipline.

The playground should be near the hostel. The hours for games should be fixed and the necessary equipment should be available in the hostel. There should be such an arrangement for games that each inmate of the hostel may get an opportunity to play some game every day. Captains or leaders should be appointed for various games. In every hostel there should be an arrangement for football, volleyball, cricket, hockey, badminton, basketball, kabaddi etc. and occasional matches should be held. Besides, indoor games like carom, chess, table tennis, etc., should also be organised. In games the individual taste of the students should be encouraged.

A committee of students for the proper management and organisation of all the activities in the hostel should be formed. Their co-operation is essential to manage the hostel well.

Organisation of the Hostel

The hostel superintendent should maintain close contact with the students in order that the atmosphere of the hostel may not get vitiated and all the students may live there as in a family. We may mention in this respect the 'home system' or the building system. According to this there should be small houses for eight to ten or twelve students. These homes should be adjacent to one another and with each group a teacher should also live. If the teacher is married the members of his family should also live there. All these students should live like the members of the teacher's family. Thus the students and the teachers will be members of one and the same family. The students should contribute towards the family life by helping out with the shopping and other household chores. This system will have the following advantages:

1. The atmosphere of the hostel will not be vitiated in any way and the students will have the feeling of living in a home.
2. The students will do their work themselves and learn the lesson of self-reliance.
3. The senior and junior students will live together and thus they will learn to treat one another in a proper and sympathetic manner.
4. The teachers will come close to the students and will be able to solve their problems.

Hostel Building

The hostel building should be such that the students may live comfortably and the superintendent may also be there to manage and inspect the hostel. The building should be such that the hostel gates may be shut and the students may not go out. For this it will be better if the hostel has a square building and is one storeyed. The room or the residence as also the office of the superintendent should be near the main gate. The hostel should not be on a busy road, nor far off from the school. In every room of the hostel there should be a sufficient number of windows so that light and air may enter the rooms. In each room there should be sufficient space for the student, and cupboards for books, etc. The room should be such as to accommodate the student's bedding, table and chair, etc., and yet leave sufficient space. The flooring should be cemented and there should be a good arrangement for water to flow out.

Besides, there should be in the hostel one reading room, play-ground and kitchen etc. The latrines should be behind the main building at some distance and the bathroom should be not very far away from it. The latrines should be clean at all times. Gardens and parks should also be attached to the hostel building.

Internal Management

The internal management of the hostel should be done through the students or committees of the students. This should include the method of the living of the students cleanliness and daily work, etc.

There should be in the hostel a fixed place for each student and it should be seen that no student changes this place. The student should keep his bed and clothes well-arranged. The articles should be purchased and games, etc., arranged with the help of the students through their committees which should consist of duly elected student members.

The superintendent should chalk out a suitable timetable for the hostel and affix this on the notice-board. Through this timetable the hours for exercise and meals, etc. should be fixed. It is necessary for the superintendent to remember that along with the timetable the other rules and regulations of the hostel should also be pasted on the notice-board or somewhere else. These regulations for good management should be as few as possible.

Registers

A few registers are required to keep a record of necessary things. These are very important for the hostel. The following registers should be maintained:

1. *Admission Register:* Names, full addresses, dates of admission and other information about the students who have been admitted in the hostel should be maintained in this register.
2. *Attendance Register:* The attendance of students at different hours of study, retiring to bed etc., should be checked. The attendance should be taken at least twice a day. This register should record the reasons for the absence of the students concerned.
3. *Register for Co-operative Activities:* A record of the committees of the students and the meetings and other activities should be maintained in this.
4. *Kitchen Register:* In this a record of the articles purchased, the rates and expenditure should be kept. This register should also indicate whether the students have paid for these articles or not.
5. *Caution-money Register:* An account of the caution-money taken from the students is to be maintained in this.
6. *Fee Register:* This will record the statements regarding the fees charged from the student and their expenditure.
7. *Property Register:* In this should be maintained an account of the property of the hostel and its utilisation. The principal should occasionally check this up.
8. *Cash Book:* This should be like the cash book of the school and it should be filled in regularly everyday showing the daily income and expenditure. Money deposited in and withdrawn from the Bank should also be shown in this.
9. *Library and Reading Room Register:* A list of books in the hostel should be maintained in this. Statements regarding the issue of books, viz., the name of the student, date of issue and return, etc. should be maintained in this. The names of newspapers and magazines subscribed for the hostel should be entered here.
10. *Visitors Book:* This should be like the visitors book of the school. The guardians of students who visit the hostel should write in this their opinions and suggestions for improvement.

Summary

Students should get an opportunity in a hostel to practise in their life what they learn in school. In a hostel co-operation and self-help should be taught. The hostel superintendent should devote his entire time to the management of the hostel.

The Necessity and Utility of Hostel: It may provide the students a suitable guardianship and atmosphere. The feeling of co-operation and self-help develops in them. The child lives there as a member of a big family. The students become disciplined. Their outlook is sympathetic. The student begins to recognise his responsibility. It helps in becoming an ideal citizen.

Hostel Superintendent and His Responsibilities: Suitable management and organisation depends upon the hostel superintendent. At this post only able and experienced teachers should be kept. They should behave like parents. The atmosphere of the hostel should not be artificial. He should treat all the students alike. The progress-report of students must be communicated to their guardians. The hostel life should not be very costly. Students may be given reasonable freedom.

General Supervision: The food provided to the students must contain all the vitamins, fats, proteins and carbohydrates.

The Standard of Living: Attention should be paid to the cleanliness in the hostels. Every possible effort should be made to keep the students free from diseases.

Health and Games: Games and other physical activities are helpful to the physical and mental health of the students. From games students acquire the qualities of co-operation, self-dependence, honesty and dutifulness.

The Organisation of the Hostel: Home and building systems may be useful for the organisation of hostel. The hostel building must be sufficiently big enough to meet the needs of the students and the hostel superintendent. There should be an arrangement for sufficient light and fresh air.

Internal Management: The standard of living of the students must be good. A suitable timetable may be drawn for students. Necessary instructions should be written on the notice-board.

Registers: The following registers should be maintained in the hostels:

Admission Register, Attendance Register, Co-operative Register, Mess Register, Fee Register, General Stock Register, Cash Book; Library and Reading Room Register and Visitors Register.

Exercises

1. Describe the necessity of a school hostel and its working.
2. What are the functions and responsibilities of a school hostel superintendent?
3. How should a school hostel be organised?

Chapter 19

The Library

The importance of a library in a school is being realised now. The work of the school is to give to the student a knowledge of necessary things and to bring about such an all-round development of the student that he is able to lead a successful life. The span of a man's life is not so big that he can learn everything through practical experience. We can learn by the various experiences gained and accumulated by our ancestors. These experiences have been recorded in various books so that they may not perish. Man saves a lot of his own time with the help of the vast store of wisdom and experience accumulated by his forefathers and handed over to him as a legacy. A knowledge of these experiences facilitates his work of acquiring new knowledge. Hence a library is a necessity for a school and sufficient attention should be directed towards its proper organisation, utilisation and development.

Utility of the Library

Students cannot acquire knowledge only through textbooks or classroom lectures. They should refer to other books also, for then only will their knowledge widen. The best thing would be that a teacher should create an interest in each student in his subject and give the names of important books for reference. In this way the students will learn to acquire knowledge themselves. The teacher should try to inculcate in the students varied interests. These varied interests cannot be fulfilled only through class lectures or textbooks. The library is of great help in the fulfilment of their wishes, ambitions and inclinations, for it provides ample opportunities for acquiring knowledge.

The knowledge gained through the class lectures of teachers may be easily forgotten after sometime but that which the student acquires himself through self-study will be remembered by him even after leaving the school. Students have different tastes at different stages of life and when he is able to read he likes to read books according to his need and taste.

The entire environment of the school contributes towards education and the library is of great help in creating a suitable environment for education. The library may help develop different taste in the student. After reading one book the desire for another is created. Thus a reading habit is formed.

The library does the work of a teacher for the students. It will not be wrong to say that the defects of classroom teaching can be rectified to a great extent through the library because the teacher cannot teach from the point of view of the interests of every student nor can he develop his various interests fully. This is possible through the library. The teacher should encourage students to read books according to their interests.

Organisation of the Library

The aims of a library may be fulfilled only when it is well organised and the selection of books is made properly. The following things should be considered while organising the library:

1. The aim of the library is to enlarge and consolidate the knowledge acquired in the classroom.
2. In a library there should be books according to the age, ability and interests of the students.
3. A library should help build up a suitable environment in the school. For this there should be such a reading room in the library where the students may sit and read.
4. A library should help develop the knowledge and intelligence of students.
5. The library should be helpful in enlarging the knowledge and helping the work of both the students and the teachers.

The utility of a library depends upon its proper organisation which includes the distribution of books, their arrangement, the situation of the library etc. A library may be properly utilised only when all this is done.

It should not be situated at such a place, where the atmosphere is not peaceful. For this it should be remembered that it is not situated near the lower classes. In schools, having double storeyed building, the library should be on the second floor.

Sufficient sitting place for the students should be provided. The room should be large enough to accommodate at least 15 per cent of the students of the school. The yearly and monthly publications should be so arranged that the students may take them out to read as they wish and then replace them. The librarian should be able to give information about the books asked for by the students.

At present a library is not properly utilised in most of the schools. The library exists only in name and the students cannot easily get books from there. Books for these libraries are purchased without any reference to the interests or abilities and standards of students. The principal does not even know what type of books are there in the school library. Besides, in most of the schools the librarian is appointed from amongst the teachers and he has to teach also. If he is busy teaching, how can he take sufficient interest in the library? He does not pay any attention towards the proper management of the library and tries limit the number of books taken by the students as far as possible. Such a library is quite useless. No taste for self-study can be developed in the students through such a library. Hence it is necessary to introduce reforms in school libraries.

It will be better if an experienced or trained person is appointed as a Librarian. If this is not possible, an interested teacher should be entrusted with this work. The teacher who is given this responsibility should get some consideration in regard to the teaching load. Besides, a teacher-librarian should be given some extra payment in proportion to the work to be done. This teacher should have all the necessary information in regard to the various subjects and books. The books should be arranged in such a manner that the student himself may know what books he should read on a particular subject. This will be possible if the books are arranged according to classes and subjects, but this can be done easily only if the teachers of particular subject also realise their responsibility. The teacher in a particular subject should assist in the arrangement of books. Apart from this the method of issuing books should be such that each student may get the desired books easily. If the assistance of some students of the class is taken, probably this job will be facilitated and the students will also get an opportunity to learn the ways of management and gain information about books. Students of higher classes can derive great benefit if the books are arranged according to subjects. The teachers of these subjects should inform the students about the books on the subject and encourage the students to read them. The distribution and issue of books should be done properly. There should be a rule of keeping a book for a fixed period of time, for then only will the students get equal opportunities.

Class-library

There should be a central library in the school, but besides this, if there are class-libraries, it will be easier for the students to get books from these. The class-teacher is familiar with all the students in the class and he can guide the students about the books suitable for them. In the class-library books should be selected according to the abilities and interests of the students of the class. Class-libraries enable the students to get books easily and to avoid a waste of time. Besides, the teacher by telling about different books, helps to develop in the students varied interests. Class-libraries will prove very useful for lower classes, because at this stage the students are not of an age to have a complete knowledge of different subjects nor do they have any interest in this. Besides, in lower classes only the class-teachers can tell the students which books on different subjects are suitable for them. In the class-library the students should be given the facility of choosing the books for themselves.

Some students get books issued from the library but they often return them unread. Hence the teacher should find out whether the student has read the book or not. It will be good if a record is maintained showing the number of books a student reads during the course of the year. All the books which a student reads should be listed on a page which should also indicate the date of issue and return. Thus the teacher will have with him an account of the books read by the students and he will be able to create a taste for reading in those students who do not have such a taste. The teacher should also see that the home task assigned by them should be such as may require the students to read books from the library.

The students should have such note-books in which they may note down the titles of the books they read, a summary of the book as also their own ideas about the same. The students should be provided with an opportunity to discuss in the class the books they have read. A student who properly reads the largest number of books in the year should be rewarded. It is very necessary for the students to make a summary of the books read, because if the important facts are not noted down they will soon be forgotten. It is necessary for the teacher also to have a knowledge of those books which the students read, for then only will he able to understand the viewpoint of the students and to participate in the discussion with them.

Classification and Arrangement of Books

The books in a library should be properly arranged and classified as they have as great an importance as the library itself. The importance does not consist in storing a large number of books as in having suitable books in a proper order. In this connection attention should be directed towards the utility of books. For this it is necessary that the teachers should consider the contents of the books. These books should be according to the capacity and ability of the students so that they may read and understand themselves. When the student is able to understand a book himself he feels encouraged to read other books as well.

The significance of a library does not lie in possessing such books of great authors which the students cannot understand, but in the collection of such books which the students of different levels can fully utilise. There should be more than one copy of the books which are useful from the point of view of the students. It is found in some schools that the teachers who are preparing for some examination get those books for the library which they themselves need and which are neither up to the capacity of the students nor of any use of them. In the school library there should be books for the teachers also but these should not be purchased from the funds for the books for students.

The following things should be considered in the collection of books:

1. The books in a library should be according to the interests, age and abilities of the students.
2. At the time of collecting books it should be remembered that they should develop the knowledge of the students.
3. The books should be such as may be easily understood by the students and may develop in them the power of thinking and reasoning.
4. The books should be useful to both the teachers and the students. After collecting the books these should be classified according to the subject, ability, interest, age and class of the students in such a way that they may be utilised. The librarian should, with the help of other teachers in different subjects and classes, write down separately in a register the names of books on different subjects and for different classes. In this way the students will easily know the names of necessary books and get them without difficulty. Thus they will also be able to make full use of the books. At present our students cannot make full use of the school library. There are several reasons for this. Firstly, the library is not well-organised and the books are not classified and arranged properly. Secondly, the students do not have any taste for reading books nor do they adopt the proper method of reading. It is necessary, in the interest of the students to remove all these defects.

The principal should purchase the necessary books for the library, because the library will prove useful only when its stock of books increases. It will be better if the schools earmark an amount for the library and do not decrease it in any way. The next question is how to decide how the books are to be ordered. For this the principal should form a committee of teachers, the librarian and a few students. In this way full attention should be directed towards enriching the library.

Reading Room

Alongwith a library a reading room is also deemed necessary. There should be sufficient place for the students to sit and read in this room. We have pointed out above the importance of light and air in a library. In the reading room there should be newspapers, magazines etc. so that the students may read them and be updated. In the reading room a copy of the school magazine consisting of articles, stories, riddles and jokes written by the students should also be kept. On reading the poems articles, stories, etc. of students, others also get an inspiration to write these. Only such magazines should be ordered for the reading room which may cater to the interests of the students and help in the formation of their character.

If along with a library there is a museum also, it will be an ideal thing. These musuems should belong to the school and articles of historical values and beautiful paintings and sculptures should be stored.

Summary

The experiences of our ancestors are collected in the form of books. Hence collection of books and good management of libraries is very important.

The Importance of Libraries: The students cannot receive all the required knowledge in classrooms. They acquire a tendency of self-study in the library. The library is useful for fulfilment of desires and ambitions.

Students do not easily forget that which is to their taste and learnt through self-efforts. The whole atmosphere of the school is related with education and a library creates a suitable atmosphere. Reading of various books makes knowledge more perfect.

The Organisation of Libraries: The situation and place of the library and the method of issuing the books should be suitable. There should be a reading room in the library. There should also be good arrangement of light and ventilation.

Some experienced and trained persons from amongst the teachers should be appointed as librarians. The library may be so organised that students may learn of their own accord how to read books. The books must be arranged according to the class and subject. The teachers of various subjects should help in this arrangement.

Class Library: This can prove more useful for students than a central library. It is easier for the students to find out books in such a library.

The teachers should see that the students read the books issued to them. The teachers should keep a record of it. The students should be encouraged to read books by announcing a reward to the best readers.

Collection of Books: Attention should also be paid towards the utility of books. The books according to the interests of students should be collected in the library. Every year the number of books in the library should be increased. Some amount may be allotted for this purpose. For the purchase of books a committee may be formed consisting of students and teachers.

Reading Room: Reading room helps the students for keeping them in touch with the current topics. Suitable news papers and magazines should be subscribed for the reading room. The handwritten magazines of the school may also be kept there.

A school museum, if maintained, will be very helpful.

Exercises

1. Describe the uses and significance of school libraries.
2. Write an essay on the defects of the present school libraries. What measures should be adopted to remove these defects?
3. What should be the main consideration in the organisation of school libraries and the collection of books?

Chapter 20

Homework

In the school the students are taught to achieve success in the struggle of life and their personalities are developed in such a way that they may, successfully facing the ordeals of life, live in society and may also contribute towards the development of the same. But the students remain in the schools for a shorter time than they spend at home and it is not possible for them to do all the required work in the school. Therefore, the homework is to help in the achievement of the aims of the school. Hence, it is not good for the school to treat itself as the be all end all of the school life. Needless to say that it is only a means among others and not an end in itself. This will prove useful only when it is suitable and care is taken before assigning it that it does not prove very cumbersome for the students but is helpful in his school work. In subjects like history, geography, language and mathematics homework becomes necessary. If the interests of the students and other aspects related to his home life are well considered while assigning the homework , it will not be cumbersome or unpleasant to them.

Two Views About Homework

Regarding the assigning of homework to the students there are two conflicting views. Some people feel that the homework makes the atmosphere of the home school-like, and as such no homework should be assigned and the students should be left free to devote their time in the home to play and do other things of their choice. It is further argued that sufficient work can be done at school in five or six hours and as such there is no need for homework. Homework simply helps one in getting through the examination and it will be futile to expect from it the fulfilment of any other objective. Too much of homework may also lead to harmful consequences. It may create in the student a habit of cramming unintelligently. This will check the development of the thinking and reasoning power in the students and will make him book worm. Homework may also affect the health of the students adversely because he feels worried to complete it and he does not get sufficient time to play or do other things.

Some other people are in favour of the homework because according to them homework is necessary for completing the school work. According to them homework teaches the student to work independently and become self-reliant.

In our opinion a middle course between these two conflicting views will be more helpful. Homework should be assigned but not so much that it may deprive the student of leisure for games or recreation.

Aims of Homework

Homework should be assigned mainly for the fulfilment of three aims:

1. First of all homework should be assigned with a view to making the student thoroughly assimilate the lessons taught at school as also to develop in him the capacity to learn new things. If the students do not revise or practise at home the lessons taught in the school the same will be forgotten after sometime.
2. Homework encourages the student towards self-study. This may be regarded as another aim. The homework should be such that it may provide an impetus to the student to enjoy self-study.
3. The third purpose of the homework is to fill in the inadequacies of classroom teaching. In the classroom teaching individual attention to each student cannot be paid. The teacher has in his mind the capacity of an average student and teaches from that viewpoint. But through homework he may assign a task to each student according to his ability and interest. The teacher can render help to the student by evaluating his homework.

The Need for Homework

Both the school and the home are responsible for the education of the child. In the school the student does not get sufficient time to complete all his work. Hence, homework becomes a necessity. If the topics read in the class are not properly assimilated and revised by the students, they are soon forgotten. Hence homework is necessary. Homework may be regarded as useful for the following reasons:

1. On examining the homework the teacher comes to know whether the lesson taught by him has been understood by the students or not. It also enables the teacher to assess the progress made by the student in that subject and the parents or the guardians of the student may also find out the progress of their ward by looking into his homework.
2. The students get an opportunity to express their own views through homework. In the classroom they do not get the time or opportunity to express their own ideas but they can do this well through homework. For example, during the teaching of some lesson in a language class, each student cannot express his ideas fluently or easily but he gets an opportunity to express his views in a beautiful and effective manner while writing essays.
3. When doing his homework the student can do his work with full interest and ability. Through this the good habit of reading other books or making use of the library may be inculcated in the students. It is needless to point out that such habits will prove very useful to them in the future.
4. If the homework is suitable it encourages the students towards self-study. They have to think for themselves, and thus through homework the power of thinking and of critical analysis is developed in them.
5. The homework enables the students to get an idea of his own progress. This is very important for the development of knowledge. This idea may create in him a feeling of satisfaction and provide an impetus towards more work.

Evidently, only that homework is suitable which fulfils the above aims.

It is necessary to consider certain issues before assigning the homework. As far as possible, little homework should be assigned. Homework is very useful for both dull and intelligent students because the former is enabled to keep pace with the class and the latter gets an opportunity to enlarge his knowledge. But it is wrong to think that the average students should not be assigned homework and that it is not useful for them. In fact homework should be assigned from the point of view of the ability, interest and circumstances of the students.

Issues to be Considered when Assigning Homework

Before assigning the homework the teacher should see whether it is desirable from the above mentioned points. It should be considered whether individual attention can be given to it and also if the students will take interest in doing it. If the students take an interest they will be encouraged to study. They will also feel that pleasure which one gets when doing a work himself. The students will take a great interest in doing something which they feel is useful. It is better if the teachers explains to the students the utility of the homework given and tries to make it useful from the students' point of view.

While assigning the homework individual differences, interests, abilities and capacities of the students should be taken into consideration. All the students of the class do not possess identical abilities nor do they have a similar capacity for work. Hence before assigning any homework it should be checked whether the student is capable of doing it. If the homework assigned is beyond the capacity of a student there will be greater possibility of it being harmful.

The teacher should also consider the family circumstances of the students while assigning homework. The student should not be given so much work that they are not be able to do it or are unable to find time to play or do other jobs. Games are necessary for health. Hence homework should not be such that it impairs the health of the student in any way. It will be bad to assign a task to a student who has an ailing relation at home or has no time to do the work or who is busy in some function or ceremony at home. Therefore, the homework should be assigned after ascertaining the family circumstances of the students.

Such a homework should not be assigned which may relate to some new thing or may involve the application of new principles. For example, it will not be good to assign a task to students in matheamtics from a new exercise, the method of which has not been explained before. Hence, the homework should be assigned on the exercises or lessons already done in the class. This does not mean that such a homework should be given for which there may be no need to read other books because in this way the students will not develop the habit of reading other books. The homework should relate to the classwork but it should require the student to read other books and not depend only on the class teaching. The teacher should while assigning the homework tell the students the name of books which may be useful for the homework. These books should not be beyond the understanding of students. It will not be necessary to read a book from the beginning to the end to do a particular piece of homework, and as such the teacher should also specify the pages to be read.

The aim of the teacher while assigning the homework should not be to enable the student to pass the examination. If the teacher assigns the homework with this aim in view, then it will not achieve the desired end.

Before assigning the homework the teacher also has to see what tasks have been assigned in other subjects by other teachers. If all the teachers assign some task in their subjects the student will have too many things to do and that will become cumbersome. In this connection the principal should see that the load of homework is not heavy on the student. If a homework enables the teacher to estimate the student's knowledge in another correlated subject it may be regarded as good. Geography and history may be correlated through the homework.

In order that the homework is useful total co-operation from the parents should be forthcoming. The guardian can see whether his ward does the homework or not.

Correcting homework is no less important than assigning it. If the task is not examined the students lose interest in it and cease attaching importance to it or they do not regard it as having any utility and take it to be a burden. Hence the task should be examined and marks awarded properly.

Different Kinds of Homework

It is not necessary that students should be given only written homework. The work should vary with the subject. Besides written work, memorising small pieces of poetry, prose extracts, or remembering the characters of some drama, drawing figures or maps. etc. may be assigned. Different lessons may be given to develop the knowledge or the artistic skill of students. Apart from this there are also appreciation lessons.

Any thing which is learnt once but not utilised later on is soon forgotten. Hence it is necessary for the development of knowledge that the thing learnt is practised at times. Therefore, in subjects like science, language, mathematics and geography such homework should be assigned that may require the student to utilise the lessons learnt. Similarly in art subjects practice is of great importance. For appreciation lessons the students should be encouraged to write poems, write prose pieces or draw. In this way different kinds of homework may be assigned for different subjects.

Harmful Homework

If the above aspects are not kept in view while assigning homework, it will not be useful. Besides, the homework assigned without considering the unsuitable home conditions of the student may prove harmful. As far as possible homework should not be given to students of lower classes and they should be left free to play at home. A student who takes tuition at home should not be assigned homework.

At present most of the teachers in our schools assign homework without considering its harmful effects. This situation leads to unhealthy consequences. The child overburdened with work, does not take an interest. He even begins to feel afraid of the homework and tries to avoid it. Hence, our teachers should assign homework with proper care.

Some of our teachers assign homework by way of punishment. Such a homework tends to create in the students a dislike for all other task.

Some teachers assign a lot of homework before holidays. This is bad because it mars the importance of holidays and the students remain worried about their homework. They spend their holidays like other working days in school and feel that it would have been better if there were no holidays. Hence, the principal should also see that too much homework is not assigned for holidays. If it is necessary, some homework may be assigned but it should be interesting and should not spoil the significance of holidays which are very important for the mental development of the children. The holidays provide mental rest to the students and they begin their work with renewed zeal when the school reopens.

Summary

The Aims of Homework: The main aim of homework be to let the students thoroughly learn the lesson taught in the school, to encourage the children towards self-study and to fill in the inadequacies of class-teaching.

The Necessity of Homework: It is needed for completing the work of the school and for strengthening the acquired knowledge. The teachers and the guardians can check on the progress of the child through homework. The children find a good opportunity to express their views. They find a good chance to work with full strength. Knowledge develops, if books other than textbooks are read. The student may measure his own progress through homework.

Some Important Points: Through homework, individual differences of the students may be attended to. It should be interesting for the students. They may feel pleasure in performing it. The homework must be fruitful and within the reach of the children. It should be given keeping in view the home circumstances of the children. Too much homework should not be allotted. Nothing new should be assigned. It should be general so that the students may stand in need of reading books other than the textbooks. The children may be informed of the list of requisite books and page numbers, therein. The homework should not aim at the passing of the examination. The reasoning power and logical power should develop by it. The teachers, consulting each other may allot the homework to the students in suitable quantity. The co-operation of the parents must be available to complete the work assigned. The homework must be corrected and marked.

Useless Homework: The homework, without taking into consideration the above points, is useless. Little children learn much through playing. To allot homework in anger or as a punishment is always harmful. Allotting too much work for the holidays will lessen the importance of holidays.

Exercises

1. Describing the aims of the homework, throw light on the necessity and importance of the same.
2. What should be considered while allotting homework to students?
3. Why is the co-operation of guardians necessary for homework?

Chapter 21

The Managing Committee and the Manager

A Managing Committee is needed to properly carry on the work of the school. In private schools the managing committee looks after all the work and is held responsible for the best management of the affairs. In our country there are many government schools also which are managed by the State. The schools under the District and Municipal Boards are managed by these bodies. These schools do not have managing committees like private schools.

According to the Education Code the private schools must have managing committee which are to be responsible for the management of the schools. The school should have an independent committee consisting of the guardians, the donors to the school establishment, and eminent educationists. Some membership fee should be fixed for this. The members of the school managing committee should elect the members of the managing body.

Constitution of the Managing Committee

Persons interested in the affairs of the school and belonging to different classes should be on this committee. In this committee the old students of the school, the guardians, representatives of the teachers, the principal, financial supporters of the school and educationist should be included in a proper ratio. The committee should be constituted in such a way that the working of the school may go on well in the best possible manner. It is needless to point out that an ideal committee will be constituted if representation is given to people of all categories.

The Manager and the Principal

The members of the managing committee will elect the president, vice-president, secretary, joint secretary and treasurer of the committee. The president of the committee will work as the manager of the school. The function of the manager will be to render assistance and co-operation to the principal. It is necessary in the interest of the school to give full liberty to the principal for organising the library, science, games, examinations, refreshments and other necessary expenditure. The manager may, if he so desires, fix with the consent of the committee the amount to be independently spent by the principal, and to spend beyond which he will have to obtain the permission of the committee. The principal should be instructed to deposit in the Savings Account the money earmarked for different departments and to inspect every day the statement in regard to the daily income and expenditure. For this he should maintain a register so that he may maintain full accounts and statement of the items under him. A school gets, from time to time, some donations and also government grants. Hence, all such money should be deposited in a bank. There should be registers for all accounts of income and expenditure and these should be inspected regularly by the inspectors. The officers of the Education Department carry on periodic inspection. That is to say accounts should be properly maintained so that no one may have any kind of suspicion or misunderstanding in this respect.

Functions of the Managing Committee

In the schools there is a provision for Provident Fund for all types of employees. The provident fund contributions should be deposited in the bank every month and it should be seen that the teachers and others are not put to any kind of financial loss. There should be a separate Pass Book for each teacher and other employees and money should be regularly deposited in this. The manager should take every precaution in this respect.

For a smooth working of the teaching work in the school there should be full co-operation between the principal and the teachers. The members of the managing committee themselves should elect the president who very often functions as the manager. It is sometimes seen that a conflict arises between the principal and the managing committee due to certain differences. Hence, it is necessary that the committee should prescribe the sphere of activity for the principal and the manager. There should be no scope for any unpleasant situation. The school is a temple of learning. So it should be the function of the managing committee to keep its atmosphere healthy.

Duties of the Managing Committee and the Manager

It is the duty, not only of the Manager, but of all the members of the committee to take full interest in the affairs of the school. If they take an interest in all the activities of the school, the school will undoubtedly make rapid progress. If the Manager is an educated and trained person, he should devote at least an hour per day to teaching. In this way he will be able to understand the problems of the teachers. He will also know the needs of the school and will try to meet them.

The manager and the members of the committee can take part in the various functions of the school and thereby help the teachers. If any member or the manager is interested in literary activities he can encourage the students to organise '*Antyakshari* contests, debates, *Kavi Sammelans, Mushairas,* music competitions, one act plays, etc. If he is interested in Red Cross and Scout activities, he may encourage such activities. In other words, the manager and the members should participate in some activities of the school according to their interests, and abilities.

Responsibility of the Managing Committee

The responsibility of the managing committee is not confined to the financial aspect of the school. In fact, it should look to the all-round development and progress of the school. It is the duty of the committee to fulfil the need and requirements of the school and to help it achieve its aims. The manager should get from the principal the various information regarding the school building, the furniture and the library. He should always try to fulfil the needs of the school.

For the benefit of the teachers the managing committee may run a co-operative society. The members of the society should elect a president, vice-president, secretary, deputy-secretary, auditor and treasurer. The society should run on the regulations of the co-operative department. Rules for the membership of the co-operative society should also be framed. Each member should make a monthly contribution and the minimum and maximum number of shares for each member should be fixed. The teachers, can, when they need, take loans from this society. The committee should lay down rules regarding the amount of loan permissible to each member, the period within which it is to be refunded and the interest to be charged.

Summary

The managing committee is responsible for all the affairs of the school.

There must be a school committee. This school committee should be authorised to elect a managing committee in which the persons of all the classes may have seats according to their strength. The principal, teacher, guardians and old students should be given a place in the managing committee.

The members of the managing committee should elect their office bearers, and the president may work as a manager. The manager should cooperate with the principal. The manager should allow the principal to spend money on games, library, science, ink, examinations and refreshment, etc. The principal should maintain separate pass books of various funds and accounts of income and expenditure. The managing committee should fully co-operate with the manager. It should also co-operate with the principal and the teachers.

The manager and the members of the managing committee should take part in the various functions of the school.

The managing committee should establish a co-operative society according to the rules of the co-operative department.

Exercises

1. What is the aim of a managing committee in a school? Describe its functions in short.
2. Describe in short the duties of the members of the managing committee and the manager.

Chapter 22

Parental Co-operation

The school is established by society to realise the ideals of education. The aim of the school is to develop the powers of the child harmoniously. Formerly, the responsibility for teaching the three Rs and imparting instruction in values necessary for life, rested mainly with the home. Due to the increase in the multifarious activities of man, the home proved incapable of discharging these obligations duly and it passed these on to the school. But the child does not spend all his time in the school where he goes only for five or six hours. Hence the time spend in school is not sufficient for education. It is necessary for the school to get the co-operation of parents. For the development of the child the co-operation between the school and home is necessary. If the school does not get the parental co-operation, a proper environment for the development of the child will not be build and the school will not be able to work fully for the good of the child. With parental co-operation the teachers will be able to know the influences on the child and the progress made by him. Thus parental co-operation is necessary for the efficient and successful working of the school.

The school will become helpless if it is cut off from society, because it is meant to discharge those obligations which were once the responsibility of the family.

Both the school and the family have similar aims. Hence, both need the help and confidence of each other. If the guardians have confidence in the school they will work for its progress and will take an interest in all the activities of the school. In this way they will give full assistance in the building up of a student's personality. The exchange of views will solve the problems of the child and afford opportunities for his development.

Responsibility of Parents

We have mentioned above that the school will become helpless without society. Both fulfil one and the same purpose. The family is a unit of society. Hence, it becomes the duty of the family and the parents of the child to cooperate with the school. They should remain informed about the management and affairs in the school. Their work does not end with sending the child to the school, but they also owe a responsibility towards his advancement. Most of the parents in our country think that their duty ends with sending the child to the school. The responsibilities of the parents in this respect are as follows:

1. The parents should see that the atmosphere of the home is not contrary to that of the school.
2. They also should look to the physical and mental development of the child and help the school in its efforts for his all-round development.
3. The parents have to see that the child does not develop any bad habit. If any problem arises in the personality of the child, they should help the school in solving it.
4. It is the duty of the parents to visit the school occasionally and find out the progress of their child from the teacher.
5. It is the responsibility of the parents to make the child ready for the school punctually. They should also see that the child does the home work assigned to him and also whether the task is suitable to the child.
6. The parents should be present at the functions of the school and also take an active part in them whenever invited to do so.

The responsibility of the parents does not end with their acquiring information about their wards. It is also their duty to take part in all the work, activities and management of the affairs of the school. They should co-operate in the work for the progress of the school and offer suggestions to the principal whenever requested to do so. This will be possible only when the parents take part in all the activities of the school. Only then will they become acquainted with the real conditions of the school. In this way the solution of the various problems facing the school will be easily available.

Methods for Getting Parental Co-operation

It becomes the prime duty of the school to make full efforts for securing parental co-operation and to organise such activities which may afford greater opportunities for bringing the parents into closer contact.

At present our schools are away from society due to the courses and methods of teaching that prevail. The atmosphere of the school is becoming unwholesome and education is drifting away from real life and thus it does not create in the child any ability to face the problems of life. In this way the atmosphere of the school and the home are becoming separated from each other. Hence, to secure parental co-operation, it is necessary that the environment of the school should be made more realistic, and whatever is taught there should have a direct relation with the life of the students. This inter-relation between education and the real life of the student will lead to a closer contact with the life of the parents, because the students and the parents are units of the same family. The schools should come closer to society and create a proper environment to secure parental co-operation through the influence of the education imparted to the students. The principal and other teachers and students of the school should often mix with society, participate in its functions and through their influence create a proper environment for parental co-operation.

The second method for establishing this contact between the parents and society is to organise social functions in the school. The principal should consider the following:

1. Organising functions in the school to afford greater opportunity to teachers and parents to exchange views and to consult each other for the better working of the school.
2. Creating in the parents a sympathetic attitude towards the work and progress of the school.
3. Treating the children with sympathy, trying to establish a close contact with them and finding opportunities to meet the parents.

For parental co-operation some functions should be organised in the school. We mention below some such functions:

Parents Day: The parents day should be observed on the occasion of the annual function of the school. All the parents should be invited to the function and special plans should be made to show to them the progress of the school during the year. Charts indicating the progress of the children should be prepared. Besides this, drawings and paintings made by the students should also be put up. The parents should be given an opportunity to see the magazines of the school. Items like plays, kavi sammelans, sports, music, etc. should be organised on this occasion. In order to keep the interest of the parents in the affairs of the school, other social items should also be organised, viz. school exhibition, health week and scouting, etc. It is needless to say that guardians should be invited on all these occasions.

The principal should apprise the parents attending any function, regarding the management of the school, its aims and ideals and the schemes under operation for the progress and advancement of the children. The principal should also invite their opinions and suggestions and solicit their co-operation in every other way. The school should maintain a register in which the parents may record their views. The parents should be informed about the condition and the circumstances of the school. Some students should be deputed to take the parents round the school on the occasion of such functions.

Parents-teachers Committee: To encourage parental co-operation a parent-teacher committee is very important. This committee should elect its president and other office-bearers. It will be better if a guardian is elected to the Presidentship of the committee. The committee should meet after two or three months and discuss the suggestions for the solution of the problems of the school. The principal should at these meetings present a report about the progress made by the school, and throw light on the new schemes and other conditions. Such a get-together will prove very useful and the principal will be able to get the views of the parents about the conditions of the school, its progress and problems. In this way a good contact will be established between the school and the parents and the school will get parental co-operation. Through these meetings the parents will also come to know about the children and will treat them accordingly at home. This system will remove many disharmonies that may exist between the atmosphere of the school and the home and will provide greater opportunities for the proper development of the child.

Organisation of Lectures and Other Functions: The school should occasionally arrange for lectures by well-known personalities. There should be in the school a students' union which may organise such lectures and other functions. There should be one teacher in this Union while other teachers should help in its functioning. The Union should be constituted by members elected by the students. The parents should be invited by the school to the functions organised by the Union.

The parents should be sent a detailed report about the progress of the child. This should not include only the examination marks but an account of all the necessary facts about the child. Along with the mental progress of the child, there should be a detailed account about his physical, social and moral development. The progress of the child cannot be estimated only from the marks secured at examinations. So only marks should not be sent to the parents. The report should have an account of the character, conduct, games, health, particular features, habits, tastes and co-operative activities of the child. This information should be sent periodically after every two or three months.

Along with the progress report, the principal should send to the parents forms to be filled in by them. Through this form the principal should get from the parents necessary information about the children and elicit their opinion in regard to the proposed schemes for the desired development of the children. There will thus be no possibility of any disharmony between the school and the parents and the school will be hopeful of getting full parental co-operation.

Parents' Membership in the Managing Committee: It will be fine if for the sake of parental co-operation one or two representatives of the parents are elected to the managing committee of the school. In this way the parents will be made to take more interest in the working of the school. The parents may be included amongst the chief members of the teachers' council or the managing committee of the school.

Summary

The Need for Parental Co-operation: The school hours are not sufficient to understand the child fully. Therefore, obtaining the co-operation of parents is necessary. The co-operation between the school and home is necessary to build up the personality of the child because without it a suitable atmosphere will not be created for the development of his personality.

The school and the family both serve the same purpose. It is easy to solve the problems of the children by exchange of ideas. This will increase the interaction between the school and the parents and it will also help in maintaining discipline among the children.

The Responsibilities of Parents: The parents have to see that the atmosphere of the school and the home are not contradictory. The following are the responsibilities and the duties of the parents:

1. To help in all-sided development of the child.
2. To prevent the child from falling into bad habits.
3. To inform the school about everything related to the child.
4. To go to the schools at intervals and to enquire about the progress of the child there.
5. To send the children to the school in time.
6. To help in the homework.
7. To participate in functions organised in the school.

The Functions of the School: Various functions should be arranged in the school. The curriculum should be directly related to the life of the students, and it should meet the needs of the society. The school should be the centre of social life. The parents should be invited to attend the annual function of the school. In the school a committee should be formed of which teachers and the parents may be members. In it matters related to the school should be considered. The mental, physical and social progress of the children should be communicated to their parents, and information regarding the children may be had from the parents.

Exercises

1. Why is parental co-operation necessary for desirable development of the child?
2. What can be the means of obtaining parental co-operation?
3. What are the difficulties which the schools have to face in obtaining parental co-operation? How can they be removed?

Chapter 23

The School a Centre of Cultural Life

The Present Condition

At present our schools are divorced from society and do not fulfil its needs. The school environment does not equip the child with the ability to successfully face the various problems of life and the teaching method does not develop the thinking and reasoning power in children. Feelings of co-operation, comradeship and brotherhood also are not inculcated in them and no special attention is paid towards the development of the feeling of community life.

Our country is predominantely an agricultural one and the number of villages is larger than that of cities. Adequate attention is not paid towards the education of villagers nor is any opportunity given to them for the development of a feeling for community life. Consequently, we do not have any spirit of community life.

Now we have begun to realise that it has become necessary that for all-round progress special attention should be paid to villages. For the villages to progress expansion of education is necessary. Schemes should be planned to develop through education the feeling of group and cultural life. Our Government has realised that the democratic experiment will not be successful without education and if our country is to advance, schools will have to co-operate in this experiment.

The Need

If democracy is to succeed school should be an ideal in the villages and become centres for co-operative, sosical and community living. If villages become such centres of social and community life, the cultural and social progress of the village will be more feasible. But for this those virtues will have to be developed in the school itself which have to be expanded over a large scale in the villages. At present the environment of the school is not suitable for such a development. Hence, a proper atmosphere should be created so that the virtues of social, cultural and community life may be developed in the children and through them in the villages.

Socialisation

Man is a social being. For the fulfilment of his needs he has to live as an indispensable part of society. Only by living in the society is his physical and mental development possible. At the time of his birth the child does not know the customs and practice of society, but he gradually learns to live according to the demands of society. The gradual learning of social ways and life is called socialisation. The socialisation of the child takes place in the school where he is taught to become an ideal member of the society. In the school the child learns how to live up to the traditions and ideals of society. Proper socialisation of the child is the aim of the school. Hence, it is necessary to develop in the school the spirit of love and brotherhood and co-operation. For this it is necessary that the school is itself a society in which all the students and the teachers live on the basis of co-operation. The environment of the school should be such that the child may feel that he is living in a family.

Developing Co-operation in the Child

First of all there should be the feeling of mutual co-operation and comradeship between the principal and teachers. Children learn more from examples than from precepts. If each activity of the teachers is based on co-operation and friendship, there is a greater possibility that these feelings will be developed in the children also.

Students' Council

There should be in the school a students' council consisting of representatives from all the classes. These should be elected by the students. The council should have an executive committee with an elected president and vice-president. The function of this council will be to organise the co-curricular activities of the school. This council should take part in the functions of the school and should organise group, social and cultural activities. It should publish the school magazine and should organise social activities like plays, sports etc.

House System and Self-Government

According to the house system all the classes of the school are divided into houses. There should be at least four such houses constituted on the basis of classes. Each house may be given a name. In this way the responsibility for the prestige of the house will be on the members of the house and they will not do anything which may bring discredit to it. The house system will greatly help in establishing discipline among the students. The problem of any act of indiscipline by any student may be put before the house to which he belongs. But in the beginning teachers will have to guide the houses which will have to work according to their directions. In this way through the house system a capacity for self-reliance and the spirit of co-operation may be inculcated in the students.

School Assembly

The school assembly is very necessary for the corporate life of the school. Before starting the teaching work the assembly of students at one place helps a great deal in creating a suitable environment for teaching and in developing the spirit of corporate living and unity. All the teachers and the principal should be present at this assembly. In this assembly convened before the beginning of the school work congregational prayers should be held. No student should show any kind of carelessness in prayers which should be distinctly pronounced. On this occasion the principal may make important announcements or give other important information to the students.

The Influence of Prayer, Motto, Flags, Uniform etc.

In strengthening the corporate life of the school, the school song, motto, flags and uniforms etc., help a great deal. If the students of the school have a uniform of their own, it will have a great influence on their organisation. If the school has a flag of its own, it will be useful, because it will strengthen their feelings of corporate living and they will remain united under the school banner. In the like manner the school should have a motto which should be written in the classrooms also. This will help in determining the tone and tradition of the school. The school flag should be unfurled on national days and other important occasions.

Plans of the Schools

In this connection the whole school works unitedly for some common ideal. All the students and teachers after due consideration start a new project for the good of the school. In this way the students get an opportunity to work jointly with others. These include the construction of a play-house, or the schemes about adult education and village reforms. Through these schemes the students will get an opportunity to understand village life and the villagers will take an interest in the work of the school.

Summary

For the progress of the country villages must be paid attention. The schools should serve as an ideal for the village. The villages should become centres of social, community and cultural life.

Socialisation: To learn to follow the customs of society is called socialisation. The child is socialised in the school. The sense of co-operation should be developed in children.

The child may live in the school like a member of the family. There should be a feeling of friendship and co-operation between the principal and the teachers. The feeling of friendship and co-operation among the children should be encouraged.

Students' Union: In students' union there must be representatives of all the classes. They should manage the various cultural activities.

Home System: It is helpful in the school and the children learn self-dependence and co-operation.

School Assembly: At first all the students should assemble at one place for prayers.

Cultural Development: Arrangement for plays, *kavi sammelans* and literary sittings should be made in the schools and villagers should be invited in them. Their help should be taken in these activities.

Teachers should develop the cultural life of the villages by their educational influence.

Exercises

1. Why should a school be a centre of the cultural life of the people?
2. How can a school be a centre of the cultural life of our villagers?

Chapter 24

School Functions

To increase the knowledge of the students and to establish contact with the public, functions are organised in a school. These functions have several aims of which the main ones are as follows:

Aims

1. To inform the public about the progress of the school.
2. To give detailed information to the public about the new educational schemes and management of the school.
3. To enhance the knowledge of the children.
4. To nullify the evil propaganda against the school and remove the doubts in the mind of the public.
5. To arrange for money required for the progress of the school.
6. To awaken a social sense in the children and to develop in them the capacity for leadership.

We can have functions of the following types:

1. School week
2. Annual day of the school
3. Educational exhibition
4. *Antyakshari* and elocution contests
5. Prize distribution
6. Staging of plays of educative value
7. Science-exhibition
8. Kavi Sammelan and Kavi Darbar
9. Programmes under the auspices of the Red Cross Society, Scout Association, Music, Sports and Literary Societies.

10. Get-together of learned men and exhibition of school magazines.
11. Old boys meetings
12. Parents meeting

School-Week

Some of the schools these days observe a school-week. In order to do this properly the principal should in consultation with all the teachers chalk out a definite programme for each day. A committee of students under the supervision of some teachers, should be constituted for this week. The organiser of the committee has to do a lot of work, so great care should be taken in electing him. There are some functions which the students cannot perform well. Hence a committee should be formed for this purpose under the supervision of a teacher. During the education week literary, cultural and athletic competitions may be organised, some plays with educational values may be staged, and Kavi Sammelan and Kavi Darbars may be organised. Many such educational acitviites may be planned. Each activity during the education week needs a president. Only a very capable person should be selected for this post so that he may be able to express correct views about education before the students and the public in a proper manner. On the last day of the school week, the elite of the town, parents and eminent educationists should be invited and the annual report should be read out. It should deal with all the aspects of the school, prizes won by the students, and the needs and requirements of the school. That is to say, the principal should throw light on all the activities of the school. In order to foster friendly relations amongst the old and the new students a meeting of the old students may be convened during the school week. The get-together of learned men is a valuable means of enhancing the knowledge of students, so this also may be arranged for during this week.

The School Annul Day and Prize Distribution

The annual day is a very important function of the school. During the education week the multifarious activities of the school are exhibited in a detailed way but on the annual day only a few selected activities are to be exhibited. Whatever activity is to be presented, it should be well-rehearsed by the students. For this occasion some interesting dialogue, or a One Act play, demonstration by the scouts group, demonstration of some physical feats or drill or any literary programme may be selected. All the items should be interesting and educative. On the annual day prize distribution also takes place, and it should be done as quickly as possible. On this occasion the elite of the vicinity, all the teachers and literary figures should be invited. The principal should present a detailed account of all the activities of the school and the importance of the school should be brought home to the minds of the persons present. It is good to select some eminent person to preside over the annual day function.

Scout Activities

Scout activities are demonstrated on the occasion of several functions of the school. To supervise the scout organisation only such a teacher who bears a good moral conduct and behaves sympathetically towards others is suitable. He who loves the children in the school as his own, should be made an incharge of the scourts. In the absence of an able scout master, the students do not take interest in the organisation nor do they understand its ideals. Hence, for the students there should be in the school a departmentally trained teacher holding a diploma from the Scout Organisation. The trained scout master will be able to create in the students the spirit of self-reliance, universal brotherhood, social service and sympathy for others. The students after joining the scout association, realise the importance of labour. The scouts work with others and the feeling of universal brotherhood and co-operation are automatically developed in them. The scouts visit different places and become acquainted with the behaviour and customs of the people. They have to face certain difficulties but they do all the work themselves. Thus they learn to solve problems in a natural manner. Through scouting the students develop the virtues of good citizenship. Thus scout training is very useful.

Educational Exhibition

The organisation of an educational exhibition is of great significance. The students come to know a lot of things through this and their general knowledge is increased. In the school exhibition the work done by the students of the school should be exhibited. The teachers should only give certain instructions in this respect, and the students should display the exhibits accordingly. These exhibits may be divided into literary, scientific and constructive groups. In the exhibition the following things may be displayed:

1. Scientific exhibits made by students, sketches etc.
2. Historical and geographical exhibits like maps, graphs and old coins.
3. Literary or journalistic exhibits.
4. Handwork exhibits of students viz., chairs, tables, carpets, paper and other useful articles.
5. Artistic exhibits, viz., good paintings of students and other related materials.
6. Other useful articles having an educative value.

The school exhibition is an invaluable means of the development of a students knowledge. If it is well organised the students will benefit a great deal.

Literary Contests and Activities

In schools elocution contests may be organised under the auspices of the literary association. These competitions create a literary taste in the students specially if they are organised on a local or provincial basis. Other literary activities like plays, debates, *kavi darbar*, etc. may also be organised. They develop in the students a capacity for work and organisation.

Museum

The school should have a museum also in which things useful for students should be stored. The museum should be maintained from the point of view of its educative value. The collection should be divided into different categories and a detailed description of the exhibits should be attached. The students should always be encouraged to collect articles having educative value. If old coins, seals, ancient monographs, manuscripts, paintings of different periods, scientific sketches, art-materials, geographical, historical and political extracts and other educative articles may be collected by the students themselves and kept in the museum, these articles will be invaluable possessions for the school. After collecting articles in the museum some eminent persons should be invited to inaugurate the museum. On this occasion important persons of the area should be invited and the importance of the school should be explained.

Constructive Work

To build up our country constructive work is needed. Our country is predominantly an agricultural one and the major portion of the population lives in villages. It is necessary for the development of the villages that the children should be devoted to social work. In every school some constructive work should be done. On such occasions work like that of cleanliness, literacy drives, building roads, making arrangements for watering of fields, planting of trees to provide shade on the roads and other activities which contribute towards the social good should be undertaken. The aim of these is to make the students realise the dignity of labour.

Co-operative Society

The aim of establishing a co-operative society is to create in the students the spirit of co-operation and self-reliance. Articles of daily necessity, viz., paper, books, pencils, scales, nibs, knives, answer books, socks, soaps, towels, etc., may be stored in the society. A student committee to manage the income and expenditure of the society should be elected by the students.

Old Boys Meeting

The old boys meeting should be held in the school. This will strengthen the bonds of affection between the old and new students.

Guardians Meeting

By organising a meeting of parents, teachers, and students all three are brought into close touch. Through such a get-together problems like indiscipline among students may be studied. It is necessary for the all-round development of the child that the teacher obtains the co-operation of the parents and it is also the duty of the parents to co-operate with the teachers.

Other Get-togethers

Get-togethers are organised in the school under the Red Cross, Music, and Sports Committees also. The meetings under the Red Cross Committee create in the students the spirit of service, and also present to the students a distinct picture of their duty towards an invalid. Music-gatherings provide a mental relaxation. Sports gatherings are organised under the sports committee. Games have an important place in education. In fact, sports are a very good means of development. The development of the virtues of co-operation, brotherhood, punctuality, etc., is possible in the sports-field. Hence, these meets should be very carefully organised in the school.

Summary

Various functions are organised in the schools for the development of the students and to establish close contact with the public.

School Week: A committee may be formed to observe this week in a convenient manner. The teachers and the students must work with mutual co-operation. The principal should allot work to students and teachers according to their interests and abilities.

The Annual Function: This is a scaled down version of the education week. Only some particular programmes may be arranged in the annual function. Some interesting debate, staging of one-act plays, scouting work, mass P.T. and other interesting programmes may be arranged for this week. Prize distribution is also arranged on this occasion.

Scouting: There should be a trained scout master. Scouts may understand the importance of labour and develop a sense of co-operation.

Educational Exhibitions: Exhibitions help in the development of the knowledge of children. The exhibits of the children should be classified subject-wise and presented in a well-decorated manner. The exhibition should be divided into literary, scientific, craft and other sections.

Mass Competitions and Literary Programmes: Antyakshari, debates and other literary competitions may be arranged to develop a literary interest in the students.

School Museum: The articles collected in the school museum should be arranged. subject-wise, and a detailed description of the article should be attached with it.

Constructive Work

1. Sanitation
2. Spreading literacy
3. Construction of roads
4. Tree planting

Old Boys Meet: It strengthens the relation of love between new and old students of the school.

Parents Meet: Meetings of the parents strengthen the closer contact between teachers, guardians and students.

Other Functions: Under the auspices of the Red Cross, music and games socieites function may be arranged from time to time.

Exercises

1. What is the importance of functions in schools? What function may be arranged in Primary, Secondary and Higher Secondary Schools? Outline a programme for a high school.
2. What are the aims of school functions? Discuss their various forms in a school.
3. Discuss the importance of an Annual Function in a school. How should it be arranged and what activities may be specially organised for it?
4. Describe an ideal form of educational exhibition and museum in a school. Also point out its utilities.
5. Criticise the current system of functions generally organised in schools and suggest an ideal system of the same.

Chapter 25

Evaluation in Education

The Need

To understand the need for evaluation in education, it is necessary that we get a clear idea of the requirements of schools. The existence of schools in fact is necessary to provide desirable experiences to children. This being so, a question naturally arises as to how these schools can prove useful in our life. It is not unnatural to demand special arrangements for it. Even when adequate arrangements for education at institutions have been made and the necessary education has been imparted to a student, the problem of to what extent the students have benefited remains to be solved. To find a solution to this problem, a need for an evaluation of the work done by children arises.

Results of Evaluation

By evaluating the success of children we arrive at a number of conclusions. So far as the child is concerned, through evaluation we know the capacity or ability of a child, and we understand how far he succeeds in making use of these. This very fact stimulates a child to show the best possible results at the time of the evaluation. Evaluation, in fact, is a warning at times to children to be careful about their work. It helps a good deal to know both the defects and the good points of children. They may be advised, at the time of evaluation, to remove their defects and show better results. The practice also proves helpful in the gradation of children and in the matter of their promotion. Besides, teachers also get an opportunity to know the type of education which has a wholesome effect upon children. Thus the teacher gets a chance to adopt better methods of teachings. In fact, we know through it the extent to which a school succeeds in achieving its goals. It facilitates the task of introducing necessary reforms and changes in a school arrangement.

Necessary Factors about Evaluation

To evaluate results efficiently, it is necessary that they are measured accurately on the basis of a healthy educational philosophy. Philosophy and science are the two essential factors which make any sort of evaluation successful. It will not be too much to say that a school without adequate provisions of evaluation ceases to progress on healthy lines. Schools, generally underrate the fact that the teaching of a group of students or its administration is as much an experiment or effort—as is the experiment, made repeatedly by us, to reach a planet. The first principle of science—understanding the relationship between cause and effect and of basing the evaluation on the results so obtained have been put into action only by a limited number of schools. Officers and other persons connected with the school who make their personal opinion the basis for an evaluation are around even today. Such an evaluation is bogus or useless. Things however do not end here. A section of the people is prepared to go to the extent of strangulating the measurement which constitutes the soul of evaluation. The evalaution to conclude can be of any use only when based on a philosophy and the science of examination.

Unreliability of Marks given by Teachers

It has been proved that marks given by teachers are not reliable. Different examiners allot different marks in the examination answer books for the same question. The same question is given good marks by some and very bad marks by others. Not only this, even the same examiner has often been found giving different marks for the same question at different times. All these lead us to the conclusion that the science of examination is still in its infancy.

How to make the Marks given by Teachers Reliable

The question naturally crops up as to how the marks given by teachers can be made reliable. This assumes greater importance because the success and failure and consequently the making and unmaking of the life of students depends largely upon these marks. Therefore, efforts should be made to achieve this objective as desired. We may consider the following points helpful in this respect.

Reform in the Examination System: It is necessary that objective tests are also introduced in order to remove some of the shortcomings of the essay type examination.

Adoption of More Rational Questions: The success and failure of students to a great extent depends upon the nature of questions asked. Therefore, utmost care should be taken at the time of setting the question. The following things should be kept in mind when framing the questions:

1. The questions set should be neither too stiff nor too easy.
2. It should be clearly mentioned if the answers are to be given in detail or in short.
3. The language of question should not be ambiguous.
4. Questions should be based on lessons prescribed in the course.
5. Questions should be so framed that students may feel attracted towards them.
6. Students should also be regularly kept informed about the time in the examination hall.
7. Desks and chairs too on certain occasions hamper writing.

Meeting of Teachers: Teachers should also exchange views at their special meetings in respect of evaluation.

Comparative Study of Markings by Different Teachers: The marking of one teacher may, on some suitable occasion, be compared with that of another. On such occasions every teacher is given a copy of the mark sheet so he may himself compare his marking with that of his colleague. In the distribution of the marksheet the teacher may give his name but the use of symbols will be better.

Normal Conditions: Teachers may be well-advised not to examine answer books in an abnormal state of mind such as anger, anxiety, excessive emotion, confusion, pain, etc. The work done in such conditions is likely to carry mistakes. They should undertake the task of evaluation in a normal mood.

Utility of Standardised Tests and Measurement

The standardised tests and measurements are capable of doing good only when they are properly used. If the right use of these is not ensured the expenditure made and the time spent on them may prove useless. New experiments are useful only when the results obtained are put into use. Experiments themselves can only analyse. They only point out the correct and the incorrect and it is up to the teacher to make necessary changes. Through experiments the differences between the interests and capacities of children are known. But this knowledge in iteself is not of much help in taking us to the desired goal unless efforts are made to meet the needs through the adoption of scientific means. Scientific experiments and tests become of some utility only when the knowledge obtained through them form the basis of our practical work.

The following points must be kept in view while constructing an objective test:

1. The problem to be taken up should be related to the school.
2. To achieve this objective, the best tests should be selected.
3. The persons who are to participate in the test programmes must have a prior training in it.
4. The material to be used in a test should be thoroughly checked and tested.
5. Necessary administrative arrangements should also be made in keeping with local conditions to carry on the test programmes smoothly.
6. The time suitable for the study of a particular problem should be decided in advance.
7. The timings of the test should be decided in advance.
8. The test results should be properly organised.
9. An inference should be drawn only after analysing the test results.

Advantages of Standardised Tests

The various advantages that we derive from standardised tests are as below:

1. The importance of standardised test is on account of their utility and adaptability for bringing about changes in forms and teaching methods. They also help in knowing about the capacity of working in the school and children. They also prove of immense help in the classification of children.

Through them we can assess the individual ability of children and can make necessary teaching arrangements for them accordingly.

2. They also have made researches possible in the educational spheres. Through these tests it also becomes possible to know what type of teaching methods will suit a particular category of children and what arrangements should be made in the school to teach different classes.
3. The teacher gets an opportunity to evaluate the lines of his own teaching methods.
4. The standardized tests also tell us about the progress made by a child. This knowledge is valuable for us in comparing the progress of one child with that of another of his age and class.
5. This system helps not only in knowing the individual progress of a child but of a group of children at any stage.
6. Through their help a comparative study of children in the same school and at the same stage is possible.
7. An impartial comparison of the working of different schools adhering to different teaching methods is also possible through these tests.

Classification of Standardized Tests

The new tests may be divided into two categories. One can be named as the general merit category and the other as diagnostic. Now the question which arises is when each of them is to be used.

The first category may be used when teachers or other school authorities desire to compare their success with other specified measurements. The second category may be applied when the success of children is to be analysed with a view to ascertaining its degree in respect of a prescribed course.

Practical Use of General Merit and Diagnostic Tests

The tests that were used originally were of the general merit type but recently people have felt attracted towards the utility of diagnostic tests and scales. It has resulted in the development and large scale use of these tests. These tests help us to know not only the performances of children but also those who are either above or below that standard.

Besides, they also provide such information which proves to be of great help in improving teaching methods. The teachers make use of these tests in the same way and in the same spirit for the benefit of children as does a doctor in the case of a patient. As a doctor tries to know the cause of ailments, decides about the line of treatment, sees its effect on the patient and is prepared to make changes when necessary, so is the case of a teacher in his dealings with his students. An example will make the point more clear.

The Example: Suppose there is a child who mispronounces words while reading a language book. Why the child does so is the primary duty of the teacher to detect. The teacher in such cases should apply the diagnostic tests and find out the real cause of defective pronunciation. He should know if it is on account of any organic defect of the child or due to his ignorance about the correct pronunciation of a particular letter. When the defect has once been ascertained, the teacher's duty is to remove it. If the defect lies in the tongue, medical help should be sought to get it removed. If it is on account of the ignorance of the child who does not know from which region of the mouth and throat a certain letter is to be pronounced, the teacher should point out the correct place. The best and the most effective way of removing the defect will be the pronunciation of the same word by the teacher himself before the child—so that he can be made to follow the same repeatedly. The teacher should particularly take care that the child practises the instructions in the right way. An occasional check should be made by him to ensure this.

Selection of Tests

It is needless to emphasise that scientific tests have occupied an important place in our modern system of education. Still the question will not be irrelevant if one asks whether all types of tests can be used to know the shortcomings and achievements of any student. In fact, a selection is to be made of the best type of tests by the teacher and the authorities associated with the school.

Which Test is Best

In this context the question naturally arises as to which test is the best. The answer to this question was not difficult to find in the early days of the scientific measuring movement, for the simple reason that there was only one method of tests or at the most one method for each subject, but the picture has entirely changed now. It is difficult to point out the best test now. We, however, may rely on certain commonly accepted principles in the matter of the selection of the best test. These are as follows:

1. The basis for tests should be scientific and worthy of measuring the work for which they have been designed.
2. Instructions in respect of application of tests and scoring, etc., should be clearly laid down.
3. The test should also help in placing children into separate categories in accordance with their achievements.
4. The tests to be selected should be cheap but certainly not useless.
5. It should also have the quality of being applied to a larger number of grades. By this the comparative study of children at different grades will be possible.
6. Tests should be of more than one form in order to make a repetition on the same child possible when a need for doing so is felt.
7. Tests should not be time and energy consuming and should make the scoring easier.

New Types of Examinations

Till recently essay type examinations had a hold over our educational system. But during the last few years a new system of examination has been evolved. The system has not only supplemented the traditional essay type examination but has also replaced it to a great degree. The structure of this new type of examination greatly resembles the standardised tests. The main difference between the two is that standardised tests are to prove their worth in practical use, but no such limiting factor exists for the new type of examination.

Hints for Constructing New Type Tests

It will not be out of place to say a few words about the points to be considered while devising new types of examinations.

1. The questions to be included in the examination papers should be of moderate and easy. It will make the evaluation of the work of children of all categories possible.
2. The first six questions of the paper should be easy enough to be solved by all examinees.
3. The questions should be selected with a view to touching all the aspects of a subject.
4. The question, causing confusion both of ideas and languages should be given no place.
5. All the questions should be short.
6. Arrangements of groups should be made for every type of question.
7. A large number of questions should be prepared on any subject so that a thousand or more of them are always in hand to be used in different forms of examinations according to need.
8. The question in the test papers should be arranged in accordance with the arrangement of lessons in the textbooks.
9. There should be clear instructions about the questions of different groups.
10. The apparent difficulty of a question should not be the basis for inclusion and rejection of the question in the examination.
11. The questions to be picked up for examination purposes, should be complete in themselves.
12. Weighing of questions on the basis of their importance and stiffness is unnecessary in the new type of examination.
13. In the allocation of marks to questions a uniform policy should be followed.
14. Pre-fixed scoring formula, except in the case of true-false questions, should be applied and the calculations of marks should be worked out accordingly.
15. The question-paper should be changed from time to time and children be examined occasionally. It saves their scoring from the influence of immediate teaching.
16. The examination questions should be printed and all the answer-books used or unused should be so preserved that the remotest possibility of the impact of recent teaching on them is removed.

Purpose of Examination—Questions and Curricula

The aims and objectives of the curriculum which has been prescribed for the children should be the major consideration in preparing all sorts of examination papers. Full benefit can be ensured to the children only by following this principle. It may also be said in other words that objectives of the prescribed courses should form the basis of all examinations.

Limitations of New Types of Examinations

A consideration of the limitations of the new type of examination will not be out of place here. The comparison of this type of examination with that of the essay type examination reveals that the former is also not free from shortcomings. Only the memory and the special aptitude of children for a subject are tested under this system. It does not provide full scope to the children to express their ideas independently on the pros and cons of a subject. Children thus do not get ample opportunity for forming their opinion on a matter in their own way. It cannot be denied that a good memory is a boon and the knowledge of facts is necessary, yet an ideal system of education will never allow its children to be turned into mere crammers of the ideas of others. Its main objective is to prepare them as active persons of independent thinking. A prerequisite for this is the opportunity for free thinking and expression of one's ideas about a thing. This opportunity, is provided to the children certainly by the essay-type examination and the new one lacks it.

New Type Examination and Standardised Tests

Certain other disadvantages of the new type of examinations come to light when it is compared with the standardised test method. Yet, it has the advantage of containing all these things which are taught to a child. The new type of examination may be used any time when desired, but the needs for standardised tests, are of a general nature. In the entire session these test should be generally taken up at a scheduled time.

Advantages of the New Type of Examination

Whatever the case may be, one cannot close one's eyes to the importance of new system of examination. The advantages derived from this may be hinted at below:

1. Children evince keen interest in the new type of examination. Some of the students even consider them to be a game and enjoy it. It is the special characteristic of the system particularly in the context where the child and his interests have been made as the central point of entire modern education.
2. The system also helps us to understand fully the shortcomings and weakness of students. It becomes easier both for the teacher and the taught to know the facets which demand greater emphasis.
3. The system may also be made comprehensive which is not possible under the old examination system, specially without spending a good deal of time.
4. The markings, too, are more reliable under the new system as they are objectively based.
5. The teacher also has to spend less time and energy over marking.
6. Ultimately we reach the conclusion that both the new and essay type methods should be adopted for all types of examinations and the proper use of standardised test should also be made according to needs.

Mental Tests

General Knowledge of Students: The above methods are of little avail for testing the general knowledge of children which, nowadays, has become necessary for every student. To achieve this objective psychologists have discovered certain tests known as mental tests. The reader may get a comprehensive idea of mental tests from any book on educational psychology.

Summary

Why Evalaution in Education: The evaluation of children's work is necessary to know what and how much they have learnt. It also gives us an opportunity to make necessary changes.

Necessary Factors of Evaluation: Evaluation must rest on philosophy and science to be useful. Negative results will be obtained by adopting a course different from this.

Evaluation by Teachers and Its Unreliability: Different teachers give different marks to the same answer of the same student.

How to Make Teachers' Marking Reliable: Steps have been taken for this. Important among these are reforms of the examination system, use of standardised tests and measurements, application of general merit and diagnostic tests and scales and the selection of the best type of examination.

New Type Examination: In the past few years a new type of examination system has been developed. It has replaced the old one to a major extent. Its structure resembles the standardised tests greatly but it is not necessary for this system to prove its practical worthiness, like that of standardised tests methods.

Framing of the New Examination: Utmost care should be taken in the matter of the selection of questions and in fixing their numbers. Proper attention is needed simultaneously on prescribed courses.

Limitation of the New System of Examinations: The new system of examinations, despite its importance in our educational system, is not completely free from defects. Its major defect is that it does not provide full scope to the students to think and express their views independently. This opportunity is, however, provided by essay-type-examinations.

Exercises

1. What is the need for evaluation in education?
2. Throw light on the unreliability of markings by teachers and explain the efforts that are being made to improve the system.
3. Discussing the development of standardised tests and measurements suggest ways for their utilisation.
4. 'It is not within the competence of a common teacher to select the best type of tests'. Give your own views in this respect and also explain the merits of a good type of examination.
5. What do you understand by new type of tests? Discuss.
6. What are the points to be kept in view while framing new type of tests?

Chapter 26

Some Main Problems of Secondary Education

India remained under the British rule for about one hundred and seventy-five years. The aim of secondary education during this rule was to turn out clerks to strengthen the foundations of British imperialism in the country. Most of the High school students remained miserably poor in the equipment for life in general and they had no alternative but to become clerks in the government or other offices.

Unfortunately in free India also, the same old educational system is still holding ground and almost the same type of students are being produced. Efforts are being made both by the Central and State governments, ever since the dawn of independence to change the pattern of education but no effective changes have been introduced so far and the students have no specific ideals before them. About eighty per cent of the students go to schools simply because their parents send them there and they choose the easiest subjects so that they may achieve success at examinations without much labour. They are absolutely blank about their future. The sole aim of the present day secondary education is to turn out students for universities.

The students spend an important period of their life in gaining secondary education. The foundations of the future life of students between 11 and 18 years of age is laid during this time. As such, this education has a great significance in the lives of students and in fact its ideal should be the development of the physical, intellectual and moral powers of the students.

India is predominantly an agricultural country and the people here are very poor, so it is a problem for many to send their children to school even up to the secondary stage. Hence, secondary education should be so planned that the students may have no difficulty later on in choosing a profession. Apart from this, the representatives of our villages constitute the Government of the country, hence, the secondary education, which the rural students can easily acquire, should be such as to inculcate in them the spirit of right citizenship, leadership and social service.

Our counry has a secular government and equal rights have been given to people of different relgiions. Consequently, it is necessary that education should be able to develop in the students such a spirit of nationalism and such a love for Indian culture that the citizens may be willing to do all that is necessary for furthering the interests of the country. Hence the ideals of secondary education may be summrised as follows:

1. *Character Building*

The first and foremost aim of secodnary education should be shaping out the character of children in an ideal manner.

2. *Professional Facility*

A large number of students often read for the sake of bettering their prospects and securing the means of livelihood. So secondary education should help in developing professional acumen also.

3. *All-round Development of the Child*

Students of different proclivities form secondary schools. Therefore, the aim should be the development of the tendencies of different children. Besides, the physical, intellectual and moral development of the children should also be brought about.

4. *Leadership Qualities*

Secondary education should develop in the students the spirit of leadership so that the reins of administration may always be in the hands of the capable persons.

It is an unfortunate fact that in our secondary schools there is a total lack of this type of education. Below we are dealing with the some main problems of secondary education.

Curriculum

The curriculum of the secondary schools appears to be unsuitable. Although efforts have been made from time to time to introduce changes in the economic, cultural and educational conditions of the country, yet nothing substantial has been done so far in regard to the curriculum of the secondary schools. The curriculum has very little concern with the future life of the students who go on acquiring education up to Intermediate, Degree and Post-graduate classes without any worthwhile aim before them. When after the completion of their education they are faced with the question of a livelihood they find themselves in a fix. This is due to the unfortunate fact that after passing their examinations the students forget most of what they have learnt, because this education has very little value in their personal and social life.

Since in India about three-fourth of the total population lives in villages, the curriculum of secondary schools should be such as to impart to the students agricultural education also. Besides, the curriculum should be comprehensive and broad based to allow the study of various subjects. In order to facilitate the students' choice of subjects according to their interests, a provision should be made for psychologists so that proper guidance can be given to them.

Discipline in Schools

Students at all levels have become indisciplined. It is a blot on their character, yet they regard this as a matter of pride. Practically everyday there are cases of indiscipline. The main causes may be summarised as follows:

1. *Deterioration of the Moral Standards of Society:* The most important factor responsible for the indiscipline among students is the deterioration of the moral standards of society. Although the students have become notorious for indiscipline, yet if we look a round we shall find the absence of discipline in every sphere of our life. In every walk of life there is visible

a deterioration of moral conduct. In the markets there is no edible commodity which is not adulterated. In like manner, we find that there are very few officers of the government who have a real sense of duty. The clerks in government offices come to office at about noon when they should reach their tables at about 10 a.m. The situation is similar in other semi-government offices also. All this has its repercussion on the students and they also behave in an indisciplined manner.

2. *Political Upheavals:* The students had taken an active part in the Indian struggle for independence and as a result of this they are prone even today to behave in the old way against their own national government.
3. *The Present Examination System:* The examination system is also a major cause of the gross indiscipline among students who take their studies non-seriously all the year round and wish to pass their examination by fair or foul means. When they are checked in their undesirable attempts they resort to misconduct and a number of teachers are either beaten or insulted during the examination days. In this the teacher finds himself between the devil and the deep sea, for if he catches a student in his unfair attempt his personal safety is at risk, and if he does not do so the student gets off scot-free whereas he himself is guilty of neglect of duty and at times even faces the risk of being dismissed.
4. *Miserable Economic Condition of the Teachers:* The economic condition of the teachers is also a factor responsible for the indiscipline among students. Due to low emoluments persons of high calibre do not join this profession and those who do remain busy with the problem of making the two ends meet. Due to this the teachers fail to command the respect of the students. The teacher of today does not regard himself as the architect of the future life of the students, nor do the students take him as such. Hence, there is an absence of love and regard among the teachers and students for each other.
5. *The Indifference of the Parents:* The students of today are not like those of the Gurukuls of old times. So they do not spend all their time in the company of teachers. On the contrary, the

students spend most of the their time in their homes. If the parents were to make a real efforts to prevent their children and wards from falling into evil ways, there will be no problem of indiscipline, for it is often seen that due to the carelessness of the parents the students pick up evil habits of frequenting picture palaces and disobeying the elders and so on.

Management and Administration

In most cases the secondary schools in many states in our country are managed by private bodies in which the government does not have a hand. Consequently, these bodies look more to their individual interests than to the interests of the schools. The horrible state of management of schools in rural areas is well-known both to the students and teachers of those schools. The teachers employed in the schools are mostly the puppets of the members of the managing committee and thus capable persons are kept out. Besides, there are other evils like low salaries and delayed payments in many schools. The financial condition of these schools is so deplorable that there is a total lack of amenities like suitable premises, libraries, reading-rooms and game-apparatuses etc.

Besides, in many states of the country a number of schools are run after the names of particular individuals or of castes and communities. Such denominational schools do not get full public cooperation and there is much competition between them and other institutions.

The general administration of the private schools is not good. The inspectors of schools do not interfere with the work of the managing bodies and they very often take their side. The teachers submit their petitions repeatedly to the inspectors but they turn a deaf ear to all these and consequently the administration also cannot help the teachers.

The managing committees of some secondary schools are usually constituted by big businessmen who have nothing to do with education and they run the schools also as a source of income. How can intelligent, capable and self-respecting teachers play second fiddle to these greedy people? Hence, only those teachers remain in these school who can just manage to carry on the work anyhow but who cannot at all serve the ends of education.

Therefore, the need of the hour is that the government should take over the management of these schools all over the country and at least three educationists and three representatives of the teacher should be on the managing committee. It is not good to leave the responsibility of education on the shoulders of uneducated and illeterate people.

Standard of Education

It has become the talk of the day that the standard of education has fallen. This is ture to a great extent but teachers alone cannot be held responsible for this. After independence the national government adopted the policy of the expansion of education which, however, adversely affected the standard. The schools in the rural areas have neither buildings, nor books nor able teachers. Those who do not get service in any other department take to the teaching profession. Due to financial straits the moral values of such teachers have gone down and they try foul means to push their students in the examinations. The salaries of these teachers are so low that no one joins the education department. There are many teachers who take to these profession only to earn their livelihood. But these conditions should not be allowed to prevail in the field of such importance as education. There should be a provision for higher salaries so that competent hands may be available. Besides, the indifference of the government towards the education department, the neglect shown by the parents towards the proper education of their wards, bad administration and the unscientific examination system lead to the deterioration of the standard.

Another important cause is the curriculum. Due to paucity of funds many schools cannot make provisions to teach a number of optional subjects. The students, therefore, do not feel interested in their studies and this leads to the deterioration of standard. Thus this type of education cannot conduce to the all-round development of the students for whom the sole object has become to pass the examinations. The students do generally forget much of what they read for examinations. The craze for cinema, cheap notes in the market and the ignorance of the parents are other factors responsible for the lowering of the standard.

The Examination System

Of all the problems of education that of the examination system is the most acute one. People are prone to judge the merits of teachers and the quality of schools on the basis of the examination results. Hence, many teachers and students generally take recourse to undesirable methods. The students read only to pass examinations and do not take the trouble to either gain real knowledge or build up their character. There are students who waste their time all the year round in undesirable activities and pass the examination by unfair means. Such students do not gain any knowledge and after passing the examinations they find themselves misfits in social life and very often become anti-social elements. It is a matter of great regret that due to financial straits some teachers also help in making the examination system all the more vicious. In return for some illegal gratification, they help the students in their unfair means at examinations. Unless the examination system is overhauled no improvement in the standard of education is possible. Hence the test of the students' abilities should be the work done by him during the year and not only at the examination.

Unless the above mentioned defects are removed Indian education cannot be improved. Secondary education is the bedrock and the future of the students depends on this for it is connected with primary and higher education as well. After secondary education students become teachers in primary schools and some of them join universities. Thus secondary education directly or indirectly affects all the aspects of society.

Summary

Some of the problems which must be solved are as follows:

1. The economic stringency of the teachers is due to their meagre salary. This stringency makes their standard of living lower. Their skill is ruined. The better teachers are not attracted to this profession. Teachers have less freedom.
2. The second problem of the schools is the scarcity of teaching equipment and appliances. The Government should spend enough to make the schools well-equipped.
3. The third problem of the schools is the scope of the curriculum. It is forced upon them by the Department.

4. The fourth problem is the lack of contact between the school and society. For the success of democracy it is necessary to make the school a smaller form of society.
5. The examination system is defective.

Managing Committee: The managing committees are generally the centres of party-politics. It adversely affects the school. The organisation of the committees is very defective. The members are influenced by favouritism. The teachers remain busy in flattering the manager and the members. The Education Department should keep a vigilant eye upon it.

The Ideals of Secondary Education; The school is a smaller form of society. The activities, which are useful for the welfare of the society, must be generally observed in schools. Education which is useful for life, should be imparted. The education in various subjects should be arranged according to the various aptitudes of the students.

Exercises

1. Express your views on modern secondary schools.
2. Discuss some of the internal and external problems of our schools.
3. How far is the administration by the Government Education Department helpful in the progress of education?

Chapter 27

The Position of Teachers

Everybody appears to be dissatisfied with the system of education that prevails today. It is generally and rightly felt that if the teachers are persons of ability and good character, having a sense of duty, their students also will have these qualities. On the other hand if the teachers are not able persons or if they do not fully know the art of teaching, or are persons who have taken to this profession because they could not get any other job, their teaching methods will be defective. Teaching is a very important job and the students are moulded by education. Hence, it is necessary for teachers to have a thorough knowledge of the art of teaching. But it is often seen at present that unsuitable persons join this profession and the work of education is not carried out properly. The teacher should have a knowledge of different subjects and should possess an ideal personality. He should be a good person in order that he may help properly develop the mental, physical and moral powers of the students. On account of the low salary no able and competent person is prepared to take the teaching profession.

Teachers and their Holidays

The teachers are responsible for making the students ideal citizens. The rise and fall of any country depends largely on education. But the society today is indifferent towards teachers. People are more prone to criticise the teachers than to realise their importance, economic conditions and their needs. Some people think that teachers have to do very little and besides they get too many holidays. This is however, quite baseless for the teachers and students.

For the poor teachers holidays are the only means of recreation. In holidays they visit their friends and relations and get some change and recreation. They do all their personal work during these holidays. They get such low salaries that at all times they are faced with the problems of keeping the pot boiling.

Social Prestige of Teachers

Today the teachers are not given any social prestige. Nowhere in society is the teacher duly respected. People have come to think that the teachers can neither do them any good nor harm. Hence, people think that it is useless to respect them. Teachers have been reduced to such a state of affairs that they are confined to their particular community and laugh and weep among themselves. There is no one else to sympathise with them.

It has often been noticed that whenever a policeman, or a *lekhpal* or any other government employee visits a village, everyone shows great respect towards them but when a teacher goes there nobody pays any attention to him.

The teachers are the guide and builders of the future citizens of our country, but very little value is attached to their work. Persons in other departments get higher salaries than teachers do. The masons who build houses, the engineers who measure the roads, the doctors who prescribe medicines, and the postmen who distribute letters, earn more than the teachers. The government employees in other departments get fat salaries, handsome travelling allowances and beautiful houses to live in, but teachers who are more able are given low salaries and there is no provision for even ordinary houses for them. A large portion of their earnings is spent on house rent. They get neither wholesome food to eat nor proper clothes to wear. This is the reason why this profession does not attract persons of high calibre. Today we find the condition of all the teachers of primary and secondary schools very pitiable.

The Teachers Community and the Management

The main cause of the pitiable condition of the teachers is the indifferences of the government. All the other needs of society are met by the government but the major portion of the burden of such an important subject as education has been left on the shoulders of the public. At present in each district of Uttar Pradesh there is at least a higher secondary school which is completely managed by the government while all the remaining ones are managed by private bodies. The condition of the teachers in these private schools is miserable although the government is fully responsible for paying full salaries to teachers. There are some such schools where there is no fixed date for the disbursement of salaries and these run into arrears for three to four months. Besides this, the services of self-respecting teachers also are not secure there. It has often been noticed that due to differences with the management the services of the principal and teachers are terminated with disregard to government rules.

Suggestions for the Reform of the Condition of Teachers

Education is the root of all our progress. Hence, the government should attach greatest significance to it. For reforming the condition of the teacher it is necessary that the government should bear the entire expenditure of education. The appointment of teachers should be made by the government in all the states of the country. The teachers should be given attractive salaries so that persons of good abilities may join this profession. The status of teachers should be regarded as the highest in society so that they may remain alert in discharging their duties. Teaching should be entrusted to such persons who have a knowledge of different subjects and a taste for teaching. Besides this, the personality of the teacher also should be an ideal one so that he may be able to develop the intellectual, physical and moral faculties of his students.

Summary

The position of teachers should be honourable, but in modern society the condition of teachers is pitiable. Teachers are not paid handsome salaries.

The public has no sympathy for the teachers. A police constable is honoured more than a teacher in the society. Holidays allowed to the teachers and the students irk the people, but in a teaching job holidays are badly needed.

Exercise

Illustrating the present condition of teachers, offer your suggestions for improving it.

Chapter 28

Health Education Scheme

Importance

Healthy individuals can make importanct contributions to development of a nation. It is one of the primary duties of every school to make proper arrangements for health-education. But schools do not pay adequate attention to this aspect of education and society as well is not quite vigilant towards this problem. Consequently, the children's health suffers. The primary purpose of education is to secure the harmonious development of the child. Unhealthy children cannot have good mental and moral development. Therefore, it is very necessary to do the needful for the health education of children.

The Aims of the Health Education Scheme

1. To acquaint each student of the school with health rules so that he may remain healthy and may impart his knowledge of health principles to others in society.
2. To inform the child about the harmful effects of smoking and drinking. To help him to contribute his share towards the maintenance of a healthy environment in the society.
3. The purpose of our education is to secure both the individual and social welfare. For this it is necessary to promote social traits in children by organising games and sports in the school. Their health will also improve through games and sports. Hence, these should be an integral part of health-education scheme in any school.

Maintenance of Health

1. *Cleanliness:* The playground, compound garden and rooms should be carefully kept clean. to have healthy environment. Attention has to paid to this everyday. Lavatories, urinals and open-drainages should be disinfected everyday.
2. *Sun Light and Air:* The rooms of the school should be so designed as to permit adequate sun light and air.
3. *The Timetable:* The school timetable should be so arranged as not to cause excessive fatigue in children.
4. *Health Examination:* Every school should make adequate arrangements for the health examination of its children. Every child should be physically examined perriodically. A school dispensary should also be maintained for the medical treatment of the ill children. Co-operation of teachers and parents is very necessary in this respect. If any child falls a victim to some contagious disease, he should be immediately segragated and a proper arrangement for his treatment should be made.

For the health of children the following points should be taken into consideration:

1. Every child should be regularly examined medically once a month or at an interval of three months. If any disease is detected in child, the parents should be informed immediately.
2. The progress of the health of the child depends upon the co-operation of teachers and parents. Adequate arrangement for medical treatment should be immediately made, some disease is detected.
3. Most of the persons are generally ignorant of health rules. Heance the principal and the teachers must take special pains to acquaint the parents with principal health rules.
4. The teachers must see that the children do not acquire any bad habit like smoking.

Education for Protection of Health

To Explain the Elements of Physiology: All the children should be acquainted with the rudiments of physiology as far as possible. The help of a medical expert may be sought to advice the children on this subject at least once a month.

Healthy Refreshment: Pure water should be made available to the students in the school. The well in the school be periodically cleaned and protected from infectious diseases. Only healthy eatables should be permitted to be sold within the school compound. The school should try to arrange nourishing refreshments for the children during the school hours.

Physical Exercises: Suitable arrangements for physical exercises, games and sports should be made in the school as these are necessary for good physical development which is a prerequisite for good mental health. Physical exercises are also likely to develop the traits of mutual co-operation, discipline, obedience and social responsibility.

Arrangement for Play: There should be a games superintendent in the school to organise games and sports. In fact, all the teachers of the school must co-operate in the organisation of these. If teachers also take an interest in games and sports, the students will be encouraged to participate in the same wholeheartedly. The following things must be kept into mind for good organisation of games and sports in the school:

1. The students should be grouped into teams according to their age, ability and desire, otherwise, they may not get an opportunity to play a certain type of game. The students themseleves should elect their leader of the team.
2. There should be a fixed timetable for games. In order to avoid monotony, different types of games should be played on different days.
3. Only a chosen few should not be given the chance to play. All the students should enjoy an equal opportunity in this respect. It is only after giving a chance to play to all that the first eleven should be chosen for any game.
4. Competitions should be organised from time to time. Inter-school competitions should also be occasionally held. But it should be seen that competitions do not generate a feeling of rivalry and jealousy.
5. The playground should be well maintained and the students must be taught how to keep equipment in order.

6. The games should be organised on a democratic basis. There should be a games-committee in the school. Each class should sent its representative to this committee. A board of games and sports should be organised by all the schools in the city or a particular area by sending their representatives. If the schools allow their students to organise and run the activities of this board, many democratic behaviours and skills will be developed in the students.
7. To give encouragement the winners should be given prizes.
8. Various types of physical feats—such as—physical exercises, school parade, class drill, race, tug of war, parallel bars, wrestling, hockey, football, cricket, bolleyball, tennis etc., should find a place in any programmes of games and sports.
9. Every school should have a gymnasium under the supervision of an efficient physical education director.
10. In the school timetable, at least one period of 40 or 45 minutes should be allowed for physical exercises or games and sports.
11. At least once a year a sportsweek should be observed. Some dignitary from outside may be invited on the occasion. Various kinds of competitions should be organised within this week. The winners should be awarded prizes. By participating in this sports week the students will learn many lessons in sports discipline.

Principles of Health Education

The school children should be adequately informed about the principles of health. In this respect the following must be explained to them:

1. The children should be explained the advantages of early rising. They should know how much time they should devote in such activities as study, play and sleep.
2. The ingredients of a balanced diet should be explained to them.
3. They should know the precautionary measures against infectious diseases.
4. They should be acquainted with the human anatomy.

5. The children should realise the importance of cleaniness.
6. They should understand the importance of pure air and water for health.
7. The teacher should watch the students very closely from time to time in order to understand how far they are observing health rules.

The Method of Health Education

The principal methods of health education are enumerated below:

1. The children should be regularly given suitable magazines and books pertaining to health. Then it should be seen to what extent they are observing the health rules laid therein. The teacher himself should observe health rules in order to present a good examples before children.
2. The mind of child is greatly influenced by the environment of the school. So all the health principles should be strictly followed in the school so that the child may also follow the same.
3. Occasionally,, some competent physician should be invited to the school to deliver lectures to students on health principles.

Mental Health

The aim of our education is to secure the all-round development of a child. Hence we should attend not only to his physical health, but to his mental health as well. The teacher occupies a very important position in furthering the harmonious development of the child. So the teacher should keep in mind the following points:

1. The teacher should pay equal attention to all the students. He should make a psychological study of the mental development of the students under his care.
2. The teacher should provide a reasonably free environment for the development of children, but no indiscipline should be tolerated. For the development of the qualities of politeness, brotherhood, friendship, co-operation and justice, the children should be encouraged to participate in social activities.
3. The co-operation of guardians should be sought so that the children do not go astray in any manner.

4. At times, lectures on the lives of great men of the world should be arranged in the school. This will help the students to imbibe some of their great qualities.

Society owes a great deal towards the achievement of sound mental health. Hence a suitable atmosphere should be maintained in the society for this purpose.

Summary

The Importance of Health Education Scheme: The aim of education is to secure the all-sided development of the child. Hence the school should pay adequate attention to health education. Our country is not rich. Hence we shall have to achieve the goals of good health within our limited resources.

Health Protection: There should be a good arrangement in schools for pure air, water, light, refreshment and medical examination.

There should be a good provision for physical exercises, games and sports in the school. All the teachers must co-operate in the organisation of games and sports.

The Method of Health Education: The students should be encouraged to read good books on health education. The teachers should present before students good examples of health habits. At times some physician should be invited to deliver lectures on health problems. The environment of the school should be healthy.

Mental Health: Good health must imply good mental health as well. The school and society must do the needful to secure the mental health of children.

Exercises

1. What are the aims of a health education scheme? Present an outline of a good health education programme for a school.
2. Explain the main principles of health protection in schools.
3. How should we organise games and sports to promote the health of children?

4. What are the advantages of games and sports? Which games and sports should be given a place in school programmes and why?
5. What is the meaning of mental health? What are the principal means of securing it?

Chapter 29

Importance, Types, Values and Essentials of Programmes of Co-curricular Activities

In the 11th chapter, we have already touched the issue of co-curricular activities. However, in this 29th and the following 30th and 31st chapters, we have explained some other aspects of co-curricular activities which should be promoted outside the school premises keeping in view their importance and values.

Co-curricular activities are not new because they happen to be as old as organized school system itself. Many of them were found in ancient days as well, in the forms or various types of competitions, such as athletics, students magazine, games of various types, debating societies, celebration of certain festivals, certain tours of places of educational importance, dramas, music, poet-meet, music, boy scouts, and girl guides. However it will have to be admitted that in the beginning, these activities were not given the importance due to them because most of the teachers concerned themselves with their teaching in the classroom situations. As a result, the teachers, in general, upto the middle of the 20th century seldom cared to recognize and accept the responsibility of what the students were doing outside their narrow subject domain. They ignored the social and physical lives of their students. But the new era in our country with the dawn of independence in 1947 ushered in a new spirit and leaders thought that the school should take upon itself the responsibility of preparing good citizens for the emerging democracy in the country. Consequently, now the schools in our land are now realising the importance of co-curricular activities along with curricular teaching in the development of our children. This awakening in the school system has led the teacher educators to incorporate in the curriculum for teacher education a place to co-curricular activities in the development of children. As a result, now we find a number of co-curricular activities in each school which are encouraged by teachers and the same are supervised by some teachers under the instructions of the principal or headmaster. The students' unions as organised in most of our schools play an important role in promoting healthy co-curricular activities under the guidance of some worthy teachers.

The kinds of co-curricular activities as we have named above, have been accepted by all promoters of healthy growth of children with the conviction that education should strive for all-round development of children. Needless to add that teaching of various subjects develop only the intellectual side of one's personality. It ignores the physical, social, aesthetic and cultural aspects of growth of children. The teacher has not only to stress the importance of knowledge and informations. The knowledge and facts are of no value in themselves unless they lead the students to think, apply and generalize and thereby help them to enrich their lives. Today the co-curricular activities are emphasized on the ground that the student is physically, mentally, socially and spiritually far more important than all the subjects put together in the curriculum. If we accept this viewpoint and endeavour for the development of children, only then we shall achieve the objective of all-round development of our children.

Importance of Knowledge, Ideals and Habits and their Relationship with Co-curricular Activities

Before we proceed to towards the purposes and values of co-curricular activities it appears necessary to remember the importance of 'knowledge', 'ideals' and 'habits' for promoting the full development of children.

Knowledge

There can be no learning without knowledge. In fact, knowledge is at the root of any learning. In fact, to some people knowledge is synonymous to education. But we have to remember that accumulation of informations and facts does not mean that one has obtained knowledge. Unless facts and informations acquired are put in action for behaving properly in all walks of life, the same are useless in the same manner as a donkey is not affected at all by the load of books that it carries on its back. So knowledge acquired must be put to good use for developing good character.

Ideals

Without ideals, an individual will find no good path for his life. Ideals give motivation and set standards for achievement. We have to set such ideals before out students which may be justified on the basis of social usefulness and which must also stand for "the greatest good of greatest number?

Habits

Importance of habits cannot be over-emphasized in the life of a good citizen. We must remember that a number of integrated and co-ordinated habits go to make an individual successful in his life. For establishing good habits, one must continually practise over and over again according to his ideals.

Co-Curricular Activities Promoting Values in the Form of Knowledge, Ideals and Habits

The role of all these essentials of education, i.e. 'knowledge' 'ideals' and 'habits' in one's life is so important that none can be omitted. If one has knowledge and ideas but is not habituated to act accordingly, he is an incomplete person. Such a person cannot choose a course of action intelligently. He cannot adapt himself to a new situation in life in a desirable manner. Till very recently the emphasis in our formal education has been upon knowledge and ideals, and not on habits which may make knowledge and ideals function in actual situations of life. For this, it is necessary that now emphasis is laid on 'doing'. One cannot be good without 'doing' the acts which stand for virtues. So now the school should try to analyse the habits of students with a view to establish a close relationship between the various aspects of his knowledge and ideals towards making them good citizens in future. Co-curricular activities offer a challenging setting for developing young students into good citizens, because they provide numerous good opportunities for picking up knowledge useful in various aspects of life, establing laudable ideals and giving actual practice for formulating such good habits of which any good citizen may be proud.

Main Purposes or Values of Co-curricular Activities

The following ones may be accepted as the main purposes or values of Co-curricular activities.

1. To enable students to be worthy and active citizens of a democracy.
2. To help students to acquire lessons in social co-operation.

3. To utilize the innate drives of students for their educational growth.
4. The develop a love in students for law and order.
5. To make the students more interested in the school life.
6. To identify the special abilities of students for developing them further.
7. To promote good discipline and tone of the school.
8. To make students self-directive.

Onwards we shall explain the meanings of these purposes and values.

1. *To enable students to be worthy and active citizens of a Democracy:* Our students have to be prepared for becoming good and active citizens of a democracy. This implies living and behaving with others democratically. For acquiring this art, one has a try to incorporate democratic ideas in his behaviour consistently. Not a single opportunity for practising this ideal should be missed. Aristotle has rightly remarked that 'there is no holiday to virtues'. Education in the art of democratic behaviour should be gradual, and it has not to be imposed. The necessity of educating the child in democratic behaviours arises because of the fact that the early life of the child has been mostly autocratic. But as the children grow parents naturally put many restrictions on them in order to make them social in various aspects of life. Young children have to be trained in good habits, because they do not always understand the meaning of worthy ideals and worthy habits. A time will come when the child will be required to have his place as a citizen. So he must be taught the responsibilities and duties of worthy citizenship in a democratic society. Without this training be cannot be a good citizen. Towards the realization of this the school should be so organised that it offers ample such opportunities and responsibilities which a citizen may be called upon in a later life to share and shoulder. Then he will be better able to utilize such opportunities and responsibilities when they happen to occur. Co-curricular activities may provide such a type training to students in schools.
2. *To help students to acquire lessons in social co-operation:* The value of worthy citizenship will be nullified if an individual does not recognize the importance of social co-operation. Social co-operation cannot be taught as a subject usually included in the curriculum. In fact, actual practice in it is necessary. Membership of a student union, games, association, debating society and dramatic club requires co-operation. Active membership in such a society or group will teach the principles of social co-operation. So the students should be

advised to participate in such school activities for learning lessons in social co-operation.

3. *To Utilize Students Innate Drives For Their Educational Growth:* Young children are born with certain innate drives which, quite naturally, propel them to be curious about things, to display what they happen to know, to initiate, to construct, to acquire and to sympathise with others at occasions. A good teacher realizes that such urges on the part of children are bad only if they are not properly utilized for their healthy growth. So he organizes a setting for affording the required opportunities to children in order to use their innate urges for their desirable growth. Co-curricular activities provide ample opportunities for capitalizing the natural urges of children for their educational growth.
4. *To Develop a Love In Children For Law And Order:* Fear is a bad tool for effecting discipline. Discipline created through fear is only temporary and it disappears at the moment when there is no fear. Teachers and headmasters who openly give threats to students in the classrooms or students' assemblies only create troubles for themselves. The best discipline is that which comes from within. An individual takes pride if he is able to set his own good ideal of conduct. This does not imply that school authorities should surrender their own obligations for enforcing discipline in students. What we actually mean is that a student should be intelligently guided to develop a sense of healthy discipline within himself. Needless to add that co-curricular activities richly provide numerous opportunities towards the realization of this coveted goal.
5. *To Make The Student More Interested In The School Life:* The student who usually participates in school games or other cultural activities in the school talks more about his "school spirit" than any other of his school fellows who are not interested in such things. He does so because he feels that he is giving more to his school, of course, in his own way. A wise man has truly remarked that "he is more blessed who gives than the one who receives." Providing opportunities through co-currioular activities will-imply encouraging students "to give' rather than 'to receive'. This feature will be very ennobling. As a result, the number of noble and good students will be increased.
6. *To Identify Special Abilities Of Students For Developing Them Further:* It is one of the main objectives of education to identify special abilities of students with a view to develop them further.

This is not always possible through teaching of various subjects in classroom situations. In the school we have not only to develop academic interests in students. In fact, we have also to promote their all sided developments, such as: physical, mental, social, culture, vocational and spiritual. Such all-round developments will be most important assets of any school organization and society. Opportunities for such kinds of development may be richly provided through co-curricular activities and also because herein a student chooses an activity for himself in commensurate with his interests, ideals and understandings. He is very much naturally encouraged in such a participation because he finds that many other children of his own age are also doing likewise. The importance of co-curricular activities in the development of character and good citizenship is very aptly stated when once a British head master of U.K. remarked that "many of our battles have been fought and won on the play-fields of Eaton and Harrow".

7. *To Promote Good Discipline And Tone Of The School:* The school has to maintain a tone and discipline of its own. Without this the community will not send its children to it for education. Parents send their children to schools because they have great faith in goodness and effectiveness of the school. For fulfilling the implied obligations on the part of the school, it is very necessary that the school consistently strives to develop its discipline and tone.. Towards this end school assemblies, cultural programmes, games and occasional educational tours will play a major role. Such activities will solidify and unify the school spirit. Then the students and teachers will be proud of the records and achievements of the school. The development of this type of school discipline and tone through co-curricular activities will of great educative value for the student.
8. *To Make Students Self- Directive:* Our students have to be taught the lessons of self-control in order that ultimately they become captains of their own souls. This will imply the development of the spirit of self-directiveness. Here once again arises the importance of knowledge, ideals and habits. A student must have the requisite knowledge in order to act accurately, he must have certain ideals in order to act in a way which is socially desirable and individually satisfying and in the third place he must develop the habit of always acting accordingly. If he is able to do so, it will mean that he has developed the power of self-directivenes. If children are over-fondled

or over-mothered at home they will lose all initiative and will become weaklings. Co-curricular activities offer numerous situations at which students may easily develop the power of self-initiative and self-direction with a view to shoulder responsibilities at their own risk.

Essentials of Co-curricular Acctivities

If co-curricular activities have to achieve their values and purposes certain essentials are have to be followed in their organization. These essentials may be called 'principles' also. We mention below some of these essential principles:

1. Co-curricular activities must be constructive.
2. Co-curricular activities must be well supervised.
3. Participation of all students is necessary in Co-Curricular activities.
4. Due respect should be given to students regarding their rights, privileges and obligations.
5. Students who have left school for good should not be allowed to participate in co-curricular activities.
6. Co-Curricular activities should be run during school hours.
7. Democratic principles are necessary in requirements for participation. In the organisation.
8. Due consideration is necessary in organization of co-curricular activities.
9. Co-curricular activities must be regarded as a part of the regular duties of teachers.
10. Co-curricular activities with a humble beginning should be developed gradually.
11. No over importance to co-curricular activities.
12. A teacher made as in-charge should be given of co-curricular activities should function as an adviser.
13. Reasonably adequate finance is necessary for co-curricular activities Onwards we shall explain the meanings of these essentials.

1. *Co-curricular Activities must be Constructive:* Co-curricular activities will not achieve their objectives, if they are not constructive in nature. During the sixth decade of the 20th century, some of the state governments in our country had banned the functioning of students' Unions in schools, colleges and universities. But this measure was considered to be impractical, as it was rightly realized that strong urges in young students must be utilized for their healthy development. So the governments in their respective states allowed the functioning of Students' Unions in a constructive manner. It

will have to be admitted that the Students' Unions in our schools have been more constructive in their approaches, because they have not been, politically motivated as we find students' unions in degree colleges and universities. In order to make school students' unions constructive in their approach some teachers should guide them intelligently in such a way as to make the students run various cultural and other co-curricular activities through their unions if they so desire. Needless to add that there must be a judicious control of teacher over the running of co-curricular activities through the students' unions. This necessity logically leads us to the second essential which is being explained below.

2. *The Co-Curricular Must Be Well Supervised:* In a small school the principal may himself choose to supervise the co-curricular activities as he has a vigilant eye over all that is going on in the school. But in a large school a team of teachers should be given the responsibility for supervising the co-curricular activities. In the absence of good supervision their purposes will be defeated.
3. *Participation of All Students Necessary But No Over Participation:* Normally all the students will not be interested in co-curricular activities. This is true of curricular activities also. We sea that some students do not pay enough attention on their studies. However, the ideal should be to encourage as many students as possible to participate in co-curricular activities. We have also to note that no student over-participates otherwise this will harm his curricular activities. Over participation by some students will naturally deprive other students for having their chance.
4. *Due Respects To Students Regarding Their Rights, Privileges And Obligation:* All the students should be regarded as honourable citizens. As such, their rights, privileged and obligations must never be overlooked If this principles is not followed in the right spirit the school has no right to exist. In fact, a school has to prepare children as good citizens of a democracy. Therefore in the conduct of co-curricular activities the rights, privileges and obligation of students must be respected.
5. *Students Who Have Left The School For Good Should Not Be Allowed To Participate In Co-curricular Activities:* The privileges and facilities available in the school are meant only for the current students of the school. So the old students must not be allowed to participate in them, because this will deprive some students of their legitimate opportunities.

6. *Co-Curricular Activities Should Be Run During School Hours:* Running the co-curricular activities during school hours will give opportunities to all students to benefit themselves from the same. Secondly, such activities run during school hours are considered as sanctioned by the school authorities. Hence they are regarded as dignified. Running of these activities during school hours must not be formalized like subject teaching. In other words, due freedom to students must be conceded to participate in the same.
7. *Democratic Principles Necessary In Requirements For Participation:* A student should be allowed to participate in co-curricular activities, if be expresses an interest for the same. For this he should not be required to show any ability. In fact, the organization of co-curricular activities is only meant to give an opportunity to develop one's ability.
8. *Due Consideration Necessary In Organization Of Co-Curricular Activities:* An organization may come up at the spur of a moment depending upon the emotional attachment of the organizers, but the same will soon disappear, if due consideration is not given in the administration and programming. But once certain activities are taken up, the same should be tried and should be given up only when some better ones have been thought of to replace them. However, frequent changes should be avoided, but this will be possible only when an activity is initiated after due consideration.
9. *Co-Curricular Activities Should Be Regarded As A Part of Regular Duties Of Teachers:* Some over-burdened teachers naturally resent if given some responsibility in the running of co-curricular activities. So in the distribution of duties in the organization of co-curricular activities, the load that a teacher is carrying must be duly considered. However, the necessity of participating in co-curricular activities must be impressed upon each teacher. But in all circumstances due recognition should be given to a teacher for whatever duty he is required to perform in the running of co-curricular activities. By doing so each teacher will regard participating in co-curricular activities as an essential part of his duty.
10. *Co-Curricular Activities With a Humble Beginning should be Developed Gradually:* It is better to make a small beginning and develop gradually than to start with a big programme and dwindle out soon. In the organization of co-curricular activities no slavish copying of what is happening in another school will be desirable. Conditions of the school, possible talents of students, and the

personnel available should determine the organization. In fact, the co-curricular activities should grow out of the life of the school itself. Therefore in view of the capacities of the students concerned the beginning should be a humble one accordingly.

11. *No Over Importance To Co-Curricular Activities:* The co-curricular activities should be organized only as supplementary educational programmes, and under no circumstances an attempt should be made to focus then as representing an adequate and complete programme of educational opportunities. In other words, the co-curricular activities must not be over-emphasized. Their main purpose should be only to utilize the other capacities of students as effectively as possible. Needless to add that a school running only co-curricular activities will be an absurd concept.
12. *A Teacher Made In-Charge Of Co-Curricular Activities To Function Only As An Adviser:* It is not easy for a teacher to function as an adviser in relation to his students, because it is but natural for him to dominate thinking that be possesses a superior wisdom and technique to do anything before the students under his control. This attitude on his part in relation to running of co-curricular activities will lead to disintegration of the same, because the students will naturally like to have their own say in matters co-curricular. Therefore, the teacher has to function only as an advisor. He must never impose his views and liking on students. It is true that the teacher is already enriched with better, judgement and more maturity, but his association with the students in relation to curricular activities should be only friendly and helpful and never dominating.
13. *Reasonably Adequate Finance Necessary For Co-Curricular Activities:* Organization of co-curricular activities will entail some expenditure. For certain items the funds required will be quite small and some will require a bigger amount. However, under no circumstances the organization of co-curricular activities should suffer on account of paucity of funds. But just as the school authorities responsible for running curricular programmes devise means for procuring the required funds, similarly, attempts should be made to organize finances for co-curricular activities, simply because they are no less educative for the young students. Needless to state that the co-operation of parents and also of the state government should be invited in this respect, by requesting them to see some of the co-curricular programmes. Some distinguished parents or friendly government officers should be particularly invited as chief guests

on some co-curricular functions. This measure is likely to create sympathy in them for helping the running of co-curricular activities.

Types of Co-curricular Activities

There may be many types of co-curricular activities such as:

1. Students' union.
2. The School Assembly in the morning or evening or whenever considered necessary by the head of the institution depending upon the appropriateness of a situation.
3. Students' clubs.
4. Dramatics and music.
5. Kavi Sammelan or Mushiara.
6. Literary societies, organizing debate or speeches by some distinguished guests.
7. Athletics and group games.
8. School exercise.
9. Organizing social events.
10. Handwritten magazines.
11. School Newspapers.
12. School Saving Banks or Sanchayika.
13. School Day Celebration.
14. Celebration of National Days.
15. Celebration of Birthdays of Great Personalities.
16. Display of Educative motion pictures.
17. The School Museum.
18. Teachers' Day.
19. Scouting and Girls Guiding.
20. N.C.C.
21. Parents Day.
22. School Exhibition.

The above are some of the few types that may be organized in a school as co-curricular activities. It may be added that the above list is not so comprehensive as to include all possible activities for students. In fact, a school may also think of some other types of co-curricular activities depending upon the particular needs and interests of students. Keeping in view of the essentials of co-curricular programmes the beginning should be quite humble. We may further observe that it may not be possible for a school to organize all the type of co-curricular activities as indicated above. So a school should try a small programme as suitable for its students and the particular surroundings they happen to come from. It is in a gradual manner than the span of co-curricular activities should be increased.

Summary

Formerly, co-curricular activities were not given due importance. But after achievement of independence in 1947 Schools in our land have become more careful about co-curricular activities as they are considered as good devices for promoting some necessary qualities in the future citizens of the state. So now our schools are organizing co-curricular activities. Co-curricular activities necessary for all-round development of children.

Importance of Knowledge, Ideals and Habits and Their Relationship with Co-curricular Activities

Co-curricular activities offer a challenging setting for developing qualities of good citizenship, and such knowledge, ideals and good habits of which any one may be proud.

Main Purposes or Values of Co-curricular Activities

1. Making students worthy citizens of a democracy
2. Acquiring lessons in social co-operation.
3. Utilizing innate drive of students for their educational growth.
4. Developing love for law and order.
5. Making students more interested in school life.
6. Identifying special abilities of students for developing them further.
7. Promoting good discipline and tone of the school.
8. Making students self- directive.

Essentials of Co-curricular Activities

1. Co-curricular activities must be constructive.
2. Co-curricular activities must be well supervised.
3. Participation of all students necessary.
4. Due respects to students regarding their rights, privileges and obligations.
5. Students who have severed their relationship with the school should not be allowed to participate.
6. Co-curricular activities should be run during school hours.
7. Democratic principles necessary in requirements for participation.

8. Due consideration necessary in organization of co-curricular activities.
9. Co-curricular activities should be accepted as a part of regular duties of teachers.
10. A humble beginning to be enlarged later.
11. No over-importance to co-curricular activities.
12. A teacher made incharge to function as an adviser.
13. Adequate finance necessary.

Types of Co-curricular Activities

May be several. The types should be chosen according to the capacity and interests of the students and local surroundings of the school.

Exercises

1. Discuss the nature of relationship of knowledge, ideals and habits in relation to co-curricular activities.
2. What are the purposes and values that co-curricular activities should be expected to promote and why?
3. Explain the essentials of co-curricular activities.
4. Describe how you will organise as a teacher any two types of co-curricular activities in a school.

Chapter 30

Importance and Organization of Dramatics, Educational Tours and Excursions

School Dramatics

A tendency in man to dramatize is as old as human race itself. In primitive people we find many forms of dramatization. Dramatization is a device through which one gives expression to intense feelings of jealousy, exultation, hate, love and mastery, etc. In his tendency to invite others a child evinces his capacity of dramatization, Through this capacity he expresses his feelings and thoughts about things and persons around him. The current concept of 'activity school' is only a recognition of the educational possibilities of the dramatic impulse in children. There are various types of literatures on dramatics. It is not possible to explain them all in this brief chapter. At best, we can emphasize here only certain principles of school dramatics. School dramatics mean only to educate the participants including students, stage managers, the audience and all types of helpers who have in any away contributed to the staging of the drama. In fact, our purpose here is only educational.

Values of School Dramatics

While discussing values of school dramatics we have to point out also to some dangers and weaknesses which should be avoided if the dramatics have to be educative to our students.

School dramatics may be utilized to raise some necessary funds for some of the co-curricular activities of the school. But in this endeavour we have to be careful about the following dangers and weaknesses of such an enterprise on the part of the school:

1. The school dramas must not emphasize how to tickle the audience instead of educating the actors and the student community in general.
2. It should be seen that benefits go to those who actually need them .
3. The school dramas should strive towards broadening of experiences of children who must not be led into highly specialized dramatic performances.

We must remember that school dramatics are not meant for public. They are solely meant to benefit the participants and also the school audience. An attempt should be made that most of the school students derive benefits from the school dramas. However, the most capable students should be allowed to participate in the dramas at which outside public may also be invited.

The school dramatics have a possibility in raising general standards of dramatic excellence. The average motion picture advertises its sex thriller to draw the attention of patrons who have not learnt to appreciate anything better. Such spectators run after only cheap movies and they feel satisfied because they have not developed aestheic sense which may demand a higher type of picture. One of the main objectives of the school is also to train its students to utilize their leisure hour in a more fruitful and educative manner. This objective may be partially achieved through presentation of well-designed dramatic performance in the school. Through such performances dramatic tastes may be developed in students. But in such an attempt, it must be seen that farcial productions are judiciously avoided, because in their preparation the box office is considered as more important than anything else. This feature leads to the working of the school for a few days in preparing students for the show. The students, under no circumstances should be encouraged to ape extravagant professional productions with the sole purpose of overcrowding the hall of performance.

Another value of the school dramatics lies in motivating the disinterested class in doing some exhilarating and educative work at the same time. It has been seen that when a few lessons are dramatized under the guidance of a skilful teacher a dull and disinterested class rises into activity which may be educative in many respects.

A teacher of any subject may use dramatizing for helping the students understand the materials fully and integrate their experiences obtained in various subjects. Preparation in dramatic presentations may provide good practice in real composition. Story lessons in history may be dramatized to a great advantage of students. Thus many historical events may be made very vivid to students. In geography lessons, models may be built, persons of various lands may be impersonated by certain students. Games may also be built around the location of states, oceans, rivers, mountains and cities and other geographical concepts. In science and mathematics students may be guided to convene their own conferences and conventions within the limits of the school. In foreign languages certain trips and foreign relationships may be dramatized. Similarly, certain lessons in commerce, economics and manual arts may be dramatized effectively in an educative manner.

Another value of the school dramatics is to develop the spirit of co-operation in the students and teachers of various subjects. This may be done through asking the help of various teachers and students to do what they can in relation to preparation of a scenery and poster. The commerce department may be requested to help in advertising and sale of tickets. Thus all the students and teachers may be called upon to help in one way or the other. This procedure will make the school dramatics a school event. Thus a higher morale and finer spirit will be felt by all concerned.

Values to the Actual Participants in the Performance

Dramatics offer an opportunity to students to discover, express and develop any talent in them for dramatization. The actor develops his vocabulary and mode of expression, confidence and poise in himself. Thus he gains both intellectually and culturally. Dramatics are equal to athletics as regards training in team work. Dramatics afford to students to experience a fuller life by appreciating the thoughts, actions, feelings and standards of others.

Values to the Community

School dramatics benefit the community also. By seeing the school dramatic performances parents become interested in better theatres and literatures. Thus they become more critical of the general movies. As a result, their tastes become more refined. Thus the school dramatics help the public to demand better motion pictures and higher types of dramatic performances. Thus, of course, indirectly the school may assume an additional responsibility for improving the literary tastes and standards of the community. Dramatics also offer an opportunity to help parents understand better their obligations to the school which teaches their children. Dramatics may indicate that an intelligent and continued support of parents is necessary if the school has to perform its task in an expected manner.

How To Organize Dramatic Performances

Club and Committees

Organisation of dramatic performances should be entrusted to an able teacher who is really interested in this type of work or to dramatic club which has been particularly set up for this purpose. This club should work under the guidance of a director who is chosen from amongst the school teachers. Interested students and teachers may be accepted as members of this club. Seleçting students for playing the roles of various characters in a drama should depend upon the already displayed proficiency in acting. A number of committees may be appointed to look after many details of staging a performance. Some of these committees many be named after the function or the item they have to deal with, namely, committee for deciding roles, committee for arranging the necessary properties and sceneries, such as, furnitures curtains, pictures and equipments of all kinds, committee for music, committee for arranging necessary costums, committee for managing the stage, committee for preparing and selling tickets, committee for publicity, committee for making payments and keeping accounts etc.

The Director

It will be better if an interested teacher is appointed as a director of the dramatic performance. During the days of preparation and actual performance at the stage the teacher-director should be relieved of his regular teaching load. The function of the director is to see that the performances are educative to the participants and to the student audience also. His concern should not be to please the parents through the school dramatics.

Selecting the Plays

Plays for performances should be chosen by a committee consisting of some teachers and senior students under the guidance of the appointed teacher-director. This committee may also consist of the main officers of the various committees which have been mentioned above. We should keep in mind the following consideration in selecting plays:-

1. The age, ability and training of the students staging the performance.
2. Author of the drama should be of recognized ability.
3. The play should be chosen keeping in view the nature, ability and culture of the audience.
4. The play should be free of undue emotional strain.

5. The play should be selected keeping in view the purpose, the performance and financial gain and entertainment.
6. The play should be chosen according to place and equipments available for staging.
7. The chosen play should be capable of being staged by the school students.

As far as possible various types, such as, farce, fantasy, comedy and musical plays should be chosen at various occasions during a year. It will be better if bedroom comedies, tragedies and plays dealing with social problems and immorality are carefully avoided in selection. The committee-in-charge should feel free to shorten or edit the play, wherever he considers it necessary.

Our discussion on school dramatics will not be complete unless we add a few words on the place of puppet show, vaudeville and pantomime.

Puppet Show

As a form of dramatics puppet show has it own unique place. It is very much liked by both young and old, but especially by young children, as to them the whole affair appear to be very strange and for some of them it is difficult to understand how the puppet is speaking and how it is moving its various limbs as symbols of certain expressions. Puppet shows may be profitably used both in primary and secondary schools just like any other type of school dramatics. These shows may be used for emphasizing personal virtues like obedience, courtesy courage, loyalty and honesty. Some able students may be guided to make the required settings, write and recite the songs or part of the speech and operate the stage settings and puppets.

Vaudeville

Vaudeville is only a lighter form of a school dramatic performance. It is principally designed for entertainment. It may consist of drill, magic, dances, short songs, style shows, skits, initiations and caricature of some well known actors of the film industry. This type of show may be easily enacted in a school because of the student of varying abilities. Such shows are very interesting and they are short and stand for varieties.

Pantomime

Pantomime is a kind of dumb show about which the audience is expected to interpret its implied meaning. It may easily be organized and enacted. A small group of students is required for rehearsing. The dramatic club of the school under the guidance of its director may easily organize some pantomimes.

Educational Tours and Excursions

School Tours

It is easy to organize tours in those schools which own their own buses. But due to the unprecedented development of means of transport, tours may be organized even by those schools which do not own their buses. Railway trains, roadways and private buses are easy means for school tours. Of course this will entail some expenditure which should be arranged from the fund meant for co-curricular activities. With the consent of the leaders of student union of the school some financial help may be drawn from the union funds. The leaders are not likely to object to this expenditure, because they will also join the tour and derive benefits like other fellow-students. Moreover, each participant may be require to contribute something to the tour expenses for meeting any eventiality. Some times a general class fund may also be raised for tour purposes and all the students are encouraged to join the tour. Normally speaking, tours mean travel to some longer distance than is done in short school trips and excursions. So in tours the problem of hotel accommodation arises. Materials for guidance in this connection may be obtained from bus company and railway journey folders and travel books. Needless to add that the expenses should be kept to the minimum by advising the students to stay in some Dharmashala or camping in their own tents at suitable places.

Places for Tours and Advance Preparation and their Conclusions

Tours should be taken up during long holidays. Places of historical, educational, religious, cultural and industrial importance may be chosen for school tours. Almost in each state in our country there are many places of such interests. The tours should be taken under the supervision of some able teacher whose character and sense of honesty is beyond reproach. Necessary preparations for the tours must be made in advance. The teacher-supervisor should see that each participant notes down the personal things that he should carry with him for the tour. The luggage of each should be so light as to permit carrying on one's own shoulder or hands easily. Each one should carry a notebook and a pen to note down his own impressions about the places of visit. Some participants may be advised to practise recitations of certain good songs and some may be advised to read some short stories for relating the same at the places of stoppages. Recitation of songs and relating of stories and ancecdotes will serve the purpose of catharsis when all of the participants get tired after the tour on a day. The attitude of give and take and mutual sympathy and co-operation will go a long way in relieving the exertions of the participants at times. When the tour is over, each participant should be required to present in writing his total impressions within a few pages. Then in a general meeting in the school the concerned students should be requested to read out their impressions for the benefit of others.

School Excursions

A school excursion is a type of co-curricular activity. An excursion is supposed to enrich classroom work in the same way as charts, maps, models, films and other illustrative materials do. Hence a school excursion should be provided for like any other device which is used for educative purposes.

Types of School Excursions

Under the first type we may include short trips to such nearly places as post office, bank, some big factory or cottage industry, a big college or some university, zoo, botanical garden, well-managed parks or some very well systematised business organisation, museums or local places of historical, cultural or religious importance. The second type is just like a tour or much longer excursion or trip which may take three, four or more days. Evidently, the first type appears to be more educative in the sense that it may easily be correlated with the school work on the same or next day. The second type of longer excursions or trips may also be made educative if they are taken up after due preparation and correlated later with the relevant school work. It may be remembered that the longer excursions must not end as sight seeing tours.

Values of Educational Excursions

Educational excursions provide first hand knowledge about many things. The students might have read about these things in their books, magazines or newspapers. But such approaches are second hand sources which bring to the students impressions of others. Educational excursions make the pictures of things and places visited very vivid. Such pictures are more lasting in their minds because they give first hand knowledge.

Secondly educational excursions provide an opportunity to students to be on the go and break the classroom monotony. During adolescence one wants to wander here and there and see new people, things, places and natural, sceneries and have new experiences which are personal and genuine.

Principles of Educational Excursions

Since educational excursions are of great values, they must be guided by certain principles. Below we are hinting at some such more important ones:-

1. *The Excursion Must Have One Definite Aim And Not Too Many:* For example, if the group of students have to be taken out for an educational excursion to Delhi, visiting of two many places in a single day will not be wise. Delhi is an ancient city and also very modern which is known as New Delhi. Within one morning or afternoon it is not possible to see all the important historical places. Then being a modern city it has many things of great educational values, such as the Parliament House, the Supreme Court, Rastrapati Bhavan, India Gate, a number of museums research institutes universities and cultural, religious and industrial centres. Similar will be the case of many other great old and modern towns in the country. So two or three morning or afternoon trips will be necessary for visiting each centre of interest. While visiting a centre, the students should be required to make their own notes. If the teacher is not able to explain certain historical and cultural points, the guidance from a formal guide will be most helpful. The notes made during the day to afternoon visit may be reviewed in the night before going to sleep. It must be remembered that the things visited should be seen thoroughly and nothing should be left for another later visit. An educational excursion should be handled as carefully as classroom activities are done
2. *Adequate Preparations Necessary:* It is not only important to tell where the students will go for a trip, but it is also important as to what and how they will see various things there. If a trip is so planned it will be most profitable. An advance preparation for a trip brings dignity and importance to it. A careful planning interests greater number of students. The various types of duties in relation to a trip may be assigned to a number committees formed for the purpose. For example, there might be separate committees for preparations, transportation and arrangements. The members of these committees will be students who will be elected for the purpose by their fellow students. Let us illustrate this formation of various committees.

Suppose a museum has to be visited. Then, the committee for arrangement will contact the director of the museum for making an appointment. The committee for transportation will arrange for the necessary conveyance. The committee for preparation will look after the necessary equipments for the visit and for breakfast, lunch and dinner. If there has to be self-cooking, or self-preparation of items for food, the necessary utensils and other requirements must be pre-arranged by this committee in advance.

If an educational excursion is so planned, it will provide a seriousness and accurateness.

3. *Educational Excursion To Be Correlated with classroom Work As Far As Practicable:* Correlation of the educational excursion with classroom work is necessary in order to enable the students to derive the best out of it. It is true that it may not be always practicable. However, an attempt by the teacher in this direction will be most praiseworthy and helpful to the students to derive the maximum benefits from the excursion.

Summary

School Dramatics

The current concept of activity school is a recognition of educational possibilities of dramatic impulse of children.

Values to the School

1. Major benefit should go mainly to the students. Not meant for public.
2. Broadening the experiences of the students.
3. To train the students to utilize their leisure hour.
4. Dramatics motivates the disinterested students into educative activity.
5. Preparation for dramatics may provide exercise in composition.
6. An opportunity to actual participants to discover, express and develop their talents for dramatization.
7. A good training in term work.
8. Parents may get interested in better movies, theatres and literatures. Thus their taste may become more refined.

How to Organize Dramatics Performances

Clubs and Committees

These are to be set up in the school for organizing dramatic performances. The club should be under the direction of a teacher-director. A number of committees should be formed for looking into the various details. These committees should be named after assigned functions.

Selecting the Plays

Plays of recognized authors should be chosen according to the age and ability of students who have to stage the show. The play should be free from great emotional strains. Selection should be made according to the equipment in the school. Bedroom comedies, tragedies and immorality should be avoided.

Puppet show, vaudeville and pantomime may also be chosen as they are of great educational values.

Educational Tours and Excursions

School Tours

Modern means of transportation have made the organization of school tours easy. Financial help may be obtained from the general fund meant for co-curricular activities, students' union funds and subscriptions from students.

1. *Place of Tours:* Places of historical, cultural, industrial, religious, and educational importances should be chosen under the guidance of an able teacher.
2. *Preparations:* Must be made in advance, luggage of each should be very light. Each should curry a notebook and a pen. Each one should be able to recite some poem or song or relate some story at the places of rest.

Educational Excursion Types

Short trips to such nearly places, as bank, museum or some historical or industrial place. Longer trips may take three or four days. Such short or long trips must not end as sight seeing prepositions. They must be correlated with the class-work.

Value of Educational Excursion

Provide first hand educative experiences. They break the classroom monotony and bring in other types of activities in students.

Principles of Educational Excursion

1. Must have a definite aim and not too many during a session.

2. Adequate preparation necessary.
3. Should be correlated with the class work.

Exercises

1. Discuss the educational importance and values of school dramatics.
2. Explain the details of organisation of dramatic performances in schools.
3. Describe the nature of the various types of dramatics performances that may be staged in a school.
4. What are the educational values of school tours? How should they be organised?
5. Discuss the various types of educational excursions that may be arranged for school students. Explain also the preparation to be made for the same.
6. Explain the values and principles of educational excursions.

Chapter 31

Hobbies, Junior Red Cross Society, N.C.C., School Assembly, School Exhibition, School Publications, Scouting, Girl Guidance and Community Service

Hobbies

Hobbies are of great importance in the life of an individual. The saying goes that a person is known by the way he keeps his leisure hours. The life of an individual may become a drudgery, if he has no hobby to occupy himself particularly at the time he is not at work. This situation becomes more serious after retirement from service.

Many retired persons are heard saying, "We do not know how to fill in our time". This situation is really very tragic. This means that such an individual has failed to develop his potentialities and he has taken his life-course as an easy one. Students in schools must be told about the great importance of hobbies in one's life. The best time for cultivating a hobby is the school period. The hobby selected by a student should be recreative and educative also. We are mentioning below the educative values of hobbies.

Values of Hobbies

1. They should provide recreation.
2. They should develop an aesthetic sense.
3. At the adolescent or adult level they are best substitutes for plays and games.

4. Some hobbies may provide some financial gains, e.s. painting, basket making or soap making are some such hobbies which may help a student to earn some money and thus feel a sense of self-importance.
5. They give a relief from monotonous work of the school.
6. If a student takes to touring as a hobby he may acquire educative historical and geographical informations.
7. Hobbies may promote creativity in students.

Types of Hobbies

Certain types of hobbies may be mentioned here for the guidance of school students.

1. Collection of stamps of various countries, pictures, seeds, flowers and leaves, etc.
2. Music—vocal or instruments.
3. Gardening.
4. Painting.
5. Sewing and embroideries.
6. Soap making, preparing candles.
7. Basket making.
8. Book binding.
9. Clay-moderling.
10. Toy making.
11. Radio & Television repairing.
12. Writing poems, essays and short stories.
13. Making pen-friends from various countries.
14. Leather work, spinning, weaving and knitting, etc.

Developing Hobbies in Students

In view of the great importance of hobbies in one's life, a school should try to encourage students to have some hobbies. In the first place, a variety of hobbies should be brought to the notice of students and importance and implications of each should be clearly explained to them. The students should be advised to choose their own hobbies in view of the facilities they may obtain at home and other relevant places. The chosen hobby must suit the temperament and aptitude of the student. For example, if a student is not interested in music, it will be futile to encourage him to develop his proficiency in music, In order to make a hobby a part of the co-curricular activities, each student should be allowed some time during the school hours for doing something at his chosen hobby. Each student at his hobby needs specific guidance from an able teacher. If such a teacher is not available in the school itself, the help of an outsider may be requisitioned for the purpose. The school should provide for the necessary finances for the hobbies chosen by students. If the students at hobbies happen to produce some saleable things the accounts of the sale proceeds must be carefully maintained.

2. Junior Red Cross Society

Red Cross Society is an international institution of great repute. This society was established in 1863 at Geneva. Its chief goal is to render help to people in trouble. Its smaller form is known as Junior Red Cross Society for school purposes. But it is a pity that now few schools have this organization in their premises. The school which establishes this society for its students places it under the charge of an able teacher who is equipped with all the preliminary necessary knowledge about health and first aid provision. Some students from each class should be chosen for the Junior Red Cross Society. Following are the three principal objectives of this society.

1. To provide care and treatment for minor diseases of children in the school. If it is reported that some student of the school has fallen ill, the leader of the society or some of its senior member is sent to the home of the sick child for doing the needful in co-operation with the parents. Under no circumstances, he should insist for a certain type of treatment, if the parents object to the same. However, he gladly offers his services to do what the parents desire for a speedy recovery of the sick child. The Junior Red Cross Society student may sit at the sick bed of the student or go to the market to make purchases for the sick fellow student under the guidance of the parents. He makes a note of whatever he does and reports the same to the teacher in-charge in the school. When there is a need all the students, turn by turn, are encouraged to render such a kind of service to sick children.

   The Junior Red Cross Society provides first aid to students in the school, if some one gets hurt on playgrounds or any where within the school premises. Towards this end the school maintains all the preliminary provisions.
2. The second principal aim of the Junior Red Cross Society is to render service to people on occasions of fairs and games. The Boys Scouts and girl guides also render this type of service in fairs, but they are not always equipped with first aid provisions.

3. The third aim of the Junior Red Cross Society is to maintain cleanliness within the school premises and do whatever is possible within its humble limits for protection of health of students in the school. Since in each class some members of the Junior Red Cross Society are present, it becomes a duty of the member to note the illness of some student, if any, in the class and report the matter to the teacher-in-charge of the society for the necessary steps. Then, the students members of the society tries to have a vigilant eye over the entire premises of the school including the compound class-rooms, verandahs, library, stores and toilets. If there is something harmful for health lying there they see that the needful is done at earliest to clean the place with the help of sweepers.

The above account indicates that the Junior Red Cross Society emphasises the humanitarian aspect of students' character. Junior Red Cross Society formed in a school principally aims at inculcating a sense of responsibility in students for helping others in need. Moreover, as we have said above this society tries to promote health by staging plays pertaining to some health problems. When infections and contagious diseases, spread this society helps the Government or Municipal Health Department in taking the necessary preventive measures. Sometimes, the society organizes lectures on health topics in the school.

The Junior Red Cross Society in a schools at times, tries to help the sick in a hospital through providing food and clothing to some patients. The society also helps the poor children in the school in purchasing some books and paying their fees.

The Red Cross Movement crosses all barriers of caste and creed, high and low and rich and poor and helps all at such times as earthquake, floods, famine and spread of epidemic diseases. It helps all alike. The entire Red Cross Society network of the world moves into action at such an hour of emergency in any country. Thus a spirit of universal fellowship is inculcated in the members of the Junior Red Cross Society in the school. So the principal and teachers of a school should try their best to run a Junior Red Cross Society in their school in order to promote the feeling of universal brotherhood in students.

3. *N.C.C.:* The short form of Natural Cadet Core is N.C.C. The Govt. of India has started the training in N.C.C. in all the Higher Seconcary Schools, Degree Colleges and Universities in the country. The chief purpose of this training is to promote a spirit of self-discipline in students and to prepare them to come to the rescue of the motherland in any emergency. A kind of military training is given to students

under this organization N.C.C. is meant both for boys and girls. It is a huge organization and its network is spread thought out the length and breadth of the country. The Central government spends crores of rupees every year on this organization. Certain military personnel is deputed from land, air and naval forces to man this organization. Accordingly, there are three principal wings of N.C.C. (1) Field Army wing (2) Air wing and (3) Navy wing. Each wing has its own uniform and separate wing flag which is hoisted at ceremonies along with the national flag Tiranga. Personnel drawn from the various forces normally serve for two years in the N.C.C. organization (with certain exceptions in which some are allowed to serve for more than two years and some remain even for five years. In each N.C.C. wing, there is an officer command, under whom there may be captains, subedar-major or Naib subedar and others:

Each wing of the N.C.C. Field, Air and Navy takes up a group of students from the schools under its jurisdiction for the necessary training. Under the training lectures are given for inculcating the necessary qualities in the students. At times the students are examined also. The students have to join parades organized by their particular wing. These parades are so organized as not to disturb the normal routine of the school teaching. During long school vacations camps are held where the cadets learn lessons in social co-operation, sympathy and self-discipline. On national days, i.e. on Independence and Republic days the cadets stage formal parades in their respective educational institutions. In the Republic Day parade in New Delhi. N.C.C. teams are sent from all over the country and in this celebration they demonstrate their ability and skill for which they have been trained during the year. Competitions are also held amongst the various teams drawn from the different corners of the land and prizes are awarded to the victorious groups.

Some parents are allergic of the N.C.C. training to their children. They think that much of the time of their wards is wasted in this affairs. Parents of girls are especially against the training of their wards, as they think that such a training will rob their daughters of some of their famine grace. So it becomes a duty on the part of teachers to grow the consciousness in parents about the great benefits that the N.C.C. training will give to their ward. So any misgiving on their part must be discouraged.

4. *The School Assembly:* A School assembly is a very important part of co-curricular activities. In a way many aspects of co-curricular

activities may originate from deliberations in the school assembly. The school assembly may develop a spirit of social co-operation. A sense of loyalty to the school is promoted by requiring all the students and teachers to assemble, together at a time. With some schools it is a common practice to assemble for prayer in the morning before starting the day work. At this assembly a teacher or the principal may speak about common programme or purposes. A school assembly should be organized with some positive purposes which may be as below:

The first purpose of a school assembly may be to heighten the religious or patriotic feelings of the students and teachers. In case of religious feeling the prayer and expression of devotion to God should be non-denominational. If this is not always possible some national song may be recited to arouse the patriotic feelings in students and teachers. The song may pertain to some universally loved great personality of the land. The prayer or the song should be accompanied by music which must not be mechanical. It must be recited feelingly.

The second purpose of the assembly may be for making certain important announcement about the day's work. Certain schools during examination days require the teachers and students to assemble at a place for listening to the examination time-table of the day and other important related instructions. At other times, in such an assembly the details about certain functions, elections, tournaments, lectures, holidays and change in the normal routine work of the school may be announced in order that the same catch the notice of all concerned.

The third purpose may be to familiarize the students with the rules and general ideals of the school in order to develop a community feeling in them. The promotion of this feeling is not possible, if various classes are isolated and all the students do not meet at times in a group. A well organized school through its assembly demonstrates its tone.

The fourth purpose of a school assembly may provide an opportunity to teachers and the principal to give lectures on some topic of general interest.

A school assembly my be used for providing news and informations about the general national interests. Certain inevitable repercussions of some international events may also be pointed out in each an assembly. The assembly may be used for motivating students for participating in certain co-curricular activities. If achievements of certain students in curricular and co-currical areas are advertised through the school assembly, it will make a great impressions on the minds of students is a whole. The achievers will also be amply rewarded by such advertisements in the assembly thinking that they have been well recognized.

The school assembly may provide an opportunity to students and teachers to come to the forefront and speak out their ideas and views about some important matter. This will create a sense of self-confidence in them which will help them in many aspects of life. The students who listen to such programmes pick up the correct habit of behaving in a group in a disciplined manner.

The organizers of the school assembly must see that the students reach and leave the place in an orderly manner. It should be seen that no student gossips and creates some kind of mischief in the assembly.

Planning the School Assembly

The school assembly should be organised by teachers and students in a co-operative manner. The programme of the assembly should represent how the school is functioning in various areas. At times, outside musicians, speakers, social leaders and actors may be invited to give demonstrations and deliver their speeches at the school assembly. This type of programme will encourage students a great deal. The consent of the head of the institution is necessary for inviting any outsider to the school assembly. It will also be profitable, if at times, inter-class contests in platform speaking or musical performances are organised for the assembly. The school assembly may be convened once or twice a month or whenever considered necessary by the principal. However, its too frequent meetings may become unprofitable. In a school assembly, the principal should not speak about the faults or weaknesses of certain students. He must also see that he does not have the major share of the time for announcing his policies and informations about certain routine matters. The function of the assembly must be instructive and inspiring to the students. So the teachers and students participating in its programmes must make good preparations.

5. *School Exhibition:* The school exhibition is of great importance in the sense that it affords an opportunity to students and teachers alike to display their best before others for emulation by each other. The academic achievements of a class as whole or of a particular student in such subjects as language, mathematics, history, geography, civics, drawing, sewing, embroidery painting, weaving, spinning, agriculture and home science etc. may be placed in the exhibition for display. The very fact that a certain item prepared by a student or teacher has been accepted as an exhibit is a great

encouragement to the maker. Various types of charts pertaining to basic concepts or developments in different subjects may be prepared for a school exhibition. This kind of preparation will afford a great training to the students and teachers both. In this process the students will be able to concretize their knowledge of various subjects.

The school exhibition may be held twice or thrice during an academic session. It will be better if it is organized particularly after the end of a long vacation, Dashahara and X'mas. In a vacation the students and teachers will be able to prepare their exhibits. Thus the teaching in the school will not be disturbed.

A portion of the funds earmarked for co-curricular activities should be allotted for the preparation of a school exhibition. The materials such as, paper, brush, clay and new pieces of cloth and other necessary items should be provided by the school, as the parents are likely to resent if their children demand extra-money for preparation of items for the school exhibition. A nominal entrance fee of ten or twenty paisa may be charged for allowing visitors to see the exhibition. The money thus collected may be utilized for preparation of items for a following school exhibition.

Exhibits for the exhibition should be chosen on merits. No partiality should be shown in this matter. Students of all classes should be encouraged to prepare something for display in the exhibition. It must be remembered that for the school exhibition things prepared by an outsider or purchased from the market must never be accepted. Due publicity should be made amongst parents and the immediate neighbourhood for coming to the school exhibition.

6. *School Publications:* School publications may be regarded as one of the most important aspects of co-curricular activities. Within the school publications we may include magazine, newspaper, handbook and year book. All these types of publications are possible only in a big school having a strength of students numbering about two thousands or so. However, in a smaller school also only one or too such publications may be attempted. A small school of about 400 or 500 students only half-yearly magazine may be considered as quite sufficient. First of all, we shall now consider below the values of such publications.

Values of School Publications

1. *Expressing the Views of Students:* Students have their own views regarding certain policies and rules of the school. The principal, at times, may say that students' views regarding the policies of the

school will be always welcome. But actually speaking, they generally frown at the suggestions given by students. The school publication is a good medium through which the students may express their views and give their suggestions.

2. *Unifying The School And Promoting A School Spirit:* The school publications provide news about achievements of students and teachers. They may also speak about the school traditions and ideals These features of the publications create a sense of solidarity and promote a school spirit.
3. *Giving Opportunity For Self-Expression And Creative Ability:* No school publication can be justified unless it provides an opportunity of self-expression and creative ability. If a student feels diffident in expressing himself, he may be encouraged to try himself out. In this way the school publications educate the students.
4. *Giving Reliable News About The School To Students, Parents And Other Schools:* Second—have information about the school activities may be misleading. The old students and parents are naturally interested about their school. Giving them correct informations about the school activities will enlist their co-operation at times.
5. *Encouraging Good Activities:* Recognizing certain activities in writing about them in the school newspapers, magazine or yearbook will lead to great encouragement to such activities. Honours won by students in music and dramatics and athletics will be highly encouraged, if they are given publicity through the school publications
6. *Developing such Virtue As Co-operation. Initiative. Sense Of Responsibility And Leadership:* The school publication should be directed to achieve such virues. In fact, it is because of such virtues in the students and teachers that school publications are ever in process.
7. *Moulding And Influencing Public Opinion About The School:* School publications focus the attention of the public on certain items pertaining to the school. Thus a desirable public opinion may be developed in favour of the school.

Functions of the School Publications

Whatever materials are included, the school publication must render some specific service, i.e. in other words, nothing should be printed for sake of printing. Information regarding various subjects may be included turn by turn because all of them may not be included in a certain publication in one issue.

7. Boy Scouting and Girl Guiding

Boy Scouting

In 1908 Lord Robert Baden Powell started the Boy Scout movement. In India it was introduced in 1911. This movement became so popular that a number of other countries also adopted it for their children. This movement aims at inculcating the spirit of humility, discipline, self-confidence, good feeling for others, self-reliance and co-operation in boys. This training meant for girls is known as girl guiding. Thus scouting and girl guiding gives great recreation to both boys and girls. It also improves their health.

It was in Bangalore that the first scout troop was organized. In the beginning, many people did not believe in its usefulness but soon within the second decade of the 20th century there were more than 3,50000 young boys and girls in this organization.

The boy scouting aims at achieving certain goals in order to make the school life of children more effective. Below we are hinting at some of the more important goals of boy scouting.

1. *Universal Brotherhood:* Scouting promotes the spirit of universal brotherhood in children. This movement looks at the whole humanity as one. It makes no distinction of caste, creed rich, poor, high, low, colour and nationality. Thus it transcends all social, religious and geographical restrictions.
2. *Love For Manual Work:* Scouting removes from the minds of children contempt for manual labour and it teaches that all should do their own work as far possible. It will have to be admitted that scouting has succeeded in achieving this goal. Now most of the students in our country and elsewhere harbour no contempt for physical labour and most of them are not shy of sweeping them rooms, cleaning their utensils and washing their own clothes
3. *To Do Something Good Everyday and Be Ever Prepared:* These have been the principal watchwords of scouting. So in its training these ideals are continually emphasized. Usefulness of scouts in fairs, a big gathering and big school functions may easily be understood, as we find that on all such occasions scouts are posted for giving the necessary guidance and help. Scope of scouts' service has been extended also to village cleaning work, and flood and earthquake relief.
4. *Spirit Of Adventure To Conquer All Difficulties:* The scouts are trained to imbibe a spirit of adventure and to go into all the details

of a problem with full determination to solve it. Outdoor activities indulged in by scouts are just an attempt to inculcate this spirit in them.

5. *To Create a Love for Nature:* Such activities of scouting as outdoor games, camp life, wandering in woods and taking up short trips are just an attempt to help the scouts to come in close touch with nature and develop an ever-abiding love for the same.

Needless to remark that scouting will be a great educational import if it is taken up in its proper perspective. Scouting teaches some such things which remain permanently imprinted on the minds of the trainees. Through scouting a restless and irresponsible adolescent may be trained into a helpful and dependable youth.

The Organization of Scouting

Scouting is meant for boys within the range of 11 to 18 years of age. The training of scouting has mainly three grades-tender fort, second class test and first class test. Boys below 18 are kept under the wolf-cub-packs. Adolescents above 18 are kept under Rover Troops. A troup consists of 32 boys. Under the supervision of a scout-master the various troop leaders function. The scouts must put on the prescribed uniforms. They have to promise to obey the scout laws. They are taught the use of ropes, sticks and techniques of rendering first aid service to the needy. At the appointed day the scouts organize camp fire, picnics and out-goings. Each scout has to learn to lead a camp life. In a way each one is trained in the various aspects of an independent living.

B-Girl Guiding

The great prospects of boy scouting attracted the notice of the womenfolk to start the same kind of movement for girls in strict accordance to their specific nature and particular requirements. Therefore Lord Baden Powel began the Girl Guide Movement.

The girl guide movement aims at inculcating womanly virtues in girls for enriching their particular personallies. This movement wants that by the time a girl finishes her school education she should be a happy, sweet, self-sacrificing and noble person meriting the love of all concerned. Like the boy scouting the girl guide also has three grades—(1) the girl guide company, meant for girls between 11 to 18 years of age (2) the Blue Bird Section for girls below 11 years of age, and (3). The Ranger company which enlists girls of over 18 years of age. Like the boy scouting, girl guiding also takes up to camp fires, rallies and excursions. The other activities of girl guides consist of nursing, cooking, first aid, games, dancing, drill and social service. A special uniform is also prescribed for girl guides.

In view of other specific functions and nature, it is needless to emphasize that these two movements should be included in the co-curricular activities of each school. In old British days boy scouting and girl guiding were more common in our schools. But after 1947 a slackness is noticed in schools for this movement. A school will not be fulfilling its obligations to its students unless it tries to inculcate in them the great ideals for the achievements of which this movement was started in the beginning of the 20th century. So it is very necessary that boy scouting and girl guiding become an essential aspect of co-curricular activities of any school.

8. Community Service

Community service programme should be an essential aspect of co-curricular activities in a school, because this will familiarise the students and teachers with the nature of communities from which they hail. The students should be encouraged to render some moral and social service to villages and mohallas adjoining to their school. Numerous opportunities are self-evident for giving some sort of community service by students. Suppose on way to school or home, a student happens to notice some pieces of glass or pieces of banana-skin spread all over a path or he finds pieces of bricks lying, in the middle of the road. Now it should be his moral and social duty to remove such impediments in order to protect the health and interests of the passers by. Similarly, many other such opportunities will appear before a student in which be may give vital service. But the consciousness of rendering such a service will dawn on him only when he is taught in the school in this direction. Below we are hinting at some kinds of community service which students under the supervision of a teacher may perform in a village or Mohalla.

1. To make a survey of a village or mohallah regarding the number of literate and illiterate persons, the number of children, adults, old persons, and women etc. Within this survey may be included the different types of occupations and industries and the number of animals, cows, bullocks, buffaloes, dogs etc. in the village or mohalla. On the basis this survey the personal, social and financial problems of the people of the area may be understood and plans may be chalked out to improve the condition of the people concerned.

2. The students may be asked to clean the compound and all the rooms of the school and to decorate the same as far as possible.
3. To organise the working of the library existing in the village or mohalla.
4. To help in construction of a community hall in the village or mohalla.
5. To clean the vicinity of the village or mohalla at least once a week.
6. To plant trees during the tree—plantation week or at other suitables time.
7. To spread literacy by teaching classes or illiterate adults in the evening.
8. At times to organize such functions in villages or Mohallas which may help the cultural advancement of the people.

Many other types of community services may be thought of depending upon the nature of students and the need of the community they belong to. Community service offers a tremendous opportunity to give lessons to students in social co-operation, sacrifice for others and duties, and obligations of a citizen.

Summary

1. Hobbies

Without a hobby the life, at times, may become a drudgery. The school period the best for cultivating hobbies.

Values of Hobbies

Recreative, aesthelic, best substitutes for play and games, financial gains also through some hobbies. Giving a relief from the monotony of life promoting creativity.

Types of Hobbies

Many as suit different individuals.

Developing Hobbies

Students should be encouraged to pick-up their own hobbies.

2. Junior Red Cross Society

Red Cross Society an international institution.

Objectives

To provide care and treatment for minor diseases of children. To provide first aid.

To render services in fairs and games. To maintain cleanliness in schools.

Emphasizes the human aspect.

Crosses all barriers of caste, creed, rich, poor, high and low.

Promoting the spirit of universal brotherhood.

3. N.C.C.

To promote a spirit of self-reliance and self-discipline. A kind of military training to students. Three wings—Field, Air and Navy. Meant for both boys and girls

Lessons in social co-operation and sympathy.

4. The School Assembly

Social, co-operation and sense of loyalty to the school are developed.

1. To heighten the feeling of students and teachers about some ennobling issue.
2. To make important announcements.
3. To familiarise the students with the ideals of the school.
4. To give lectures on topics of general interest.
5. To motivate students to participate in some good activities.
6. To advertise the achievements of students.

Planning the School Assembly

Should represent how the school is functioning.

Outsiders may also be invited at times.

5. School Exhibitions

An opportunity to the students and teachers to display their best achievements. Should be organized twice or thrice a year. Exhibits should be chosen on merits and they must be prepared by students and teachers.

6. School Publications

Magazines, newspaper, handbook and yearbook.

Values

1. Expressing views of students.
2. Unifying the school and promoting a school spirit.
3. Giving opportunity for self-expression and creative ability.
4. Giving reliable news about the school.
5. Encouraging good activities.

6. Virtues of co-operation. initiative, leadership and sense of responsibility.
7. Moulding and influencing public opinion.

7. Boy Scouting and Girl Guiding

A. Boy Scouting

Aims. Spirit of humily, discipline, self-confidence, self-reliance universal brotherhood. love for normal work. To do something good every day. To be ever prepared. To promote a spirit of adventure. To create a love for nature.

Meant for boys within 11 to 18 years of age. Three grades-tender fort. second class test and first class test wolf cub packs and Rover Troops. Prescribed uniform. To obey the scout laws. The use of ropes and sticks.

B. Girl Guides

A Prescribed uniform. To promote womanly virtues. 1. The girl guide company. 2. Blue Bird section. 3. The Rangers Company.

Nursing, cooking, first aid, games, dancing, drill and social service.

8. Community Service

Familiarising the students and teachers with the nature of the community.

Some moral and social service to villages and mohallas should be rendered.

The students should be taught in the above direction.

Certain Types of Community Services

1. To make a survey of a village or mohalla.
2. To understand the problems of people.
3. To clean the school compound, villages and mohallas at times.
4. To organise a library in a village.
5. Constancting community hall.
6. To repair broken walls, paths and roads.
7. To plant trees.
8. To organize social functions.

Exercises

1. Discuss the importance of hobbies in the life. of an individual. How can a school help develop them in students ?

2. Describe the functions of Junior Red Cross Society and its importance for a school.
3. Explain the utility of N.C.C. as an aspect of co-curricular activity in a school.
4. What should be the nature and function of a school assembly and why ?
5. Explain the importance of school exhibitions.
6. What are the functions and nature of school publications ?
7. Describe the importance of boy scouting and girl guiding in the development of character of boys and girls.
8. Describe the nature and function of community service to be run by a school.

Index